The Vedānta-Sūtras
of
Narayana Guru

The Vedānta-Sūtras of Narayana Guru

with an English translation
of the original Sanskrit
and Commentary

Swami Muni Narayana Prasad

DK
PRINTWORLD
Publishers of Indian Traditions

Cataloging in Publication Data — DK
[Courtesy: D.K. Agencies (P) Ltd. <docinfo@dkagencies.com>]

Narayana Prasad, *Muni*, 1938-
The Vedānta-sūtras of Narayana Guru : with an English translation of the original Sanskrit and commentary / Swami Muni Narayana Prasad. — 2nd rev. ed.
p. cm.
Includes text of Vedanta sutras by Narayana Guru in Sanskrit (Devanagari and roman).
Includes bibliographical references and index.
ISBN 13: 9788124606575

1. Vedanta. 2. Narayana Guru, 1856-1928. Vedānta sūtra. I. Narayana Guru, 1856-1928. Vedānta sūtra. English & Sanskrit. II. Title.

DDC 181.48 22

First published in India, 1997
Reprinted, 2003
Second revised edition, 2013
ISBN 13: 978-81-246-0657-5 ISBN 10: 81-246-0657-9

Printed and published by:
D.K. Printworld (P) Ltd.
Regd. Office: 'Vedaśrī', F-395, Sudarshan Park
(Metro Station: Ramesh Nagar)
New Delhi – 110 015
Phones: (011) 2545 3975; 2546 6019 *Fax*: (011) 2546 5926
e-mail: indology@dkprintworld.com
Website: www.dkprintworld.com

Prologue

NARAYANA Guru lived in India in the last phase of the nineteenth century and the first quarter of the twentieth century CE. Both in the Sanskrit language and in two regional languages of India, Malayalam and Tamil, he presented his vision of the Self with an astounding clarity and in minimum words. In India's ancient spiritual tradition, he added a new chapter which can, in effect, lead all seekers of wisdom towards a new era.

The hierarchical presentation of the Science of the Absolute was formulated in pre-Vedic India. That science grew into a way of life and became the contemplative foundation of Indian civilization interlinking the periods before and after Christ. In India, spiritual thoughts began with Āgamas (ancient predictions), followed by Nigamas, a period of deductions. Then came the dawn of the pre-Vedic period and the Saṁhitās of the four Vedas (the compendium of *mantra*s or formulae neatly arranged by the Veda-knowers).

The votaries of the Vedas were very pragmatic people. They wanted to experience whatever was suggested in the Saṁhitās. The Saṁhitās were mainly preserved by learned families keen on acquiring wisdom. Out of the Vedas arose instructive injunctions on applying the formulae of the Vedas in the daily life of people. The literature that came to be formed in that period is called the Brāhmaṇas. In childhood, adolescence and youth, young Indians memorized the Vedic chants and in their transition from youth to middle age they were very enthusiastic in experiencing whatever was passed on to them by their elders.

Naturally when age advanced, the allure of hedonistic pleasures withered away and people became rather tired of living in crowded families. They were now engaged in contemplative thoughts and there was a natural desire to become more familiar with the promise of a hidden treasure in the secret core of one's own Self. Thus a new literature arose introducing the disillusioned person to a deeper search, which came to be known as the Āraṇyakas. In their solitary search, the recluses came closer to truth, as if they were sitting at the feet of truth itself. This marked the transition from the Āraṇyakas to the Upaniṣads. We can confidently say that this, inevitably, exposed a person of mature wisdom to an actual peak experience of truth and reality.

The growth of Vedic literature in India came almost to a finale a few centuries before Jesus Christ. Then historical changes in India brought a lacuna in the zest for spiritual truth. People began to lose the key to understanding Vedic and Vedāntic lore. The need arose to recapture the lost heritage. That brought India to a very vociferous age of commentaries and elucidations of the wisdom-filled visions of past masters. This new historical need was initiated by the commentators called *bhāṣyakāra*s. Among them, Śaṅkara, Rāmānuja and Madhva were the foremost. The *bhāṣya* period was followed by a new decadence in spiritual search and understanding. But in literature a surge in activities relating to poetics, logistics and pragmatics followed.

Thus several centuries elapsed. India almost descended to a level of total confusion and became alienated from whatever was valuable to her spirit. It was at such a time that Narayana Guru appeared to reawaken people with the clarion call of a seer of the modern age. He spoke in the same language of *ṛṣis* like Yājñavalkya and the authors of the pre-Vedic Āgamas who prevailed in the form of Śaivite *Tevāram* and Vaiṣṇavite *Nālāyira Prabandham*. Like Lord Buddha, Narayana Guru mainly used the layman's language prevalent in his area, Malayalam. To revive the glory and significance of the lost heritage, he also wrote compositions in Sanskrit. His *Vedānta Sūtras* are on par with Bādarāyaṇa's *Brahma Sūtras*.

My spiritual brother and friend, Swami Muni Narayana Prasad, trained and instructed by my own teacher, Nataraja Guru, presents in this commentary an elucidation of Narayana Guru's aphoristic vision of the Self. I reproduce here a representative portion of Swami Prasad's learned exposition to introduce the reader to the clarity and insight of the *bhāṣyakāra*, Swami Muni Narayana Prasad:

Sūtra* 5 : *tad idam sad asad iti

tat	:	That
idam	:	(the world) here
sat	:	(considerable) as existence and
asat	:	non-existence
iti	:	as

That, as the world here, is (considerable) as existence and non-existence.

This *sūtra* answers the question asked in the second part of *sūtra* 2 : ". . . from what standpoints may it be considered?"

The luminous world of appearances exists as an expression of self-effulgent *ātman* and so it was emphasized that the world, having *ātman* as its sole content and substance, is also real. Now, however, Narayana Guru discriminates between "That" and "this world" as Reality (*sat*) and appearance (*asat*).

The constituents of the world are its ever-changing forms: emerging, being sustained for a while, and then dissolving back into the mystery from which they appeared. In this they are analogous to gold ornaments which may be continually melted down and changed into other forms without any intrinsic change in their essential composition or substance. In Vedānta the Real is considered to be that which exists eternally, unchanged through all its changing expressions. In this particular sense the Guru refers to the relative, transitory forms of the world as *asat* and its unchanging substance, *ātman*, as *sat*. To consider the world as *asat*, thus, is not to deny its actuality. To know things as they appear to be is *yathārtha-jñāna* (factual knowledge) and to know what is fundamentally real in all appearances is *paramārtha-jñāna* (knowledge of the ultimate).

The world of *prakṛti*, Nature, the field of action, is present as an immense variety of specific forms, qualities and transactional events; but these are only sparkings of the self-effulgent Self. An enlightened knower of Reality perceives the relative, multiple, transitory forms of the world as unreal in themselves though real as forms assumed by their one pervasive substance . . ."

I am very much pleased to endorse this commentary in which the Muni clearly avoids exegesis and relies more on his own personal conviction. With this beautiful elucidation Swami Prasad places Narayana Guru on par with the Upaniṣadic *ṛṣi*s and the *sūtrakāra*s like Bādarāyaṇa and Jaimini, Gautama and Kaṇāda, Kapila and Patañjali. My congratulations and blessings to the commentator and to the collaborator of this commentary, Mr Dan Arbeid (Dānadayānidhi).

auṁ tad eva sat

Nitya Chaitanya Yati

Preface

A COMMON factor linking living beings on earth is that they naturally turn away from painful experiences. In human beings this natural impulse to turn from painful towards more pleasurable states is expressed as a quest for happiness. Man, however, uniquely among living species, has the ability to question the meaning of happiness and the meaning of his own being.

In the cultures of both East and West such questions have always provoked philosophical thought and religious expressions which in earlier times were one and the same thing. They became two, in the West, only after the so-called "dark ages" when a general aversion developed, especially among thinkers, towards religion in the aftermath of the Inquisition. In the East, however, they have remained inseparable. Therefore Indian religious scriptures are, in essence, philosophical works.

In the West the different schools of philosophy derive from different sources. But the schools of Indian philosophy all derive from one primary source, the Vedas. Each of these schools places emphasis on particular aspects of the Vedas. Nyāya gives primacy to the categories of existence, Vaiśeṣika to the nature of basic substances, Sāṁkhya to the evolutionary aspect of nature, Yoga to practical discipline, Pūrva Mīmāṁsā to Vedic rituals, and Uttara Mīmāṁsā, or Vedānta as it is more commonly known, to the acquisition of knowledge of Ultimate Reality. All these schools, however, have the attainment of enlightenment as their common objective. None of them claim to have originated the teachings they propound. None of the proponents is thought to be the originator of the school he is associated with. The origin of each is attributed to a line of masters stretching back to the mists of the past ages. Each current master therefore claims to be only the most recent exponent of an already-existing teaching.

Historians consider that India's wisdom attained its maturity in Vedānta. It is perhaps for that reason that a number of specific sub-schools developed from it; those of Śaṅkara, Rāmānuja, Madhva, Vallabha, Nimbārka and Caitanya, to name the most prominent of them. These, in fact, are not distinct schools of different thoughts but are different interpretations of one and the same message of the Upaniṣads propounded in the *Brahma-Sūtras* of Bādarāyaṇa. Their different interpretations had, however, in the long passage of time, rendered the message of the Upaniṣadic *ṛṣi*s vague and difficult to understand, so that a simple and direct restatement of it became necessary.

This necessity was fulfilled by Narayana Guru with his teachings and his written works. His *Vedānta-Sūtras* are his most succinct expression of the original Upaniṣadic teaching of non-dual Reality. They do not comprise a linear progression of ideas and concepts concerning Reality, but expand from a central assertion — that one Self alone exists and it is that Absolute Reality. As the circle expands from that central point the centre is regarded from different standpoints, each throwing some fresh light on the nature of the seeker and the self-enquiry.

The Guru's concluding *sūtra* is a reassertion of his opening statement and it is the major point reiterated throughout this commentary. It is a teaching coming from an ancient source to which a great body of scripture, literature and commentary is attached, all providing some particular points of view regarding the existence of *Brahman*. It is a teaching of truth that may be known in self-luminous inner-awareness, a truth expressible in three words from the *Chāndogya Upaniṣad* — *tat tvam asi* — meaning, That Thou Art.

Narayana Guru's disciple, successor and founder of Narayana Gurukula, Dr Natarajan, who became Nataraja Guru, translated much of the Guru's work into English and wrote commentaries on it. But these *sutras* did not come to light until 1978, after Nataraja Guru's death in 1973, and so he did not have the opportunity to write a commentary on them. As a disciple of Nataraja Guru and at the instance of Guru Nitya Chaitanya Yati, the present guru and head of Narayana Gurukula, it became my lot to undertake that task.

I wrote the original commentary in my mother tongue, the Malayalam language, and then translated it myself into English, or "Manglish" (mangled Malayalam/English) as our friend Dan Arbeid, the UK representative of Narayana Gurukula, prefers to call it. As part of his own dedicated service to the cause of spreading Narayana Guru's teaching, he has retranslated it into "Queen's English." It is not the Indian custom to express thanks verbally as it separates, as it were, the thanker and the thanked — a separation opposed to the essence of the *advaita* philosophy of this work. Dan Arbeid's contribution is sincerely appreciated in that light.

A further work I have undertaken, as a companion to this one, is a comparative study of the Vedānta interpretations of Śaṅkara, Rāmānuja and Madhva. That study as well as this commentary of the *Vedānta-Sūtras* are dedicated to the Guru with the hope that they will further his endeavours and assist the reader/seeker towards Vedānta's goal.

Varkala, India **Swami Muni Narayana Prasad**
October 1996

Contents

Introduction

ALL life is one; only its living forms are multiple. That in which they live, breathe and have their being and which lives and breathes in them, is one unbounded, timeless existence. It is the reality underlying life and all else. To know this one causal reality and its wondrous self-revelation in its effects constitutes wisdom.

To seek, find and know the real nature of oneself and the world is the ultimate human achievement transcending and subsuming all others where individualized life experience is concerned. Its attainment corrects the errors of man throughout his history in understanding existence, and the mistaken views of dogmatic religion and mechanistic materialism which have conditioned his mind and kept from him the knowledge of his true nature. Gaining that knowledge brings him the gifts of wisdom which enable him to live free of fear, desire and anger, fulfilled in life and at peace with himself and the world.

This wisdom, too, is one. Through the course of human history there have always been some few enlightened visionaries, a few saints and seers, whose mission has been to restore to light the perennial knowledge of ultimate reality which, over the long passage of time, becomes lost to view. The interpretations of their vision have, of course, been expressed in the particular language and context of the time, culture, religion and social environment in which they lived. Inevitably, those expressions have differed very much, but they have all proclaimed the same oneness of reality.

Narayana Guru was one such exceptional seer and sage, a knower of reality gifted with mystic insight. His background is that of India's Hindu culture. He was born in 1854 in a village near Trivandrum in the south-west Indian state of Travancore, now part of modern Kerala. His father, a teacher, was a scholarly man versed in Astronomy, Sanskrit and Ayurvedic medicine; his mother was a simple, graceful, kindly woman endowed with beauty and sensibility.[1] Nanu, as he was then called, was acquainted with the Hindu scriptures and with the expressions of perennial wisdom contained in them at an early age. In his youth he mastered Sanskrit and became conversant with the doctrines of the Vedānta philosophy expounded by the great Upaniṣadic *ṛṣi*s (seers). While still a young man he took the path of *saṁnyāsa* (renunciation) and undertook the austere life of a mendicant monk. In early middle age he attained enlightenment and quietly began to teach.[2] He was soon recognized to be a very great *guru* by an ever-growing number of devotees. His life and teachings soon began to assert an enormous and enduring influence in south India inspiring many great social, economic and educational improvements there, especially for the lowly poor and oppressed of Travancore. He died in Travancore in 1928. We know him today, first and foremost, as a spiritual teacher in the Vedānta tradition, a Vedāntic *ṛṣi*. His teaching is a revision and restatement of Vedānta's central message of the non-dual nature of existence. As Dr Paul Deussen so eloquently puts it in his *Outline of the Vedanta System*: "On the tree of Indian wisdom, there is no fairer flower than the Upaniṣads and no finer fruit than the Vedānta philosophy."[3]

---

1. *Life and Teachings of Narayana Guru*, Nataraja Guru, published by Narayana Gurukula Foundation, Varkala, 1990, pp. 253-54.
2. Ibid., p. 17.
3. Preface, *Outline of the Vedanta System*, Dr Paul Deussen, Cambridge, Mass, U.S.A.

Vedānta is one of the six systems of Indian philosophy which may together be described as a staircase of six flights in the edifice of human understanding. It is the topmost flight of that ascent leading the seeker of wisdom to a conclusive certainty concerning the two most fundamental questions of life: "Who am I?" and "Whence this world?" Gaining that knowledge brings the gift of self-fulfilment (*ānanda*) and awareness that the final goal of wisdom-seeking has been attained. Thus Vedānta may truly be said to be the finest fruit from the fairest flower on the tree of India's wisdom.

Originally the word Vedānta was a name applied to the Upaniṣads in general, the Upaniṣads being the concluding sections of the Vedas, India's four most ancient scriptures. Later the name came to be used more specifically to indicate the philosophy derived from the Upaniṣads. The word combines two Sanskrit words, *veda* meaning knowledge, and *anta* meaning end or conclusion. It therefore means the end or culmination of knowledge.

The Upaniṣads, the *Brahma-Sūtras* and the *Bhagavad-Gītā* together constitute the doctrinal foundations of Vedānta. The *Brahma-Sūtras* are a systematic exposition of the essential teachings of the Upaniṣads through logic and reasoned argument. The *Bhagavad-Gītā* is a section of the epic *Mahābhārata* in the form of a dialogue between Kr̥ṣṇa, an *avatāra* and supreme wisdom teacher, and his disciple Arjuna, a princely warrior. It, too, proclaims the essential teaching of the Upaniṣads. The Upaniṣads are, therefore, seen to be the primary sources of Vedānta.

The work known as the *Brahma-Sūtras* is attributed to the *r̥ṣi* Bādarāyaṇa. It is not certain when the work known as Bādarāyaṇa's *Brahma-Sūtras* was composed, but it is generally held to be more than two thousand years old. That it predates the *Bhagavad-Gītā* is clear from references to it in the latter work[4] and, as has been observed, the many commentaries on it during this long period of time. It stands as the seminal source of all polemics developed in the later history of Vedānta, especially after the time of Śaṅkara in the first millennium. The polemical form of its text influenced later commentators to adopt that style of presentation in their own work. Subsequently, during the course of many years, different schools of Vedānta came into being which based themselves on the interpretations of particular commentators. Each school disputed the views of the other schools, finding support for its own views by appropriately citing verses and passages from selected scriptures. Their disputes were carried on to later periods, during which a large and controversial body of literature was generated. This growing body of literature had the greatest contribution from the schools of the *Advaita* (non-dualism) of Śaṅkara, the *Viśiṣṭādvaita* (qualified non-dualism) of Rāmānuja, and the *Dvaita* (dualism) of Madhva. In all, there are some twenty-one definitive commentaries on the *Brahma-Sūtras*, each claiming to represent the meaning intended by Bādarāyaṇa. These, with their conflicting arguments, succeed in thoroughly confusing the modern student of Vedānta. Actually, in their eagerness to project and justify their own points of view, the different commentators and their followers, in course of time, ended up obscuring the very clarity and purity of the vision of the Upaniṣadic *ṛṣis*. Such was the state of Vedāntic speculation towards the end of the nineteenth century and the early part of the twentieth century.

It was at that time, in the latter years of the British Raj, that Narayana Guru undertook the task of re-evaluating and restating the Vedānta as appropriate to a modern age of science and technology. Although essentially an *advaitin* (non-dualist) he did not solely subscribe to and support the Śaṅkara school of non-dual philosophy, nor did he oppose the teachings of

4. *Bhagavad-Gītā*, Chapter 13, v. 4.

other schools. Indeed, some of the hymns he composed are apparently dualistic, and yet they convey his non-dual vision. He saw that Absolute Reality comprehends the immanent and the transcendent together, and that both duality and non-duality are valid perceptions from different standpoints. His comprehensive vision and contemplative insight reconciles the superficial disagreements between the different Vedāntic schools. It restores the pristine vision of the Upaniṣadic *ṛṣis*. In this age of scientific revelations his revision and restatement of Vedānta is all the more relevant and timely.

Unlike earlier propounders of Vedānta, Narayana Guru did not add to the plethora of commentaries on Bādarāyaṇa's *Brahma-Sūtras*; nor did he write commentaries on any other Vedāntic source-book. Instead he wrote original works which removed the accumulated dust of centuries of misunderstanding obscuring the clear light of Vedānta's central message. Among these works, in the form of mystico-philosophical poems in his native Malayalam language, are the *Ātmopadeśa-Śatakam* (One Hundred Verses of Self-Instruction), *Advaita-Dīpikā* (The Lamp of Non-Duality), *Aṛivu* (Consciousness) and *Daivadaśakam* (Ten Verses to God). He has, to his credit, a translation of the *Īśa Upaniṣad* in Malayalam. The Guru's poetic genius is such that this latter Malayalam work, like the Sanskrit original, is often chanted as a *mantra* (sacred formula of instruction). His Sanskrit works include the *Darśana-Mālā* (Garland of Visions of the Absolute), the *Brahmavidyā-Pañcakam* (Five Verses on the Science of the Absolute) and numerous hymns. Whether in Malayalam, Sanskrit, or, sometimes, Tamil, his writings articulate his vision with great poetic beauty. They culminate in the highly cryptical Sanskrit composition which is the subject of this book, the *Vedānta-Sūtras*. This work, which is not in the polemical style of Bādarāyaṇa's *Brahma-Sūtras*, is a simple, original, aphoristic restatement of the essential teachings of the Upaniṣads.

And Narayana Guru is the only latter-day interpreter to present the Vedānta philosophy in a fresh and original *sūtra* form. The *Vedānta-Sūtras* of Narayana Guru thus have a unique place in Indian philosophy as the first *sūtra* expression of Vedānta since Bādarāyaṇa.

Sūtra composition developed as a literary style in the Sanskrit language of ancient India, perhaps because it rendered a text easier to learn by heart. Such a way of learning was necessary at a time when written work was not generally available and teachings were handed down by word of mouth. Even these days, despite the availability of written records, the tradition of learning an entire text by heart continues among Sanskrit scholars. The six systems of Indian philosophy, which must have been composed at that early time, were all originally systematized in the form of *sūtra*s. The popular treatise on Sanskrit grammar by Pāṇiṇi is in *sūtra* form and even some ritualistic instructions, such as the *Gṛhya-Sūtras*, are in that literary style.

The literal meaning of the word *sūtra* is a thread which strings something together, as, for example, a thread that strings together the beads of a rosary. As a literary style it is a way of presenting great concepts in an economical manner, through short, cogent sentences. The whole work in this style may be called a *sūtra* and each of its separate aphorisms may also be referred to as a *sūtra*. The origin of this literary style is generally attributed to the method of teaching prevalent in India's ancient *gurukula*s.

The word *gurukula* literally means *guru*'s home, or *guru*'s family, and it is the name applied to a community of a wisdom-teacher and his students. In earlier times these were mostly forest dwellings of a *guru* and his handful of disciples. The *guru*, in teaching, would use a few key words which, later, enabled the students to recall the details of a lesson. Such key words would have meaning only for those who attended the class. *Sūtras* are, in a like manner, the key words which string together a wide specturm of meanings comprehensible only to those who are familiar with the fundamental teaching, or those who are guided by clear commentary.

Sūtra commentators, especially of philosophical works, have invariably added expressions of their own vision in their endeavour to clarify the original meaning. Such expressions, with their individual colouring, have been the principal cause of conflict in different interpretations of the *Brahma-Sūtras*. Commentators have also been influenced by the times and conditions in which they lived. Śaṅkara, in his revision of Vedānta, was confronted by Buddhist nihilism and, later, Rāmānuja and Madhva were faced with the increasing tide of Islamic influence flooding in from the Middle-East. The influence of personal and historical factors is therefore inevitable in the work of *sūtra* commentators and it is possible that it may even overlay and obscure the intended meaning of the original. Commentators, being contemplative thinkers with their own insight, have sometimes adapted their personal vision to that of the work being interpreted. They have also sometimes distorted the vision of the original to fit in their own with it. As a consequence there are some contentious elements in nearly all the commentaries on Bādarāyaṇa's *Brahma-Sūtras*.

It is not claimed that this commentary on Narayana Guru's *Vedānta-Sūtras* does not have any such pitfalls. However, this work may have steered clear of many pitfalls owing to the fact that the Guru did not live in the distant past. His *Vedānta-Sūtras* do not stand as his only work and what he expresses in them through aphorisms, has been fully expounded in his other more extensive compositions. The meaning of his *Vedānta-Sūtras* may therefore be clarified in the light of these other works. In this commentary, therefore, allusion will be made to them and to parallel meanings indicated in the *Bhagavad-Gītā* and the Upaniṣads. Reference will also be made to the prevailing views of modern science though these, unlike the perennial truths of Vedānta, may in time change or simply be discarded.

The 24 Sūtras

SŪTRA 1

अथ यदात्मनो जिज्ञासुस्तदिदं ब्रह्मैवाहम ॥

atha yad ātmano jijñāsus tad idaṁ brahmaivāham ॥

Now then! that which the seeker of the Self desires, it is this: *Brahman* (the Absolute) indeed am I.

SŪTRA 2

किं तस्य लक्षणमस्य च कति गणनयेति ॥

kiṁ tasya lakṣaṇam asya ca kati gaṇanayeti ॥

What defines it and from what standpoints may it be considered?

SŪTRA 3

तज्ज्योतिः ॥

tajjyotiḥ ॥

That, effulgence is.

SŪTRA 4

तेनेदं प्रज्वलितम् ॥

tenedaṁ prajvalitam ॥

Because of "That" this (world) properly shines existent.

SŪTRA 5

तदिदं सदसदिति ॥

tad idaṁ sad asad iti ॥

That, as the world here, is (considerable) as existence and non-existence.

SŪTRA 6

भूयो सतस्सदसदिति ॥

bhūyo sataḥ sad asad iti ॥

Again, it is from Existence that existence and non-existence emerge.

SŪTRA 7

सच्छब्दादयो सदभावश्चेति ॥

sac chabdādayo sad abhāvaśceti ॥

Such words as existence imply their opposites as well.

SŪTRA 8

पूर्वं सदिदमनुसृत्य चक्षुरादयश्चैकं चेति ॥

pūrvaṁ sad idam anusṛtya cakṣurādayaś caikaṁ ceti ॥

In the beginning this was Existence, followed by the apparent existence of senses and mind.

SŪTRA 9

ज्ञातृज्ञानयोरन्योन्यविषयविषयित्वान्मिथुनत्वमिति ॥

jñātṛ jñānayor anyonya viṣaya viṣayitvān mithunatvam iti ॥

Knower and knowledge are paired, mutually subject and object.

SŪTRA 10

एवं ज्ञानज्ञेयविभागे ॥

evaṁ jñāna jñeya vibhāge ॥

So too, with the division of knowledge and known.

SŪTRA 11

एकैकं रुद्रत्वमासीदिति ॥

ekaikaṁ rudratvam āsīd iti ॥

Each apart has always been a cause of sorrow.

SŪTRA 12

ब्रह्मैवाहं तदिदं ब्रह्मैवाहमस्मि ॥

brahmaivāhaṁ tad idaṁ brahmaivāham asmi ॥

Brahman indeed am I. That indeed is this world. *Brahman* indeed I am.

SŪTRA 13

अतीतागामिनोरसत्त्वं यतः यदेतदन्विच्छत ॥

atītāgāminor asattvaṁ yataḥ yad etad anvicchata ॥

By which everything past and future is non-existent, seek that continuously.

SŪTRA 14

परिमाणं ततः ॥

parimāṇaṁ tataḥ ॥

There is measurement because of "That."

SŪTRA 15

सदसतोरन्योन्यकार्यकारणत्वात् ॥

sad asator anyonya kārya kāraṇatvāt ॥

Because Existence and appearance are mutually cause and effect.

SŪTRA 16

अहं ममेति विज्ञातो मत्तो नान्यः ॥

ahaṁ mameti vijñāto matto nānyaḥ ॥

That which is known as "I" and "mine" is not other than the Self.

SŪTRA 17

तद्वत्तस्मात् ॥

tadvat tasmāt ॥

Likewise not other than That.

SŪTRA 18

दृग्दृश्ययोः समानकालीनत्वात् ॥

dṛg dṛśyayoḥ samāna kālīnatvāt ॥

Because of the simultaneity of subject and object.

SŪTRA 19

सुखैकत्वात् ॥

sukhaikatvāt ॥

Because of the unity of happiness.

SŪTRA 20

व्यापकतया दिशामस्तित्वात् ॥

vyāpakatayā diśām astitvāt ॥

Because of the extensive existence of directions.

SŪTRA 21

अणुमहदवयवतारतम्यस्याभावात् ॥

aṇu-mahad-avayava-tāratamyasyābhāvāt ॥

Because of the absence of physically comparable atomicity and immensity.

SŪTRA 22

असतोऽव्यापकत्वात् ॥

asato 'vyāpakatvāt ॥

Because non-existence cannot be pervasive.

SŪTRA 23

आत्मान्यत्किञ्चिन्नास्ति ॥

ātmānyat kiñcinnāsti ॥

Other than *ātman* (the Self) nothing exists.

SŪTRA 24

तस्मात् तस्य सत्वाच्च ॥

tasmāt tasya satvāc ca ॥

Therefore other than the Existence of "That," nothing.

Sūtra 1

अथ यदात्मनो जिज्ञासुस्तदिदं ब्रह्मैवाहम ॥

atha yad ātmano jijñāsus tad idam brahmaivāham.

atha	:	now then
yat	:	that which (is desired)
jijñāsuḥ	:	by a seeker
ātmanaḥ	:	of the Self
tat	:	it is
idam	:	this
aham	:	I (am)
brahma	:	*Brahman*
eva	:	indeed

Now then! that which the seeker of the Self desires, it is this: *Brahman* (the Absolute) indeed am I.

VEDĀNTA, in common with all other systems of Indian philosophy, has a predetermined objective. It is this, above all else, which differentiates Indian philosophy from its Western counterpart. This objective is the attainment of the highest human value of self-knowledge. It means, to realize and to experience that one's own self is not different from *Brahman*, the Absolute. Such realization brings the gift which in Vedānta is called *mokṣa* or *mukti* (liberation).

In this first *sūtra* Narayana Guru conceptualizes Vedānta's objective with the words, *brahma eva aham* (*brahmaivāham*)

"*Brahman* indeed am I" and declares it to be the goal of the seeker.

The attainment of any goal is accomplished only through effective means. The search for self-knowledge is itself the effective means by which this goal is attained. This also is indicated in the first *sūtra* by the words *ātmanaḥ jijñāsuḥ* (seeker of the Self).

The ends and means of Vedānta, thus, are made clear in the very first *sūtra*.

Atha

It is customary for Indian writers to begin any serious work with an explicit or implied invocation. Narayana Guru, in nearly all his major compositions, has a preference for implicit invocation. In Indian tradition the letter *a* signifies *Brahman*. This *sūtra* work begins with the word *atha* and so an invocation is implied in the first letter of the word.

In opening this work with the word *atha*, Narayana Guru is adopting an ancient convention of Indian *sūtra* writers. The *Brahma-Sūtras* of Bādarāyaṇa begin with the words *athāto brahmajijñāsā*, (Now then, let us have the desire to know *Brahman*). Jaimini's *Pūrva-Mīmāṁsā-Sūtras* begin with *athāto dharmajijñāsā* (Now then, let us have the desire to know righteousness). The first *sūtra* of Patañjali's *Yoga-Sūtras* is *atha yogānuśāsanam* (Now then begins the instruction on Yoga). By way of this tradition *atha* has come to indicate the beginning of a *sūtra* text.

The literal meaning of the word *atha* is "now then," but in *sūtra* literature it also indicates continuation of a preceding matter. In this way the meaning of words in *sūtra* literature is maximized and the number of words used minimized.

Śaṅkara's Prerequisites

The search for knowledge of the Absolute requires certain conditions to initially exist for its successful undertaking. The question of what those conditions should be has been a bone of contention between the various schools of Vedānta, especially between those of Śaṅkara and Rāmānuja. Śaṅkara believed that the seeker should acquire certain personal attributes to fit him for the search. Rāmānuja held that a detailed knowledge of the Vedas and their rituals was necessary.

According to Śaṅkara there are four personal prerequisites which collectively are known as *sādhana catuṣṭaya sampatti* (to have acquired four personal disciplines). These are *nitya anitya viveka* (the ability to discriminate between that which never changes and that which is transient), *vairāgya* (detachment from worldly pleasures), *śamādi ṣaḍguṇa sampatti* (to have gained the six qualities of self-discipline), and *mumukṣutva* (the intense desire for liberation). The six qualities of self-discipline are: *śama* (calmness; the ability to resist worldly temptations), *dama* (self-restraint; the ability to restrain the senses from attachment to objects), *uparati* (self-dependence; non-dependence on external opinions and influences), *titikṣā* (endurance; the inner strength to endure troubles and difficulties without vengefulness or self-pity), *śraddhā* (faith; to have full faith that the scriptures and the teachings of one's *guru* disclose the object of one's seeking), and *samādhāna* (resolution; to have one's mind fixed on the attainment of the wisdom of the Absolute, even when engaged in day-to-day activities).

This does not necessarily mean that the wisdom of the Absolute is only for reclusive monks and those prepared to renounce worldly concerns, activities and responsibilities in a one-way pursuit of that goal. It is also attainable by those engaged in their respective worldly activities provided they have the sense of discrimination and the resolution to conduct their lives in ways conducive to its achievement. It is not by denying the nature of the physical organism but through its regulation that the goal, denoted in this first *sūtra* as "*Brahman* indeed am I," may be attained. The body, mind and intellect may continue their natural functions, but with these so ordered as to be supportive of the seeker's aspiration. To achieve this it is necessary to develop a sense of continual, detached witnessing of these functions. They will not then overshadow the mind and hold it subservient to sensory experience. This is expressed in the following verses of the *Bhagavad-Gītā*:

> He who sits, with organs of action restrained,
> mentally dwelling on objects of the senses,
> self-deluded, he is said to be a hypocrite.
> But he who, controlling the senses by the mind,
> engages the organs of action without attachment,
> he excels in the Yoga of action, O Arjuna.[1]

Rāmānuja's Prerequisites

Rāmānuja expresses a view quite at variance with that of Śaṅkara. Perhaps because he was faced with the increasing Islamic influence of Muslim invaders, he turned to Vedic orthodoxy to prepare those wishing to undertake the path indicated by the word *atha*. In his view, a thorough knowledge of the Vedas — their substance and their prescribed practices — was an indispensable prerequisite to the pursuit of Vedānta's goal. These four most ancient scriptures of India are known respectively as the *Ṛgveda, Sāmaveda, Yajurveda* and *Atharvaveda*. They are chiefly comprised of hymns, rituals and invocations addressed to various Vedic deities. They also embody knowledge of the laws governing the manifest existence. But in their study and in the practice of their rituals, the seeker

1. *Bhagavad-Gītā*, III.6-7.

will eventually despair of them as a means of knowing *Brahman* and will turn to the Upaniṣads for better guidance. In that light and in the light of the knowledge they embody, Rāmānuja considers a sound knowledge of the Vedas to be a necessary preliminary to the study and path of Vedānta.

Narayana Guru's View of Prerequisites

Narayana Guru's views are akin to those of Śaṅkara but, as the Guru expresses them, the four prerequisites described above represent progressive stages of the aspirant's personal development. There are those who have a natural aptitude for discrimination and those who through instruction, contemplation and their own resolution acquire an ability to discriminate. Such people, aware of the transient nature of other values, will seek for that which does not pass away. They will look for an enlightened teacher to aid them in their search. The Guru portrays this situation in the first verse of his *Brahmavidyā-Pañcakam*:

> Discriminating between the eternal
> and the transient, the well instructed one
> attaining detachment, duly well adorned
> with the six initial conditions
> of calmness, self-restraint and so on,
> and keenly desirous of liberation here on earth,
> then greets with prostration a *Brahman*-knowing *guru*,
> who, pleased by this proper attention and service,
> becomes favourably disposed.
> Thereafter, he should ask of such a *guru*:
> O master, who am I, whence this world?
> Teach me this, O great one.

The Five Senses

In the first verse of what is perhaps his best known work, the *Ātmopadeśa-Śatakam,* Narayana Guru says of the senses:

> With the five eyes (senses) restrained
> one should search and with repeated
> prostration one should chant*

In the eighth verse of the same work he says:

> Perched on a perishable body and enjoying the five fruits, sound and the like, the five birds fly back and forth, continually changing places. That radiant inner awareness should fill one's entire being and cut them down.

With our senses, the five flying birds, we normally engage only the externals of the objects of perception. Their forms and qualities may seem substantial but the senses do not reveal their underlying Reality. To know that Reality one has to seek a way of knowing which transcends sensory perceptions. Such a way of knowing is found in the transparency of inner awareness. It is the inner awareness gained in meditation when the senses are disengaged from their objects, and the mind, released from outer activity, is able to turn inwards and settle into itself.

In waking consciousness it is the nature of the senses to be open to receive the impressions with which mind creates its picture of an external world. The mind is bombarded by a continuous stream of external stimuli which overshadow the inner reality of the effulgent Self and obscure the knowledge that it is that Self which assumes the form of the senses and their objects. It is the nature of the mind to turn towards the pleasurable. But such is the value of the inner reality that mind will readily turn away from external influences to enjoy its greater pleasure.

Atha, in a Modern Age

Narayana Guru was however, aware that in the modern age in which he was propounding his revaluation of Vedānta, it

* The chanting of sacred scriptures is traditional in India.

was not sufficient merely to become competent in the pre-*atha* ways described. *Atha* has another value too in this age. So affected are we by the ever-increasing stresses and demands of our time and its lack of spiritual values that we are forced to seek a way out of our predicament. We reach a point of "now then" what is to be done? Then, for the competent, the search for self-knowledge may begin.

Whatever they conceive it to be, all individuals seek satisfaction in life. None are solitary beings; every living thing lives with others as part of a total life system. Within that life system human beings strive for fulfilment and self-contentment. The state of self-contentment can only be gained by harmonizing the discontented self with the world — a world generally perceived to be external, as the other and as even hostile. Oneself and the world need to be seen together as a unified reality. It should be the aim of education to provide this proper understanding (that oneself and the world are not separate nor separable). Man, learning this, may be led to a state of inner peace and peace with his fellow beings. But modern education concerns itself only with perceived external realities and does not lead to self-knowledge. Without self-knowledge the world and "oneself" are perceived as separate and attempts to harmonize the two will fail. When the psyche, the "I," is studied in modern psychology it is viewed as an object. In reality, it is the subject and knower of objects. All our sciences constitute knowledge of "bits" of an external world of infinite particles, waves and mysterious forces. "Now then" (*atha*) — let us desire knowledge of the whole!

The Indisputable Experience of Oneself

Experiencing oneself as a living conscious being is the most immediate and intimate knowledge one has of existence. The knowledge that one exists is indisputable; but what is it knowledge of? It certainly posits a self-aware living organism to which a particular name and particular attributes are attached. But being given, or taking, another name does not change the nature of an organism; so its reality is not in its name nor in any other assumed or attached identity. It may consider itself to be the son or daughter of so and so and the parent of someone else, with this or that profession and status in society. However, these only indicate its activities and relationships and not its underlying nature. It may be a native of this or that country and of this or that race, but these too are superficialities and not its reality. Examining such notions of one's identity reveals that through them one knows nothing of one's own inner reality, let alone that of other entities perceived as having external existences.

In order to know the reality of anything at all it is necessary to know the reality of oneself; to have self-knowledge. It is this knowledge which brings inner peace, fulfilment and self-contentment; the Self-knowledge which in Vedānta is called *ātma-jñāna*. Without it even the most erudite, elevated, wealthy and sophisticated people do not escape the traumas, pains and conflicts of corporeal life. Gaining knowledge of the Self resolves inner problems and only through such knowledge can outer problems and conflicts too be resolved. Man without knowledge of his real nature and being feels himself to be separate from others and from the world. He lives "in" the world as if it were somewhere else — alien and outside himself. So he feels he has to contend with the forces of nature. He feels confined within the boundary of his skin, a solitary, transitory creature, closely identified with a perishable body, the inevitable death of which is a fearful prospect. Indeed, there have been cultures, as in ancient Egypt, which preserved dead bodies in anticipation of their future resurrection. Even now, in some countries, there are those who at great expense contract to have the dead bodies of themselves and their loved ones deep-frozen for such an eventuality.

Yet man intuitively feels that he is something more than just an impermanent organism; that he possesses a soul. This, however, he sees as a sort of in-dwelling shadowy replica of "himself" which he hopes will survive his death and somehow get itself out of the body. About the nature of this surviving entity and its future habitation, he is even more vague than of his incarnate existence here. He longs for immortality and seeks assurances from religion, spiritualism, mysticism, philosophy and so forth. But as he conceives immortality to be only a future indistinct possibility he sets himself to more tangible and attainable earthly goals of wealth, a successful career, status in society and the gratification of his appetites. They are goals which, if attained, he will eventually have to relinquish and they are appetites which, not feeding his inner needs, will leave a nagging dissatisfaction. Such is man's predicament when he is ignorant of his own reality.

Jijñāsā, The Desire for Wisdom

The word *jijñāsā* means "desire for wisdom." One who has that desire is called a *jijñāsuḥ* (seeker). The seeker's desire for wisdom is not based on vanity or mere fancy but is an intense aspiration to know Reality. The intensity of that aspiration generates an element of resolute self-discipline known as *tapas,* a word which literally means "heating up." The search for reality requires *jijñāsā*, resolution, discrimination and the faith that it is an attainable goal; it should not be deflected by dogma, creed, or by any other preconceived ideas or "isms."

Meaning of "Guru"

The seeker may be aided in his search by a teacher who has already attained the sought-for goal. Such an enlightened teacher is known as a *guru,* literally "one who dispels darkness." A *guru* may provide lengthy, detailed instructions, indicate a path through a single cryptic utterance, or teach through silence. The word *brahmaivāham* with which Narayana Guru concludes this first *sūtra* is one of the *mahāvākyas* (great dicta) of Vedānta. The others are: *tat tvam asi* (that thou art), *aham brahma asmi* (I am *Brahman*), *ayam ātmā brahma* (this Self is *Brahman*), and *prajñānam brahma* (*Brahman* is pure Consciousness). Whatever the mode of instruction the seeker needs to reflect deeply on what he hears. The hearing of a *guru*'s instruction is called *śravaṇa* and reflection on it is called *manana*. This reflection convinces the seeker of the truthfulness of the *guru*'s teaching which is confirmed in the seeker's experience in meditation known as *nididhyāsana*.

Narayana Guru's Emphasis on Ātman

Without any polemical arguments or ambiguity, Narayana Guru states in these *sūtras* that the underlying reality is one absolute, unbounded and eternal existence, the nature of which is immortal-bliss-consciousness. In his assertions he restates the inner content of Vedāntic wisdom and the ancient teaching of Bādarāyaṇa. The Guru differs from Bādarāyaṇa, however, in one subtle but very important particular. Whereas Bādarāyaṇa defines Vedānta's objective to be the realization of *Brahman* (the Absolute), the Guru shifts the emphasis to the realization of *ātman* (the Self). This shift is especially noticeable in his philosophical poems in Malayalam. In the best known of these, the *Ātmopadeśa-Śatakam* (One Hundred Verses of Self-Instruction), he expounds Vedānta with all its theoretical and practical implications without using the word *Brahman* at all. The same is true of his works entitled *Advaita-Dīpikā* (Lamp of Non-duality) and *Aṛivu* (Consciousness). In these works he expounds *Brahmavidyā* (the Science of the Absolute) by simply and ingeniously replacing the word *Brahman* with *ātman*, or with the Tamil or Malayalam words meaning "substance," "core," "consciousness" and so on. This is not owing to an unwillingness to use the word *Brahman*, which he uses in his

Sanskrit compositions, viz., *Brahmavidyā-Pañcakam* (Science of the Absolute in Five Verses), and *Darśana-Mālā* (Garland of Visions). His emphasis is on the search for reality as the search for oneself. This "oneself" realized as *ātman* (the One Self) culminates in the knowledge that it is identical with *Brahman* (the Absolute).

The entire edifice of Vedānta is erected upon these two words, *Brahman* and *ātman*. Their connotations and nuances will be examined in later commentary. Here, it suffices if *ātman* is understood as meaning the "I" (*aham*) of the first *sūtra* in which it indicates the underlying Reality of oneself, the one Self identical with *Brahman* — the underlying Absolute Reality of absolutely everything.

The word *Brahman* conceptualizes an all-encompassing Absolute Reality which, unless it is realized in one's own life, remains conceptual and therefore questionable. Philosophies have arisen in India which have not admitted such a concept. Neither Buddhist nihilism nor Sāṁkhya dualism, for example, accepted the reality of an underlying Absolute. Confronting their views Śaṅkara had to argue the case for its existence. In his commentary on Bādarāyaṇa's first *sūtra* he says:

> *Brahman* which is all-knowing and endowed with all powers, whose essential nature is eternal purity, intelligence and freedom, exists.[2]

He further argued for the existence of *Brahman* as the one Self with the following words:

> Moreover the existence of *Brahman* is known on the ground of its being the Self of everyone.[3]

2. *The Vedānta-Sūtras of Bādarāyaṇa*, with the commentary by Śaṅkara, tr. by George Thibaut, New York: Dover Publications Inc., 1962, p. 14.

3. Ibid., p. 14.

A critical enquiry into any philosophical concept should be based upon unshakeable ground. The concept *Brahman*, if unrealized as intimate personal experience, does not present such firm foundation. Narayana Guru therefore preferred to erect the expressions of his monumental thought and vision on the ground of the incontrovertible existence of oneself.

This approach is indicated in the *Bṛhadāraṇyaka Upaniṣad*, where the illustrious *ṛṣi* Yājñavalkya, talking to his wife Maitreyi, states:

ātmā vā are draṣṭavyo śrotavyo mantavyo
nididhyāsitavyaḥ maitreyi

O Maitreyi, the Self verily is to be visualized, to be heard of, to be reflected on, and to be meditated upon.[4]

Every individual experiences his or her own self-existence and whilst the existence of an all-emcompassing Absolute may be questioned, one's own self-existence cannot be denied. Searching for the real nature and content of one's self-evident existence and realizing it as *ātman* is also the realization of Absolute Reality, called *Brahman*.

The desire to know *Brahman* (*brahma-jijñāsā*) is an objective only, but the desire to know *ātman* (*ātma-jijñāsā*) implies both the goal and the means of its attainment. Narayana Guru therefore emphasizes the seeking of *ātman* rather than of *Brahman*, as that enquiry into the nature of oneself which leads to the conclusion:

Brahman indeed am I.

---

4. *Bṛhadāraṇyaka Upaniṣad*, IV.5.6.

Sūtra 2

किं तस्य लक्षणमस्य च कति गणनयेति ॥

kim tasya lakṣaṇam asya ca kati gaṇanayeti ॥

kim	:	what is
lakṣaṇam	:	the defining characteristic
tasya	:	of that
ca	:	and
kati	:	how many
gaṇanayā	:	by consideration
asya	:	of this
iti	:	thus

What defines it and from what standpoints may it be considered?

AN idea or theory is made credible and proved by defining it (*lakṣaṇam*), classifying it (*vibhāga*) and finally verifying it (*parīkṣā*) in the fires of reason (*yukti*) and direct experience (*anubhava*). The first two of these tests, definition and classification, are applied in this second *sūtra*. Verification through reason and experience will be considered later in this work.

Defining the Goal

The goal defined in these *sūtras* is to know *Brahman* (the Absolute), by seeking and attaining knowledge of *ātman* (the Self). The goal of any search has to be clearly defined if it is to be successfully attained. In Sanskrit the definition of an object or objective is called *lakṣaṇam*, a word derived from the root *lakṣ*, meaning to make something perceivable or to mark something out. The word *lakṣaṇam* therefore implies a precise description of something so as to make it perceivable, directly or indirectly, as distinct from other perceptions. The word is sometimes also used in the sense of science as, in the Indian view, science (*śāstra*) should have a well-defined objective.

A proper definition will always clarify the object's essential content (*svarūpa lakṣaṇam*) and differentiating characteristics (*vyāvartaka lakṣaṇam*). As an object may have characteristics in common with others, a description of its general characteristics will not constitute a precise definition. The characteristics particular to that object alone have to be discerned and described without omitting any of them. This is how the definition (*lakṣaṇam*) of a thing is conceived in Indian thought.

The words *kati gaṇanayā* literally mean "How many, on counting in?" In this *sūtra* context they cannot mean "How many selves are there?" for the conclusion reached is that one Self alone has existence and nothing exists apart from it. *Gaṇanā* is understood to mean "proper consideration" and *gaṇanayā*, "on proper consideration." So the question the *sūtra* asks can only mean, "How many standpoints are there from which *ātman* may be properly considered?"

Perspectives of Reality

Science, philosophy and religion all seek, or propound, their conclusive understanding of the reality underlying the perceived world. Their theories and conclusions give rise to many different schools, groupings, sects and creeds, whose beliefs depend upon the positions from which they view reality. The views may be fervently held or fanatically adhered to but Reality remains unaffected by any views attached to it.

Perception of anything at all from one viewpoint is always incomplete. When a percept is examined from a single position, only partial knowledge of it is gained. To gain more knowledge the object of attention must be inspected from two or more different standpoints. For example, both sides of a coin must be inspected to know its value. A magnet generates its mysterious magnetic field between opposite poles, and therefore the knowledge of either one of these implies the existence of the other; so do all qualities imply their opposites. Hot implies cold, light implies dark and pleasure implies pain. All such pairs of opposites are the polarities linking degrees of difference in a spectrum of related values. Even without direct knowledge of imperceptible values, their existence may be inferred by perception of their counterparts. This is also possible in the enquiry into the Ultimate Reality.

In the Indian tradition the method of uniting the two aspects of paired values is known as *yoga-buddhi*, the word *yoga* meaning union and *buddhi* meaning understanding. It is the *yoga* proclaimed in the *Bhagavad-Gītā* and the Upaniṣads and the method known in the West from the time of Plato as "dialectics." Narayana Guru makes use of *yoga-buddhi* in his compositions and, in this *Vedānta-Sūtra* text, considers Reality from the two perspectives of *sat* (existence) and *asat* (non-existence).

Seeking Cause

Modern science seeks explanations **for** perceived phenomena through experiments and calculations based upon data derived **from** perceived phenomena. Scientific enquiry is inevitably bound by the limitations of the technology, hypothesis and methodology upon which the enquiry is based. It is further bound by the preconceptions associated with it and the subjectivity of the observing scientist. Such enquiry is, therefore, more or less empirical.

It may be observed, for example, that one catches cold on getting drenched in the rain. It is natural then to assume that getting drenched in the rain is the cause of catching cold. However, it is also observed that another may get drenched in the rain and not catch cold. This suggests that catching cold may have other causes. In attempting to establish whether getting drenched in the rain is the cause of catching cold, scientifically collated data, based upon observed effects, may provide an answer of sorts but will never reveal an indisputable primary cause.

The data derived, in this case, are based upon the hypothesis that getting drenched in the rain could be the cause of catching cold. The further observation that on getting drenched one does catch cold and another does not may be attributed to some difference in the physical nature of the observed subjects. The physical body, however, is an aspect of nature's total system which also includes the rain. So it might be thought that rain may be **a** cause and, finally, that nature itself is **the** cause of catching cold. The ultimate conclusion is that there is one underlying primary cause of all effects.

The science of modern physics, seeking explanations for the existence of the world, looks far out at the macrocosm and sees unimaginable numbers of galaxies, of unimaginable numbers of stars, at unimaginable distances, speeding away from each other in an ever-expanding universe. It looks deep into the microcosm and finds that the nature of matter at its sub-atomic level is not assertable as particle or wave motion, matter or energy and that its location too is uncertain. This being so, it now includes an "uncertainty principle" in its calculations. Both directions dissolve in the same shimmering infinity and the notion that matter, evolving from matter, is the cause of matter, is no more scientific than the religious belief that the world, in some past time, was created by a being called God.

Mind and Matter

In the modern science of psychology, consciousness is generally thought to arise from the functioning of the physical organ called brain. Brain is therefore thought to be the **cause** of consciousness. The observation that physical damage to brain affects the functioning of mind confirms the belief that brain is the source of mind. Yet it is also observable that stimuli, triggering physical dysfunction, may be of an entirely non-physical nature. The sudden shock of hearing unexpected news, for example, may **cause** a brainstorm, or bring about a heart-attack. Brain is brainless without mind and mind mindless without brain. The faulty perception of mind and matter as separate entities creates the perplexing problem of relating them as cause and effect. Does matter cause mind or does mind cause matter? The realization that they are two functional aspects of one non-dual reality resolves that problem.

Narayana Guru does not see mind and matter as two separable entities. He visualizes mind as one pole and the physical body (extending to the boundless matter of the universe) as the other pole of inseparably-paired values. He sees them simply as two aspects of the creative self-expression of non-dual *ātman*. The Guru expresses the view that to question whether mind is the cause of matter or matter the cause of mind is as meaningless as asking whether the earth exists as particles or particles exist as the earth. The same reality, when viewed from different standpoints, appears to be earth or appears to be particles. Similarly, mind and matter are simply two aspects of one underlying reality. In Verse 74 of the *Ātmopadeśa-Śatakam* the Guru says:

> Particles there are innumerable in the earth and this earth does not exist apart from particles. Matter similarly abides in mind and mind in matter. When cogitated on, they are simply One.

He says in the second verse of *Ātmopadeśa-Śatakam*:

> Mind, senses, body and the many perceived worlds, all, when contemplated, embody the divine form of the Supreme Sun, shining in the sky of transcendence. This should be known through unremitting search.

The "Supreme Sun" of this verse is the self-effulgent *ātman* and what is to be known through "unremitting search" is that mind, senses, body and the many perceived worlds constitute its manifest form.

Confirmation of Theories

Scientific theories are based upon perceived phenomena and preconceived notions — on the perception of matter, for example, and the notion that matter causes mind and matter. As such, scientific theories are subject to revision or, with the acquisition of further data, to complete rejection. They can never provide a final, absolute explanation for existence. In Indian thought, a theory is confirmed and proved as certitude (*pramā*) only when it meets two requirements: one, that it is a new idea of something previously unknown and, secondly, that there is no possibility of it being refuted by any other idea.

It was not Narayana Guru's purpose to examine the prevailing "isms" or theories. His preference was for knowledge that is not conditioned by any popular preconceptions. He was therefore able to determine the standpoints from which reality should be considered in order to arrive at unprejudiced certitude.

That such was his intention is clearly revealed in his *Darśana-Mālā* (Garland of Visions), an original contribution to Vedāntic literature in the Sanskrit language. *Darśana* is a word used to denote "a system of philosophy" but its etymological meaning is "vision" or "visualization." In this work the Guru expresses his vision of non-dual Reality from ten different standpoints and shows how the one Reality may be intuitively perceived from these different positions. Each perspective has a particular colouration yet contributes to the overall vision of non-dual Reality. In this *sūtra* text the Guru limits the number of these perspectives to two and, in so doing, conforms to traditional *sūtra* economy.

Tasya and Asya

The words *tasya* (of that) and *asya* (of this), in this second *sūtra*, both refer to the same Self. Considered as an object of enquiry (as if it were an external entity) the Self seems a distant goal that can be reached only through strenuous effort. But the Self searched for is none other than "oneself," the nearest and most intimate reality of everyone. So the *Īśa Upaniṣad* referring to the Self says:

> It moves, yet moves not.
> It is far, yet is very close.
> It is within all this,
> and also without all this.[1]

Considered as object and therefore externalized, the Self can only be referred to as "that." As subject, that is, as "oneself," it becomes "this." The goal of self-enquiry is the realization — I am "that," known also to be "this." So in posing the question, "From what standpoints may it be considered," Narayana Guru refers to "it," the Self, as *asya*.

The final certitude, the goal of this enquiry, is the experience of a transparent Reality which can be said to be neither "this" nor "that" but which transcends both. In the concluding verse of the *Ātmopadeśa-Śatakam* the Guru says:

> Neither "that" nor "this"
> nor the content of existence am I,

---

1. The *Īśa Upaniṣad*, 5.

but "Existence Consciousness Elixir-Immortal."
Attaining clarity, thus emboldened,
discarding preference for being or non-being;
one should gently, gently merge in *sat auṁ*.

Sūtra 3

तज्ज्योतिः ॥

tajjyotiḥ ॥

tat	:	That
jyotiḥ	:	effulgence is

That, effulgence is.

ALL human beings with a well-functioning nervous system have awareness of their own existence. This awareness is revealed by meditative self-enquiry to be self-luminous. That is to say, it is visible by its own light and does not require illumination from outside to make it apparent. Nor does it need anything outside itself for its confirmation. It cannot be of the essence of darkness, for then there would be no I-sense, no knowledge, only non-aware nothingness. The Guru therefore states that *ātman* is effulgence. Of the essence of light, it is self-luminous and shines forth. In Verse 18 of *Ātmopadeśa-Śatakam* he says:

> "I" is not darkness in essence;
> were it so we would have remained
> unaware of ourselves as "I" "I."
> For the reason that we are aware of ourselves,
> do declare to all that "I" (the Self)
> is not darkness in essence.

Narayana Guru defines the Self as effulgence, light.

In the common understanding of light, certain of its

properties may be asserted. It is known to be radiation from a "light-source." It travels in oscillating straight lines at the enormously high but finite speed of 186,000 miles per second.[1] It may polarize in passing through certain diaphanous structures in its path and it breaks into a spectrum of rainbow colours of different wavelengths, some of which (ultraviolet and infrared) cannot be seen by human eyes, when passing through a prism. It is subject to the gravitational pull and so exhibits characteristics of particled mass. The sun and the stars from which light begins its journey are vast nuclear reactors shining in infinite space. The current theory of astro-physics declares that they were formed from dust clouds created in a big-bang at an infinitely dense point in time estimated to be between ten and twenty thousand million years ago.[2] What it was that banged or where it banged or what was there before that is not, however, explained in that theory. In a religious, mystical or poetic sense, it is just as valid to declare that the sun and stars are torches given by God, the divine light-source, for us to see and delight in. The light radiating from them illuminates, paints with colour and makes visible the bodies in its path but is itself invisible. It passes through the pupil to the retina where it triggers the brain to produce images of an external world, a world thus brought out of darkness. These brain-made images are seen in one's conscious awareness; the light, the seeing and the seen are in consciousness, in "oneself." The light of Consciousness dispels darkness and sees. So the Guru says *tat*, the self-luminous Seer, is effulgence.

Inseparability of Consciousness and Self

Consciousness and Self are regarded as two separable entities by those for whom the effulgence of the self-evident "oneself"

1. *A Brief History of Time*, Stephen Hawking, London: Bantam Press, 1988. *The Universe at Large*, Hermann Bondi, Heinemann, The Science Study Series.

2. Ibid.

is veiled by ignorance. "Oneself" is not perceived as **being** consciousness, but as **having** consciousness. The theories of modern psychology, of the relationship of the "one" to the "other," are postulated on that faulty premise. With the removal of the veil of ignorance, the self-transparency of awareness is revealed and it is seen that Consciousness and Self are one. In the penultimate verse of the *Ātmopadeśa-Śatakam,* the Guru says:

> Consciousness and Self are one
> for one of unveiled awareness.
> Others will have contrary arguments.
> Were consciousness and Self different
> there would be none to know of this Consciousness.

The Words "Brahman," "Ātman" and "Tat"

The Self is referred to in this *sūtra* as *tat* (That). In Vedāntic terminology the word *tat* refers to *Brahman,* and it has to be understood in that sense here. It is not dialectically inconsistent to refer to the Self as *tat,* as in the final certitude, expressed as "*Brahman* indeed am I," both Self and *Brahman* are understood to be one and the same, and the only Reality. Therefore, *tat* should be understood as defining both *ātman* as the Self and *Brahman* as the Absolute.

In the previous *sūtra* it was stated that a precise definition of an object will clarify its essential content and its differentiating characteristics. But the Self, *ātman/Brahman,* all-encompassing and all-pervading Reality, cannot be defined with characteristics differentiating it from the "other" as there is no other apart from it. Therefore, in this *sūtra*'s definition, there is no duality of *svarūpa lakṣaṇam* and *vyāvartaka lakṣaṇam,* but just "That, effulgence is."

The one invisible, pervasive Reality is signified by the Sanskrit word *Brahman,* derived from the root *bṛh* meaning "to grow." *Brahman* then is the ever-growing Reality, manifest here as an ever-expanding universe. In contrast to this immense and seemingly impersonal view of Reality is the intimate, pervasive reality of "oneself" denoted by the word *ātman*. Both words, *Brahman* and *ātman*, are to be understood, in a metaphysical sense, as two perspectives of the one Reality. The realization of this one invisible, indivisible and indestructible pervasive Reality of everything as oneself is Vedānta's goal.

In India's scriptures, the word *ātman* has acquired various shades of meaning. In ordinary usage it means only "I" or oneself, as in the word *ātmaja* meaning son (literally, one born of oneself). In a religious sense it is a synonym for *jīva*, soul, especially in such secondary scriptures as the Purāṇas (legends) and the *Itihāsa*s (epics). It means "I" in a philosophical sense also, as the real content of oneself, and thus to know *ātman* means to know the reality that constitutes oneself. In another philosophical context the word is understood to indicate the consciousness that functions as the knower (*jñātā*), the doer (*kartā*) and the enjoyer (*bhoktā*). Metaphysically, the word means the reality that pervades all phenomena.

Different Upaniṣadic *ṛṣi*s shade the word with different nuances in different contexts. The word, thus, has a range of meanings depending on the context in which it is used. But the differences are not to be taken as having universal validity. Unless the particular context in which the word *ātman* is used in an Upaniṣad is clearly comprehended, it may be misunderstood and may then misrepresent the essential teaching of that Upaniṣad.

Ātman is one of the rare words in Sanskrit having a number of possible etymological derivations. Sanskrit nouns are derived from verb roots and the noun *ātmā* is derived from the roots *ad*, *at* and *āt*. The root *ad* means to eat or enjoy. In the sense of that root *ātman* means the eater or enjoyer and implies the knower and doer too. An entirely different sense is derived from the root *at*, meaning, to be in a state of constant progression. In that sense *ātman* implies the ever-changing creative progression of unchanging Reality. The third root *āt* means "to be pervasive" and, in this sense, *ātman* means the pervading content of all forms whatsoever. This pervading substance is the one material and instrumental cause of all the phenomena of the world of apparent existences, of which "I am" is an integral aspect. These apparent existences of the phenomenal world include both its physical and mental aspects. Both are facets of *ātman* and are modes of the creative self-expression of one, underlying, Absolute Reality. They are analogous to the complementary negative and positive poles of one magnet.

A Vedāntic verse, attributed to no one in particular, defines *ātman* as follows:

> It extends itself as everything,
> It absorbs everything into itself,
> It enjoys objects here,
> It is the perennial substance of the world.
> For these reasons it is glorified as *ātmā*.[3]

A machine made of steel is composed of steel substance. But steel has no form of its own and can only take on the forms it is made to assume. Even when a machine is broken up or melted down its steel substance continues to exist and can be given other forms. Whilst these forms too may in turn be destroyed the steel underlying them continues to exist. Only the forms of steel substance are seen; without form steel is invisible. Conversely without steel there can be no steel forms. Likewise, *ātman* the pervasive substance of all manifest forms, physical and mental, is invisible, apparent only through the forms it takes.

---

3. *yac cāpnoti yad ādatte*
yac cātti viṣayān iha
yac cāsya santato bhāvaḥ
tasmād ātmeti gīyate

One of the Upaniṣads, the *Chāndogya Upaniṣad*, notes the following:

> Just as, my dear, by one clod of clay all that is made of clay becomes known, the modification being only a name arising from speech, while the truth is that it is just clay.
>
> Just as, my dear, by one nugget of gold all that is made of gold becomes known, the modification being only a name arising from speech, while the truth is that it is just gold.
>
> Just as, my dear, by one pair of nail-scissors all that is made of iron becomes known, the modification being only a name arising in speech, while the truth is that it is just iron. Thus, my dear, is that teaching.[4]

Jīva, Jīvātman and Paramātman

The common misconception that *ātman* is a synonym for *jīva* obscures the metaphysical sense of the word *ātman* given in the paragraph above. *Jīva*, understood as an indwelling and animating principle of living beings, is a concept readily acceptable to most people, especially to those with religious views. In Indian thought philosophy and religion are indivisible. Therefore the shift, over time, from the philosophical to the theological sense of *ātman* was not generally noticed or seriously considered. It is the view of the multiplicity of souls held by the theological schools of Vaiṣṇavism and Śaivism which has been most responsible for that shift. In later Vedānta, especially after Śaṅkara, it resulted in the emergence of the concepts of *jīvātman* and *paramātman*, signifying respectively individual soul and universal or supeme soul. These two words do not appear in any of the major Upaniṣads nor in the *Bhagavad-Gītā* and although the *Bhagavad-Gītā* mentions the word *jīva* four times, it is used in a sense not at all related to the concept of *jīvātman*.

---

4. *Chāndogya Upaniṣad*, VI.1.4-6.

Most of the introductory textbooks of the Śaṅkara School of Vedānta use the word *jīva-brahmaikya* (the oneness of soul and *Brahman*) to express the vision of Vedānta, but the word *ātma-brahmaikya* (the oneness of Self and *Brahman*) would have been a more correct expression of that vision. The words *jīvo brahmeti nāparaḥ* (the soul is nothing other than *Brahman*) are often repeated in these textbooks, which, in the understanding of the Śaṅkara School, means that in an individual being, the soul only is real and the body (perceived as non-Self, separate from the soul) is unreal. This, despite the fact that Śaṅkara asserts:

> The soul and all the worlds are Brahman indeed.
> Such is the summary of the teaching of Vedānta.[5]

It should be clearly understood that Vedānta's concept of *ātman*, the pervasive reality of all that appears (gross, subtle, physical, vital and mental), does not exclude the body. Only non-existent nothingness is unreal.

In discriminating between Self and non-Self, Śaṅkara examines the perceptions of gross-body, subtle-body and causal-body and concludes that having no existence apart from the Self they are, if considered apart, non-Self. He saw that the transcendental inner content of every individual living being (*jīva*) is the Self which, in this context, he referred to as *jīvātman*. Misunderstanding his use of the word, his followers took "inner content" to mean an individual, indwelling soul. This error arose from confusing Śaṅkara's vision with his methodology. At an initial stage of his thinking he discriminates between Self and non-Self as a methodological device to show that both are aspects of one non-dual Self. This subtle distinction between the methodology and axiology of Śaṅkara's thought was lost on his followers and they began to identify *ātman* with *jīva*, obscuring the truth that *ātman* is also the reality of the matter considered by them as unreal. The view of a multiplicity of

5. *Vivekacūḍāmaṇi*, v. 478.

individual souls having individual, separate and independent realities is contrary to the teaching of *Advaita-Vedānta* which holds that one Self alone exists and there are no others. Coupled with the erroneous view of the existence of individual souls is the equally erroneous view that multiplicity, arising from one ultimate reality, is appearance only and hence unreal. Appearances too are *Brahman*.

If the concept of *jīva* has a place at all in Vedānta it can only be in its literal sense of *prāṇadhāraṇa*, respiration, "to be in a vitally functioning state." That which sustains this function is called *jīva*. The etymological meaning of *jīva* is "that which survives through breathing" (*jīva-prāṇadhāraṇe*), i.e., a living being. It is, therefore, a purely biological concept. *Ātman*, the pervasive reality in every breathing organism may, in that sense, be called *jīvātman*.

The concepts of *jīvātman* and *paramātman* which emerged from the Śaṅkara school caused much confusion in latter-day Vedānta and so obscured its central teaching that it became virtually impossible to present Vedānta without reference to them. Only Narayana Guru, in his revaluation, avoids the use of those twin concepts, a feature which makes his work unique among post-Śaṅkara Vedānta propounders. The Guru's avoidance of the *jīvātman* and *paramātman* concepts is all the more significant in that they are uniquely those of the Śaṅkara Advaita School. Other schools simply treat *jīva* and *ātman* as synonyms.

It was not Narayana Guru's intention to present his revision of *Advaita-Vedānta* as a rebuttal of the views of other propounders; his primary concern was to restore the clear vision of the Upaniṣadic *ṛṣi*s. It is regrettable that adherents of the traditional view of Vedānta, based upon Śaṅkara's commentaries, may not be open to the originality and clarity of his vision and his restatement of fundamental Vedānta philosophy.

The Nature of "I"

In the spirit of the age of science in which he lived, Narayana Guru, in Verses 10 and 11 of *Ātmopadeśa-Śatakam*, presents an experimental situation which, in precis, is as follows:

> Two men are sitting in the dark. One asks, "Who is there?," to which he receives the reply, "It is I, who are you?" He too answers "It is I."

The question then is to know the real nature and substance of the "I" common to both. In the dark, unaware of anything external, each is aware of his own self-existence, his "I." Progressing from this, the Guru, in Verse 27 of the same work, defines that "I" of common awareness:

> Sitting in the dark, that which is aware of itself is *ātman*, Consciousness Itself, manifesting as names and forms, as mind and senses, as actions and the doer of actions. Behold, what great magic!

Ātman is the consciousness that, even in darkness, is conscious of itself in the light of its own existence. It is this consciousness, which, as Vedānta reveals, is the pervasive substance of each and every being and everything else.

Though blind, we are aware of self-existence; even when deaf, self-awareness remains. If all five senses are withdrawn from their objects and there is no awareness at all of externals, even then awareness of self-existence would continue. That self-effulgent self-awareness, devoid of externals, pure and unconditioned, is *ātman*, the Self of all and everything.

Ātman, Dweller and Dwelling

Any attempt to locate the seat of *ātman* is compared to the gropings of a blind man for a non-existent black cat in darkness. It has no abode yet dwells in, and as, all that is. It dwells even in, and as, the mind that searches for it. It is the dweller and is also the dwelling. The *Bhagavad-Gītā* says:

> He who dwells in the body of everyone
> is eternal and invulnerable, O Bhārata;
> therefore you should not grieve for
> any creature whatsoever.[6]

In some of the Upaniṣads, it is said that *ātman* dwells in a cave within living beings. The cave is to be understood figuratively as the inner mystery of living beings. The *Taittirīya Upaniṣad* says:

> One who knows it as dwelling in the transcendental space within the cave (*guha*), fulfils all desires and attains *Brahman* the all-knowing.[7]

The same Upaniṣad later defines *Brahman* as follows:

> That verily from which all these beings are born,
> that by which when born they live,
> that into which on departing they enter,
> seek for *It*. That is Brahman.[8]

The figurative cave indicates the indistinct abode of the Self which, though in darkness, is fully aware of itself and so, paradoxically, is itself effulgent — *tat jyotiḥ*.

One who is unenlightened, though a seeker, is ignorant. Ignorance is a sort of darkness, yet even the most ignorant are aware of their own self-existence. One has only to be awakened to the perception that one's awareness **is** the Self, to gain the knowledge that the Self **alone** exists and is the underlying reality of all phenomena. Unconditioned Pure Consciousness is without subject-object duality. Awareness of something "other" is of the nature of subject-object duality.

---

6. *Bhagavad-Gītā*, II.30.
7. *Taittirīya Upaniṣad*, II.1.
8. Ibid., III.1.

It is through its own creative urge that from Consciousness knowledge arises and with it the subject-object duality of knower and known. Knowing this is the culmination of knowledge indicated by Vedānta.

That, *tat*, is defined as Effulgence, Effulgence as Consciousness, and Consciousness as Self-Aware-Existence. Each of these is a specific definition of the One-Absolute-Reality which Vedānta refers to as *ātman* and *Brahman*. Whether understood by those two Sanskrit words or by *sat-cit-ānanda* or by the word God, it is the same ultimate Creative-Intelligence, the Being of all beings, in which all knowledge is known.

In identifying and emphasizing *ātman/Brahman* as the self-effulgence of Consciousness, Narayana Guru is restating definitions in certain of the Vedāntic scriptures, such as the following from the *Chāndogya* and *Bṛhadāraṇyaka Upaniṣad*s respectively:

> Of the form of transcendental effulgence.[9]
>
> That God is the light of lights worshipped by mortals as the Immortal.[10]

The *Bhagavad-Gītā* says:

> The light even of lights
> it is said to be
> beyond darkness.[11]

The Guru's definition of *ātman* as effulgence therefore is in keeping with scriptural references as well as direct experience. In some of his other works he uses the words *svayam prakāśam* and *svaprakāśaḥ*, meaning self-luminous and self-illuminating, to emphasize it as self-effulgent.

---

9. *Chāndogya Upaniṣad*, VIII.3-4.
10. *Bṛhadāraṇyaka Upaniṣad*, IV.4.16.
11. *Bhagavad-Gītā*, XIII.17.

Sat-Cit-Ānanda

The most usual definition of *Brahman* is *saccidānanda* (*sat-cit-ānanda*). It is not a definition found in any major Upaniṣad though it does occur in some of the later, minor Upaniṣads; nor is it to be found in the *Bhagavad-Gītā*. It is a concept of a later time developed by combining definitions from two Upaniṣads. These are *satyam jñānam anantam brahma* of the *Taittirīya Upaniṣad* and *satyam jñānam anantam ānandam brahma* from the *Sarvasāra Upaniṣad*. The former means, "*Brahman* is Reality, Consciousness and Infinitude," and the latter means "*Brahman* is Reality, Consciousness, Infinitude and *ānanda*." When these two definitions were merged *satyam* (truth, reality) became simply *sat* (existence, being). The word *anantam* (infinitude) was dropped as its sense is implicit in *sat*. The word *jñānam*, which connotes knowledge, was replaced by *cit*, more precisely meaning "Pure Unconditioned Consciousness," that is Consciousness with no "other" to be conscious of.

Narayana Guru expresses *ātman/Brahman* as *saccidānandam*, explicitly or implicitly, in many of his compositions. In his work entitled *Daivadaśakam* (Ten Verses to God), he addresses God as *satyam jñānam ānandam* (another version of *sat-cit-ānanda*). The words *sat* and *satyam* are often interchanged as synonyms, though in the latter there are connotations of appearance and morality. The Guru concludes the second chapter of his *Darśana-Mālā* with the words: *sarvam hi saccidānandam neha nānāsti kiñcana* (everything here indeed is *sat-cit-ānanda* and there is nothing else existing). The final verse of *Ātmopadeśa-Śatakam* refers to *ātman* as *saccidāmṛtam* (Existence-Consciousness-Elixir/Immortal). Narayana Guru's vision embraces all these terms in his definition of *tat* as effulgence.

SAT

The word *sat* does not simply mean existence in a general sense, but implies the one Existence which is infinite, unchanging, indestructible and indivisible. The *Bhagavad-Gītā* says:

> Weapons cannot cleave him, nor fire burn him;
> water cannot wet him, nor wind dry him away.
> He is uncleavable, he cannot be burned,
> he cannot be wetted, nor yet can he be
> dried. He is eternal, all-prevading,
> stable, immovable, ever the same.[12]

The *Sarvasāra Upaniṣad* defines *sat* as follows:

> Existence is the indestructible one; that which endures, incapable of being destroyed. In those which are destroyable, due to spatiality, temporality and materiality, is the indestructible. It is known as *sat*.[13]

The changing phenomenal forms of manifest existence, the forms of all transitory beings and all temporal appearances, cannot be said to be the unchanging *sat*. Only the underlying never-changing reality assuming those forms is *sat*. In the *Brahmavidyā-Pañcakam*, Narayana Guru describes *sat* in these words:

> That which pervades everything, living and non-living, as pots and plates and such are pervaded by clay. That, of which the creative upsurging from within is this world, this world in essence is the same. That unborn essence of Existence, into which all on dissolution are absorbed and continue. Understand that as the Real (*satyam*), to which those of uncontaminated understanding make prostrations to attain Immortality.[14]

Invisible *sat* is not only imperceptible to sight but also to all other senses. Mind cannot conceive it; it transcends mind. The invisible nature of *sat* has never been perceived by anyone at all through the senses, nor has it ever been understood in the

---

12. *Bhagavad-Gītā,* II.23-24.
13. *Sarvasāra Upaniṣad,* III.
14. *Brahmavidyā-Pañcakam,* v. 3.

human mind, yet its invisible existence is known through its visible effects as without it nothing visible can appear. Just as a steel pin cannot appear without the substance of steel, so the forms of existence cannot appear without the substance of existence. The knowledge of *sat* is located only in consciousness and is itself a manifestation of consciousness. Existence without consciousness cannot be known even to itself and so has no reality. Consciousness without existence has no being. Being only in consciousness, *sat* **is** Consciousness, which is called *cit* in Sanskrit and that existing *cit* therefore **is** *sat*.

CIT

In Verse 50 of the *Ātmopadeśa-Śatakam*, following a detailed and progressive analysis of the common "I" "I" identity, Narayana Guru reveals that all is not other than *cit*, Pure-Unconditioned-Consciousness. He says:

> Earth, water, air and fire, space and I-sense, knowledge and mind, waves and ocean, in short everything — these, in the awakened, are transformed as *cit*.

The visible world is the world perceived by the senses. With the eyes we see only a small semi-circle called the visual field. The world outside that field is a logical extension conceived by mind. Its existence is taken for granted on the supposition that it can be reached and actualized in experience. In the very small field of the senses objects are first cognized, then encountered again, and are re-cognized. The recognition of anything implies prior knowledge of its existence. When not in awareness, that pre-knowledge must exist in a "somewhere" from where it can return to awareness. That somewhere, in Western psychology, is called the "sub-conscious" and its seat is thought to be the brain, where memories are supposedly stored much as information is stored on a computer disc. That may indeed be so in mechanistic terms but machines, whilst able to store information, are not themselves intelligent; they do not know the information they store. Knowledge is nowhere else but in consciousness; it may be known in an aware mind or it may transcend mind's perception. Knowledge must exist before it can be known and must be known before it can be re-known, re-cognized.

A bottle cannot be recognized as a bottle unless the knowledge "bottle" already exists in consciousness. In other words, a bottle is perceived to be a bottle only when the concept of bottle is already in mind; the recognition comes when we identify its known qualities of shape, colour, transparency, function and so on.

A rose is recognized by its distinctive form, colour, fragrance and other particular qualities. Only the distinguishing characteristics of bottle and rose are perceived; bottle and rose as entities in themselves are invisible. Bottle, rose and all else, perceived by mind as having external existence, exist nowhere but in Consciousness, *cit*. Mind is nothing but a functional mode of that very same Consciousness.

Thus the visible world is created in individual minds as constantly changing mental images of constantly changing sensory inputs. Yet each mind feels assured that it is identical with the world in the minds of others. In reality the mental images in the mind of an individual being are not accessible to any other individual. All experiences are configurations of consciousness, manifestations of the infinite *cit*.

In Verse 32 of the *Ātmopadeśa-Śatakam* Narayana Guru observes as follows:

> It is not the substance but attributes only that are seen, the substance remains invisible. As the world in which all attributes are perceived is invisible, it has no existence except as a configuration of *cit*: do understand.

In his *Advaita-Dīpikā* he illustrates this with an analogy:

The cloth here is but cotton threads,
These in turn are seen to be nothing but fibres,
these fibres nothing but an aggregate of elements.
Speculated on thus, just as water seen in a mirage,
it may be traced to its source in *cit*.
Cit is indeed the ultimate Reality.[15]

In his *Darśana-Mālā* the Guru says:

> Nothing other than *cit* manifests itself, therefore other than *cit* nothing exists. That which does not manifest itself is non-existent, neither does the non-existent manifest itself.[16]

Sometimes, Narayana Guru uses the word *pratipat* as a synonym for *cit*. The human mind, in its cyclical modes of waking, dreaming and deep-sleep, has *pratipat* as its underlying reality. The self-luminous awareness which each individual identifies as "I" is nothing other than that. When Indians put their hands together to greet one another with a respectful *praṇām*, it is the *pratipat* in both they are acknowledging. Referring to *cit* as the creative *pratipat*, the Guru says:

> Having created this world through *prakṛti*, that which enters it and by which the created world is sustained from within, because of which one becomes an individual being, enjoying distinct objects, and because of which "I" becomes *prājña* in deep-sleep, a minute part of which scintillates in everyone as "I" sense, in respect of which we greet each other. That consciousness, *pratipat*, that perfect one, art thou indeed, do hear![17]

ĀNANDA

Ānanda is a Sanskrit word with no satisfactory equivalent in English. It is usually given as Happiness with a capital H or

15. *Advaita-Dīpikā*, v. 3.
16. *Darśana-Mālā*, II.8.
17. *Brahmavidyā-Pañcakam*, v. 4.

Bliss with a capital B, but neither of these words are adequate to communicate its subtle nuances. In an individual consciousness there is always an element of sensation, emotion or mood, informing the individual of the value of different perceptions. Such value perceptions arise from the *ānanda* aspect of the Self. Ultimate *ānanda*, the *ānanda* of *sat cit*, is the absolute value sensing state of *ātman* in which there is nothing other than *ātman* to be sensed. It is the state of absolute fullness, in which there is nothing lacking, nothing other to be desired, a state of Self's contentment in Itself alone. Perhaps "Supreme Unconditioned Contentment" is as close to expressing this *ānanda* as is possible in English.

By knowing what is real in oneself, what is real in all becomes known; the knowledge of oneself becomes knowledge of all. Enlightenment, *ātmajñāna*, wisdom of the Self, thus becomes *brahmajñāna*, wisdom of the Absolute. Its attainment is the culmination of the search for Self-knowledge and brings release from the bondage of unfulfilled longings. Attachments to worldly gains and sensory pleasures are loosened, and stability and equanimity in meeting the many ups and downs of life are attained. That fulfilment is an expression of *ānanda*, called *priyam*, dearness, meaning the dearest of all.

Confusion and conflicts arise only in the diverse objects involved in the expression of *ānanda*. Underlying all confusions and all conflicts is *ānanda*'s harmony, *ānanda*'s dearness. The Guru says:

> Dearness is one in kind, the confusion of "this is dear to me," "that is dear to you," "something else is dear to a third," arises only in respect to the objects of dearness.[18]

That which exists, *saccidānanda*, is not inert. It is Creative

18. *Ātmopadeśa-Śatakam*, v. 21.

Intelligence which, through its own impulse, manifests itself as a world of ever-changing forms and qualities. This self-expression of *sat-cit-ānanda* is known as *prakṛti*. The prefix *pra* means "in the proper way" and *kṛti* means "action." The etymological meaning of *prakṛti* therefore is "properly conducted action." It is usually translated as "Nature" and frequently referred to as "Mother Nature."

In *prakṛti*, Mother Nature's realm of manifest relative existence, *ānanda*, imbuing everything with value, is the link connecting the entire system of life. No living creature exists by itself or is independent of others; each individual is dependent on others for reproduction, nourishment and maintenance. Each transitory life, mysteriously appearing, staying for a while and then disappearing, is connected in an incessant flow from source back to source. It is the creative self-expression of *ānanda*, called *prakṛti*, "Nature," or "the world." In the *Darśana-Mālā*, Narayana Guru says:

> *Ānanda* alone exists and manifests itself, nothing else has existence. Everything is *ānanda* in essence; without *ānanda* nothing exists.[19]

He continues:

> All is *saccidānanda*.
> No multiple realities exist here.
> One who sees multiplicity
> goes from death to death.[20]

The "effulgence" of Narayana Guru's definition of *tat* is the effulgence of *sat-cit-ānanda*.

---

19. *Darśana-Mālā*, II.9.

20. Ibid., II.10.

Sūtra 4

तेनेदं प्रज्वलितम् ॥

tenedaṁ prajvalitam ॥

tena	:	By That
idam	:	this world
prajvalitam	:	is illumined

By That this world is illumined.

HAVING defined *ātman* as self-effulgent Consciousness and the pervading reality of "oneself," Narayana Guru now defines it to be the cause, effect, substance, illuminator and the only pervading reality of the world.

The world can only be said to exist through its constituent entities, living and non-living. As all these are of transitory nature the emergence of this world, of transient ever-changing phenomena, must also augur its eventual dissolution. The existence of this continually changing world must have a changeless reality as its basis. That unchanging reality, the basis, cause, and substance of the ever-changing world, is what Vedānta calls *ātman*, the Self.

It is *ātman* which assumes the phenomenal phases of birth, life and death, known in Sanskrit as *sṛṣṭi, sthiti* and *saṁhāra* or *laya*. Indian philosophy recognizes six distinct phases in life. These are: *asti* (being), *janma* (birth), *vṛddhi* (growth), *pariṇāma* (transformation), *apakṣaya* (decline), and *vināśa* (dissolution).

As nothing can emerge from nothingness, an indeterminate beingness (*asti*) is considered to be anterior to birth, which is simply to say that in order to be born something must first exist. It is this unborn being which appears in the changing phases of life, itself undergoing no intrinsic change. Even after the final phase of dissolution it continues to exist. The *Bhagavad-Gītā* declares:

> These bodies are known to have an end;
> the dweller in the body is eternal,
> imperishable, infinite.[1]

Casting off the body, like a worn-out garment, it completes a life cycle and donning the garb of a new body begins a new life cycle. With this perspective, life is understood in the Vedānta philosophy as a beginningless and endless cyclic process, the substance of which is *ātman*. As the H_2O molecule remains unchanged through all its many transformations as water, steam, ice, snow, cloud, rain, river and ocean, so *ātman* continues unchanged in all the many changing forms of the world. Narayana Guru makes this explicit in his *Darśana-Mālā*:

> That which causes the six phases, existence, birth, growth, transformation, decline and dissolution, is none other than the actionless Self.[2]

Cause and Effect

The theory of causation states that the appearance of anything at all is an effect which must have some underlying cause. In Sanskrit, an effect is called *kārya* and cause, *kāraṇa*. In Western philosophy causes are differentiated as the material cause, efficient cause, formal cause and final cause. The Indian tradition recognizes only the first two of these; the latter two are considered to be subsumed in efficient cause, called *nimitta-*

1. *Bhagavad-Gītā*, II.18.
2. *Darśana-Mālā*, VI.8.

kāraṇa. Material cause is called *upādāna-kāraṇa* and implies the substance from which objects are formed as, for instance, clay from which clay pots are formed. Of these, the potter, his visualization, his tools and his work, together constitute the *nimitta-kāraṇa*. The material cause of the world is *ātman* and, there being no other reality, *ātman* is also the efficient cause. In this sense *ātman* is called the *abhinna-nimittopādāna-kāraṇa*, a composite word which encompasses both causal meanings.

The ocean appearing as waves undergoes no intrinsic change; similarly *ātman* appearing as the world undergoes no intrinsic change. Cause appearing as effect without undergoing any intrinsic change is called *vivarta* in Sanskrit. The theory of the illusory appearance of the world is called *vivarta-vāda*, the suffix *vāda* indicating a prevailing theory. Narayana Guru expresses this in Verse 3 of the *Ātmopadeśa-Śatakam*:

> All that is seen here as external existence is illusory. The elements fire, space and such, when pondered upon, should be understood, like lines of waves arising from ocean's treasury of water, to have no separate reality.

Effect, following cause, becomes cause of following effect and both are as sequential frames in an unwinding reel of film of the same picture show. As no creation takes place in this concept of the world's being it is known in the Vedānta philosophy as *ajāta-vāda* (the theory of non-creation).

Admitting this view the Guru, in his *Darśana-Mālā*, observes as follows:

> Apart from cause there is no effect.
> Therefore all this world is unreal.
> For the unreal how can there be an origin?
> and of the unoriginated, what dissolution?[3]

When, in the context of this verse, the Guru says "all this

3. *Darśana-Mālā*, II.2.

world is unreal" he means only that it has no reality apart from its essence. He does not deny that it is actual and experienced as such; just as waves have no reality apart from the ocean, but as a configuration of the ocean are actual and experienceable. Vedānta is not, as it is sometimes misconstrued to be, a denial of life's actualities. In Verse 88 of the *Ātmopadeśa-Śatakam,* Narayana Guru says:

> Everything is real in itself;
> one who grasps this basic truth
> understands that all this is One.
> If through apperception this is not known
> *māyā,* the great enemy, causes much confusion.

The ancient Indian theory of evolution, called *pariṇāma-vāda,* is in marked contrast to *vivarta-vāda*. It postulates that space evolved from *ātman* (the original cause), air evolved from space, fire from air, water from fire, earth from water and so on. The most familiar modern concept of evolution is the Darwinian theory of the origin of species, which postulates a struggle for survival and survival of the fittest. It is a theory of the evolution of specific living forms that deals with mainly their transformations rather than their creation or origin.

Vedānta does not subscribe to such theories of gradual, consecutive creation. It perceives the constant transformation of forms as an expression of the continually unfolding creative impulse of the Self. If creation is admitted at all, it is the instantaneous creation called *yugapat-sṛṣṭi* which equates to the appearance of the world at the moment of waking from sleep. Narayana Guru in his *Darśana-Mālā* says:

> Not at all from the sun by stages did the world come to be, but appeared all at once from the Self, instantaneously, as if by its own vision on waking from deep sleep.[4]

4. *Darśana-Mālā,* I.9.

Evolutionary theories postulate that cause undergoes intrinsic changes, as milk, for example, curdles to become something which plainly is different from milk. In the contrary perspective of *vivarta-vāda* changes of form, having only one underlying reality, are regarded as illusory. The primal cause alone, undergoing no intrinsic change, is considered real. Effects, having no substantial separate existence, are considered as unreal. Consequently *vivarta-vāda* is also known as *sat-kāraṇa-vāda* (the theory that cause alone is real). This is not the view of *sat-kārya-vāda* which considers that effects, not different from cause, are also real. Narayana Guru expresses that view in the *Darśana-Mālā*:

> Not different from cause, how can effect be existent? And how, for the same reason, can there be non-existence of cause?[5]

The one primal cause of the world is the Self, *ātman*. The unending chain of transformations emanating from it, alternately perceived as cause and effect, are not different in reality and cannot therefore be considered *anātmā* (non-Self), as is the mistaken view of a good many post-Śaṅkara Vedāntins. If the world is to be considered non-Self, it can only be as a means of differentiating apparent from transcendent reality and as an aid in the seeker's aspiration for self-knowledge. Śaṅkara himself made good use of that device. Through it, the seeker finally realizes that what, at the beginning of his enquiry, was considered *anātmā* (non-Self) and as illusory appearance, is nothing other than *ātman* appearing as the world. The world, non-existent apart from the Self, is an expression of the Self and therefore is not unreal. The Guru says in his *Darśana-Mālā*:

> The world, both gross and subtle in nature,
> emerged from *cit*.

5. *Darśana-Mālā*, II.4.

> If its existence is affirmed it exists as *sat.*
> If denied, it exists as *cit.*[6]

The words *sat* and *cit* simply indicate two different aspects of the one *ātman*. And so, seen from either perspective, *ātman* is the world's one Causal Substance.

For no other purpose than its own innocent pleasure a child will use whatever is at hand to create an imaginary play-world. It is an expression of the child's creative imagination given external form. Similarly the child emerges and has being as an aspect of the creative self-expression of *ātman*, rising as a joyous impulse of its own *ānanda*. It is the same *ānanda* which sparkles and reverberates in the child and urges on its creative play.

The child's self-expression creates a world often not comprehended by the conditioned minds of its elders. In the same way the creative self-expression of *ātman* projects a world of infinite forms and qualities not comprehended in minds conditioned by erroneous historical, cultural and religious views. The cosmic impulse of creative self-expression is perceived in Vedānta to be the *līlā* (joyous sport) of *ātman*, actualizing and expanding its *ānanda* through innumerable manifestations.

It is *ānanda* which links all manifest entities in the total structure of the world and connects all living organisms in ecological interdependence. A fruit tree blossoms and provides nectar for the honey bees which reciprocate its hospitality by pollinating its flowers and ensuring its progeny. The tree fruits and is fulfilled in providing sweet nourishment to all manners of creatures, who carry off its seeds which germinate and grow elsewhere. The soil in which the trees grow, the air, water and sunlight give their gifts to the earth's family and all are thus sustained and fulfil their purposes. An invisible thread of *ānanda* joins every minute particle of the world in

6. *Darśana-Mālā*, II.1.

ineffable, structural perfection. In the *Bhagavad-Gītā*, Kṛṣṇa, as *ānanda* incarnate, tells Arjuna:

> This universe is strung upon me as pearls on a thread, O Wealth-Winner. I am the taste in water, the radiance in moon and sun, the Word *AUṀ* in all the Vedas, sound in the air and manhood in men. The scent in earth am I, the heat in fire and the life in all born beings. Know me to be the eternal seed of all birth, the understanding of those who understand and the splendour of the splendid.[7]

Narayana Guru reveals this holy secret in the *Ātmopadeśa-Śatakam*:

> To know itself and its own nature here, *cit* transforms itself as specific manifestations, such as earth and other elements; which are like the tip of an ever-glowing firewood stick spiralling up, back and forth and turning round.[8]

Tapas

Sat, *cit* and *ānanda* are inseparable aspects of the Self. The why and how of manifestation are equally inseparable. The creative impulse of pure unconditioned *saccidānanda* necessary for it to manifest itself as the conscious mind and the world of forms and qualities, is portrayed in some of the Upaniṣads as a sort of *tapas*. The word has the literal meaning of heating up or brooding over, and is generally understood to mean the spiritual practice of self-imposed austerities. In this view the world came into being through the brooding over of the Self, as if by the hatching of an egg.

The *Taittirīya Upaniṣad* describes the process as follows:

> He desired; let me become many, let me be born. He underwent *tapas*. Having undergone *tapas* he created all this, whatever is here. Having created it he entered therein, indeed. Having entered it, he became both the actual and

7. *Bhagavad-Gītā*, VII.7-10.

8. *Ātmopadeśa-Śatakam*, v. 33.

the beyond, the defined and the undefined; both the founded and the unfounded, understanding and non-understanding, the true and the untrue. As the Real, he became whatever is real here. That is why all here are considered to be real.[9]

The Self, having manifested the world through *tapas*, looks at it and finds Itself as its only Reality. Through self-actualization it realizes its Self in *ānanda*.

The *tapas* of the all-pervading *Brahman* and the *tapas* practised by seekers for spiritual discipline are as two sides of a coin. The cosmic *tapas* realizes the Self through becoming the world; the *tapas* of the seeker realizes the world as the Self. The impulse of Creative Intelligence arises from its source in *ātman* to seek knowledge of Itself through its own creation. Man, one of these creations, searches for knowledge of his source and returns to it in the mystic union of Self-realization. So the circle of *tapas* is completed and the *līlā*, the joyous game of the Self, is fulfilled. The *Bhagavad-Gītā* depicts that *līlā* in the following words:

By virtue of my own nature I emanate this
whole aggregate of beings again and again.
Powerless they are and subject to the
compulsion of my *prakr̥ti*.[10]

Under my sway nature gives birth to
all things, living and not living. Through this,
O Son of Kunti, the world revolves.[11]

Prakr̥ti

Nature, *prakr̥ti*, is not separate from the Self but is the creative impulse of the Self to manifest and diversify. Inherent in *prakr̥ti*

9. *Taittirīya-Upaniṣad*, II.6.

10. *Bhagavad-Gītā*, IX.8.

11. Ibid., IX.10.

is action (*kṛti*) without which there can be no "Nature." Nature is the field of action, the field of actualization and the field of change. In Indian tradition, it is the field of the *guṇas*, the three modalities of Nature called *sattva* (pure, clear, supportive and neutral), *rajas* (active, forceful, positive) and *tamas* (dark, inert, resistant and negative). Nature is the actionless Self giving rise to action through these modalities. Narayana Guru defines it with the following words:

> That which spontaneously performs the
> diversifying actions of the *guṇas*;
> it is called *prakṛti*.[12]

Karma

Another word for *kṛti* is *karma*, meaning action or work. *Karma* is defined in the *Bhagavad-Gītā* as the specific creative urge inherent in *akṣaram brahma paramam* (the "Imperishable Supreme Absolute"), which causes the emergence of beings.[13]

Actions, although apparently performed by individual beings, are in reality those of the Self in Nature's field of *māyā*. Narayana Guru describes this in the *Darśana-Mālā*:

> Though unattached to actions, the Self indeed
> performs *karma* through *māyā*.
> Like the function of self-luminous *taijasa*
> while in sleep.[14]

The word *taijasa* literally means "that which is bright and luminous." In Indian psychology *taijasa* is the name given to the functional state of unconsciousness in which dreams arise and are perceived in sleep.

Vedānta views *karma* as belonging to the Self alone and

12. *Darśana-Mālā*, IV.10.
13. *Bhagavad-Gītā*, VIII.3.
14. Ibid., IV.1.

not to individual beings. The mistaken belief that each born being has individual *karma* has taken root deeply in Indian minds. It causes people to take upon themselves a heavy but quite imaginary kārmic burden. The *Bhagavad-Gītā* says of this:

> The Supreme Lord creates neither the authorship
> of action in beings, nor their *karma*,
> nor the link between *karma* and its fruits.
> It is carried out by His own innate urge
> manifesting as all these.[15]

All of man's creativity, his cities and magnificent buildings, his music and dance, his works of art and his wondrous machines and technology, all are expressions of the one creative Self. Man's creativity is a subtle aspect of those infinite Self-expressions, as also are the free will and self-enquiry which enable him to probe into the very source of his being and to know himself as both creature and creator. There are no contradictions in this view, merely different perspectives of the same reality. Many seeming contradictions are reconciled in Vedānta, a philosophy propounding that both this and that are real, and not that either this or that is real.

All man's notions of his authorship and responsibility in *prakṛti*'s field are modes and functions of the one and the same *prakṛti* in him and all beings. Realizing this enables him to offer back to *prakṛti* that which he wrongly took as his own and free himself from *karma-bandha*, the bondage to action and its fruits. It is the offering back symbolized by the *yajña* (burnt sacrifice), the most important of Vedic rites. Giving up that burden is *mokṣa*, the liberation longed for by seekers of the Self. It is not a philosophical concept, nor is it a matter of religious faith, nor a conclusion reached through reason and logic; it is a simple fact, a state of being which one may intimately experience. Through it one can continue to act and enjoy the

15. *Bhagavad-Gītā*, V.14.

fruits of Nature's actions without their previous binding attachments. Those who take upon themselves the authorship of action remain in bondage. The *Bhagavad-Gītā* says:

> Actions in every case are performed by
> the *guṇa*s of nature. He who is deluded
> by a sense of "I" holds himself the doer.[16]

One freed of the delusion of "I am the doer" sees in his actions the functioning of Nature's modalities, the *guṇa*s, and is released from their binding influence. One, then, does not become careless in actions or irresponsible in the performance of them. Freed of ego's false sense of responsibility he develops a higher sense of responsibility to that which acts through him. He will wish to offer back his actions, with reverence and devotion, to the Real Doer of actions. A greater love and respect for all other living beings will grow in him and his actions will reflect his desire for their good. He will act and enjoy without harming, without desiring and without attachments. It is in that light that *niṣkāma-karma*, the desireless action of the *Bhagavad-Gītā*, is to be understood.

All phases of creation, maintenance and dissolution, whether of an individual being or the whole world, involve *karma*. This incessant flow of action, the creative process, is analogous to waves rising on the surface of an ocean which appear for a while, and then fall and disappear back into the ocean. Before their appearance, during their apparent existence and after they are gone, all that really exists is the water of their substance. The birth, life and death of waves are merely changing configurations appearing on the surface of the changeless ocean. So the birth, life and death of all beings are the transitory configurations appearing on the surface of the changeless ocean of Infinite Reality. Narayana Guru calls this Reality *samvit-sāgara* (the ocean of Consciousness). In his words:

16. *Bhagavad-Gītā*, III.27.

Like waves rising on the ocean,
bodies one by one, incessantly
arise and then merge back.
Ah! where is an end to this?
It is simply the ceaseless *karma* inherent
in the primal ocean of Consciousness.[17]

Māyā

The great mystery of the world's appearance and its ever-changing forms is expressed in the Vedāntic concept of *māyā*. It is the mystery of the Self emerging as the world, veiled by the world. Through *māyā* the externals of the world and all its numberless separate aspects are perceived as real, whilst its underlying single Reality is not perceived.

As the watery ocean does not remain without waves, so the ocean of Unconditioned Consciousness does not remain inactive. Its potential for activity is unbounded, and so immense and potent it is that it manifests itself in infinite expressions, as everything. It is all physical elements, all qualities, the totality we call the world. It is the numerous worlds of ancient mythology and modern astronomy; the worlds imagined and the worlds perceived. It is all the phenomena, physical and mental, in all the worlds. It is mind and mind's functions and all its conceptions. It is the ceaseless flux of the Self's reality. It is the endless *māyā* in Consciousness. The Guru says:

In the waveless ocean is endless *māyā*,
immense, potent, assuming beginningless
and endless effects, as water and its taste,
as all the worlds of ever changing forms.[18]

The Vedāntic concepts of *māyā* (illusion) and *avidyā* (nescience) are contentious issues among commentators of Bādarāyaṇa's

17. *Ātmopadeśa-Śatakam*, v. 56.

18. Ibid., Verse 57.

Brahma-Sūtras, which overshadow the meaning of that work and obscure the author's vision. It is noticeable that Narayana Guru, in his *Vedānta-Sūtras*, avoids the use of those controversial concepts and expresses a pure, pristine vision of Vedānta without introducing them at all.

All that is perceived in the relative field of phenomenal existence as creation, sustenance, dissolution, birth, life and death is the *līlā*, the endless play of, and in, the transcendent Consciousness of *ātman*. The Guru states:

> Know all this as the divine sport of *cit*,
> without beginning and endlessly playing;
> within itself.[19]

That, which is both appearance and substance, which is called *ātman, sat-cit-ānanda, Brahman*, is the one and only Absolute Reality. Self-effulgent, it is the source of all light and all illumination. So it is that Narayana Guru says: *tenedam prajvalitam* (By That this world is illumined).

Yet the Guru does not consider the world to be merely an illuminated reflection of the Effulgent Self. Some schools of Vedānta, particularly that of Madhva, view soul as a reflection (*pratibimba*) of *Brahman*, the original (*bimba*). Such a view can only be relevant when it is considered that Ultimate Reality (*Brahman*) and apparent reality (*māyā*, the world) are separate and distinct. A reflection implies a separately reflecting original; but being a form assumed by the original, the world and its original are not separate. The world though illusory while appearing to be self-contained and distinct is not removed from Reality and is not unreal. It is neither the reflection of an original nor is it itself an original.

Narayana Guru expresses this paradoxical existence in the following words:

---

19. *Ātmopadeśa-Śatakam*, Verse 34.

> There can be no shadow without an originating form.
> No such form exists of which the world is a shadow.
> Neither shadow nor original, it is like the image
> of a snake painted by a talented artist.[20]

An image pre-existing in the mind of a talented painter and projected by him on to the canvas may be seen as a work of art. A viewer, while perceiving its material existence to be paint and canvas, may also discern the life and creative intelligence of the artist behind it. The image may be painted so realistically that if it is, for example, an image of a snake it may invoke fear in the mind of a viewer who fears snakes. Whatever the image is perceived to be, the minds of the artist and viewer are united in its vision. In the union of that shared vision the artist communicates both his existence and creativity and thus the work of art fulfils its purpose. So too, when the mind of the world's Creator (God, the Self) and the mind of the world's perceiver (man, the seeker) are united in a vision of the world, then God's presence and creative intelligence are communicated and the world's purpose is fulfilled.

That which is seen as separate and real may appear threatening and cause fear in the mind of the perceiver. The famous Vedāntic analogy of a rope in a dimly-lit place appearing to be a snake is an example of that situation. As fear is generated by that which is seen as separate from "oneself," the world seen as a separate reality may be frightening. When its reality is not other than oneself (the one Self), it is also realised that there is nothing other to fear and fearfulness disappears. Such fearlessness is gained with the realization of *Brahman*.

Physical science has examined matter from its outmost substantial appearance to its molecular structure, elemental atoms, to the level of sub-atomic particles. Beyond this, a union

20. *Ātmopadeśa-Śatakam*, Verse 85.

of three forces, called "quarks," has been discerned and the limits of perceptible substance have been reached. Science has revealed that matter is a form of energy, a revelation which is expressed in Albert Einstein's famous formula $E = mc^2$. Although the fundamental nature of matter/energy has not been scientifically established, it is known that it can be endlessly transformed but cannot be destroyed. A fundamental particle can, for example, be caused to transform to the energy of an atomic explosion but, existing, cannot be made to cease to exist. Indestructible and appearing in its innumerable forms as the world, matter/energy is the manifestation of energetically vibrating Consciousness itself.

The world is experienced both objectively and subjectively, as external existence and inner perception. The Guru likens this to two creepers growing together over a tree and concealing it with their dense foliage:

> From *cit* emerges a sense of "I" and
> with it a sense of "this." Like two
> vines they spread over the tree of *māyā*
> and hide it from view.[21]

Phenomena, emanating from Self-Effulgent Reality, are not merely seen in Its light but, in essence, are of Its light. All is *ātman*, all is Effulgence: *tenedam prajvalitam.*

---

21. *Ātmopadeśa-Śatakam*, Verse 51.

Sūtra 5

तदिदं सदसदिति ॥

tad idam sad asad iti ॥

tat	:	That
idam	:	this (the world) (considerable)
sat	:	(as) existent
asat	:	non-existent
iti	:	as

That, as the world here, is (considerable) as existent and non-existent.

THIS *sūtra* answers the question asked in the second part of *sūtra* 2: ". . . from what standpoints may it be considered?"

The luminous world of appearances exists as an expression of Self-effulgent *ātman* and so it was emphasized that the world, having *ātman* as its sole content and substance, is also real. Now, however, Narayana Guru discriminates between "That" and "this world" as Reality (*sat*) and appearance (*asat*).

The constituents of the world are its ever-changing transient forms — emerging, sustained for a while, then dissolving back into the mystery from which they appeared. In this they are analogous to gold ornaments which may be continually melted down and changed into other forms without any intrinsic change in their gold substance. In Vedānta the Real is considered to be that which exists eternally, unchanged through all its changing expressions. In this particular sense, the Guru refers to the relative, transitory forms of the world as *asat* and its unchanging substance, *ātman*, as *sat*. To consider the world as *asat*, in this sense, is not to deny its actuality. To know things as they appear to be is *yathārtha-jñāna* (factual knowledge) and to know what is fundamentally real in all appearances is *paramārtha-jñāna* (knowledge of the ultimate).

The world of *prakṛti*, Nature, the field of action, is present as an immense variety of specific forms, qualities and transactional events; but these are only as sparkings of the self-effulgent Self. An enlightened knower of Reality perceives the relative, multiple, transitory forms of the world as unreal in themselves and real as forms assumed by their one pervasive substance.

From Outer to Inner

Such a vision of Reality requires the attention to be turned from the outer world of sense perceptions to the inner realm of oneself through the practice called meditation. Meditation is not a process of introspection involving self-judgement. It is not to inspect one's inner functions — the automatic physical, mental and emotional functions of thinking, intellect, mood, breathing, pulsating and feeling. Nor is it to examine the personality, the worldly person of gender, age, nationality, language, endowments, relationships, status, name and character. All these belong to Nature's field of the *guṇa*s, that is, the field of time, space, action, multiplicity and all the pairs of opposites. This practice of meditation, the turning of attention from outer to inner perception, is not in order to contemplate the great themes of existence — the whats, whys and hows, of life on this earth. It is rather to gain release from all involvement with sense objects (the "fruits of the five birds") and transcending these come to the field of non-duality. The nature of mind is such that it is able to dip into this field of unconditioned consciousness (awareness without subject-object duality) and merge with it. In Indian tradition this merging of mind with its source is *yoga*, a word meaning union. It implies the union of the Absolute and Relative fields of Existence, the union of *sat* and *asat*. It is the union which, in the *Bhagavad-Gītā*, Kṛṣṇa, the supreme *yogī*, urges Arjuna, his disciple, to attain:

> The Vedas' concern is with the three *guṇa*s.
> Be without the three *guṇa*s, O Arjuna, freed
> from duality, ever established in purity,
> steadfast in the well-being of *yoga*
> possessed of the Self.[1]

The practice of uniting the mind with its source is highly beneficial. Just as the colour of a cloth is strengthened by being continually dipped into dye, so the mind is strengthened when continually dipped into the field of transcendent Consciousness. Because of the nature of the body such dips are usually brief awareness being drawn out of the transcendent and recaptured by such auto-biotic functions as thinking and breathing, as well as by outside sensory stimuli. But returning from that transcendental field, the mind is refreshed and imbued with something of its value. Such frequent dips of the mind in self-effulgent, non-dual transcendental awareness, washes away the darkness of ignorance and the grime of life's fears and stresses. Then, even when fully engaged in the transactions, turbulences and changes of this human life on earth, an inner stability and peace is gained. With the growing realization of one's oneness with the unchanging Reality a sense of detached witnessing develops, as does the ability to discriminate between transient and eternal values. One is not led to a denial of life's actualities, but gains a greater ability to contend with those actualities,

1. *Bhagavad-Gītā*, II.45.

with equanimity, resolution and, in the fully enlightened, a sense of perfect freedom.

As a bonfire emits sparks which have no other reality than their bonfire-source, so the Self emits, as it were, countless sparks from Itself which appear as the world. The world is experienced as a spark of the Self's knowledge of itself by one of enlightened perception. The Guru says in the *Ātmopadeśa-Śatakam*:

> From *cit* countless sparks are emitted, seemingly existent though non-existent, and the world gleams as a result. Nothing exists apart from *cit*. Do have such an awareness and it will bestow the final realization of Oneness.[2]

This "final realization of Oneness" resolves all problems. Problems exist only when they are perceived as belonging to individual beings. When understood as belonging to the field of the *guṇa*s, they cease to be the individual's problems.

Adhyāsa

As in the example of the rope identified as a snake in dim light, the projection of a non-existent form onto an existent reality is known in Vedānta as *adhyāsa*. The Self, *ātman*, finds expression in the countless forms and qualities of ceaseless creations from Itself. All specific knowledges, all forms and qualities, all actions, all experiences and feelings, whether perceived as existing externally or internally, whether known in the waking, dreaming or deep-sleep states of consciousness or even in the fourth, the transcendental state called *turīya*, are configurations superimposed on a substratum of Unconditioned Pure Consciousness. That substratum, Unconditioned Pure Consciousness Itself, is the one ineffable, Existent Reality. It is only to be experienced when all superimposed configurations have been transcended or

2. *Ātmopadeśa-Śatakam*, v. 89.

integrated. Whatever is superimposed upon it has no separate existence, just as the image of snake projected on rope, or wave projected on ocean, or ornament projected on gold has no existence apart from its substratum. Whatever is conditioned and superimposed on the substratum of Consciousness is *asat*; only the unconditioned, non-superimposed substratum itself is *sat*. Whatever is thought of, spoken of, or conceived to be, is superimposed and conditioned. What is not superimposed and not conditioned is unthinkable, ineffable and inconceivable Reality, referred to in the Upaniṣads simply as *auṁ* or as *auṁ tat sat* (*auṁ* is That, the Real).

Narayana Guru, concluding the chapter called *Bhāna-Darśana* (Vision of the Functional Modes of Consciousness) of the *Darśana-Mālā*, says:

> What is manifest, that is superimposed and conditioned. What is not superimposed and not conditioned, that is the unmanifest. Whatever is superimposed and conditioned is *asat*. What is not superimposed and not conditioned; That indeed is *sat*.[3]

Existent or Non-Existent World

Inconceivable and ineffable Reality cannot be subjected to critical enquiry. Transcendent, without form, invisible to all the senses, it cannot be picked up or be weighed and measured. It is possible, however, to examine the two conditioned views of it from two opposing perspectives. As it is possible to know the existence of the positive pole of a magnet by knowing its negative pole, so by knowing the conditioned, *asat*, the world, one may gain awareness of the unconditioned, *sat*, the world's Reality.

The question, "Is the world existent or non-existent" may

3. *Darśana-Mālā*, IV.10.

be answered in two ways. We know it to be an emanation of the Self and know that the Self is its only existent substance. In that sense, it is real. We know it to have no existence of its own, apart from the Self. In that sense, it is unreal. The Upaniṣads tell us:

> Having created it, into it indeed he entered.[4]

The creation of the world and the entry of the Self into it does not take place in a temporal and sequential sense but simultaneously. The Guru expresses this view when in his *Brahmavidyā-Pañcakam* he says:

> Having created this world through *prakṛti*, that which enters it and by which the created world is sustained from within . . .[5]

Ontologically, the Self alone exists. Therefore the world, having no existence of its own, is considered unreal, *asat*. Yet although one may question the world's existence one's own existence is irrefutable. It is in fact from the questioner's undeniable existence that the questioning arises. He seeks to know Reality by knowing what is Real in himself and realizes that what is Real in himself is the same Reality in all entities. In that sense, the perceived world is considered Real, *sat*.

Even when understood in a philosophical sense to be illusory, the world's existence is undeniable in actual experience. The sailor's understanding that waves have no existence apart from the ocean does not lessen their force in a sea-storm. Even with the understanding that the world has no existence of its own, it continues to be perceived with all its actualities. The Guru emphasizes this in his *Advaita-Dīpikā*, in the following verses:

> Even when, by the dawning of discriminating awareness, it is reduced to having no existence of its own, the world will

4. *Taittirīya Upaniṣad*, II.6.
5. *Brahmavidyā-Pañcakam*, v. 4.

> still be perceived by the senses. As when the confusion about directions is clarified, the perceiver continues to see directions erroneously.
>
> The world does not exist really, still all gleams as before even when destroyed by the clarity of discrimination. Even with the certainty that there is no water in a mirage; it continues to gleam as before.[6]

It is not through denial of the world's actualities that the truth of Existence is comprehended, but through a vision of those actualities as the natural expression of Existence.

Bhāva

It has been stated that the one underlying Reality is formless and invisible. As such it is simply an abstract principle. It has to assume tangible form to gain actuality and value. It is an immutable law of Being that eternal substance does not exist without manifesting as apparent form. Abstract Reality has not existed as an actuality anywhere, nor at any time, without taking form. Whilst it is eternal and unchanging, the forms it assumes are ever-changing and transient. Conversely, no transient form can appear without a changeless basis. That which itself is eternal, changeless and formless, eternally appears in transient, ever-changing forms. That invisible, eternal Reality is called *sat*; its appearance in transient forms is called *bhāva*.

In the context of Vedānta, *sat* is *Brahman* and *bhāva* is the world. *Brahman* does not exist without assuming the form of the world. The world has no existence apart from *Brahman*. Thus the perceptions of *sat* and *bhāva* are merely two conceptual aspects of the one non-dual Reality.

Graphically expressed, if the eternally existing substance is represented by a vertical axis, then the world of ever-

6. *Advaita-Dīpikā*, vv. 9 and 10.

changing appearances can be represented by a transversing horizontal line.

Non-duality is represented by the meeting point which is neither vertical nor horizontal:

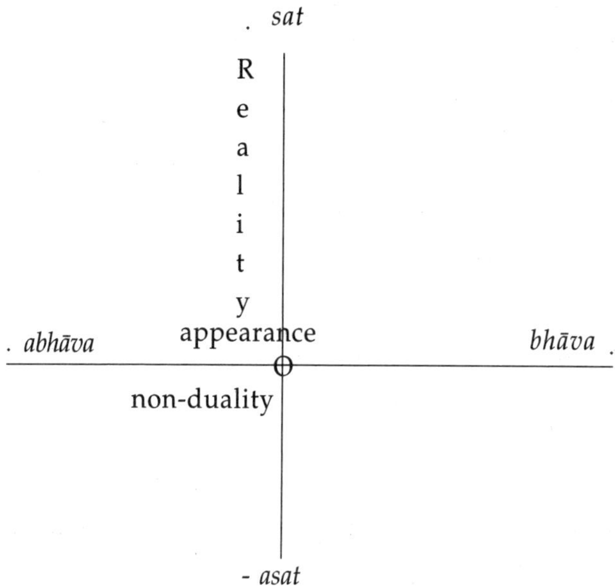

In defining the reality of the ever-changing world in terms of its unchanging substance it is called *Brahman*. In defining *Brahman* in terms of its actualities it is called the world (*bhāva*). The distinction between "this world" and *Brahman* is only a concept in the mind of the unenlightened perceiver. The truth, that Reality is one only, is ever veiled by the erroneous conceptual duality in unenlightened minds. The non-duality of the world and *Brahman* is known by seers of Reality, the true philosophers called *tattva-darśī*s in Sanskrit. The secret of true philosophy, *darśana*, is expounded in the *Bhagavad-Gītā*:

> The unreal cannot manifest.
> The Real never ceases to manifest.
> The inherent truth of these two has

> thus been perceived by the seers of
> ultimate Reality.[7]

The very enquiry into non-dual Reality causes it to be perceived as a division of *sat* and *bhāva*. It is analogous to the enquiry of modern physics into the material substance of the world which causes it to appear as particle or wave.

The possibility of such errors of perception is universal and is known as *māyā*. It is *māyā* which must be transcended by seekers of Reality; but Vedānta warns that even the attempt to transcend *māyā* is conditioned by *māyā*.

The *Taittirīya Upaniṣad* expresses the inseparability of *Brahman* and oneself with these words:

> Verily, one does become unreal if he considers *Brahman* as non-existent. If he knows, *Brahman* is what really exists; such a one becomes known as the Existent.[8]

The comprehensive search for the undivided Self, originating from the perception of an apparent world, is therefore to be accomplished by considering the world from twin perspectives and realizing that it is neither *sat* nor *asat*, but is *sat* and *asat* both.

---

7. *Bhagavad-Gītā*, II.16.

8. *Taittirīya Upaniṣad*, II.6.

Sūtra 6

भूयो सतस्सदसदिति ॥

bhūyo sataḥ sad asad iti ॥

bhūyaḥ	:	again
sataḥ	:	from Reality
sat	:	Existence
asat	:	non-Existence
iti	:	thus

Again, it is from Existence that existence and non-existence emerge.

EXISTENCE and appearance are the dual aspects of non-dual Reality referred to earlier as *sat-cit-ānanda*. In the graph of the previous *sūtra* commentary, the neutral zero point unfolded itself as four limbs each having its own specific characteristics. Similarly the one transcendent Absolute (*param-brahma*) unfolds itself and gives rise to perceptions of *sat* (the real) and *asat* (the unreal).

The neutral Absolute by its own *karma* unfolds itself as *sat* and *asat* as if by a transformation within itself, whilst Itself remains unchanged. The Guru in the *Ātmopadeśa-Śatakam* describes the process as follows:

> On the surface of a pool wafted on incessantly by wind emerge rows and rows of ripples; likewise the constant

> wafting of the wind of fiction transforms the inner content of the Self into endless forms.[1]

The seeker too is such a ripple, looking within himself as he flows along on the surface of Being. In Indian tradition the world he experiences and takes for granted is an aggregate of five basic metaphysical elements symbolized as space, air, fire, water and earth. The real content of the world is *cit* and in the verse following the one quoted above the Guru poetically describes how *cit* assumes the form of these elements:

> The transcendent is space. Vibrating energy the wind. Knowledge is fire. Senses water and sense objects are earth. Thus the five ever blaze. Their mysterious Reality is One Alone.[2]

All things considered to be external entities are merely modes of *cit*, the one existent Consciousness. Its nature is such that it has the ability to transform itself as anything whatsoever. In unbounded space there is room for everything to exist. So it is that Consciousness is said to be like space, the most subtle of the five elements. Its inherent potential is like a wind, blowing on a horizontal plane and causing the emergence of the world; it is therefore linked to wind. Actualizing itself as specific items of knowledge, that is to say, the contact of mind and its senses with their objects, it is like a burning fire of countless darting flames and, in this sense, it is seen as fire. Mind and senses are equated with water and earth, the two most gross of the five elements, which together provide the basis for the appearance of the world and the emergence of life from it. The world emerging as a transitory appearance of non-apparent Eternal-Pure-Consciousness can, therefore, be considered as both real and unreal.

---

1. *Ātmopadeśa-Śatakam*, v. 76.
2. Ibid., v. 77.

Akṣaram and Kartā

The creative impulse within the Self, a continuous becoming, is understood as *karma* (action). Inherent in the creative expression of the Self every entity appearing to have separate existence as an aspect of the world, has within it the same creative urge. Functioning in diverse and distinct ways, *ātman*, the indestructible, everlasting substance of all entities, is sometimes called *akṣaram* (the "Imperishable"). All actions, all *karma*s, therefore belong to the one imperishable *ātman* and not to the apparent entities and beings resulting from its *karma*.

Alone among the world's entities human beings have intellect, free will, sense of responsibility, moral sense and other such attributes. The human being exists as an expression of the creative impulse of the Imperishable Reality, but unmindful of that fact he holds himself as the doer (*kartā*) of the actions occurring through his unconscious agency. He feels too that the results of actions belong to him, as the enjoyer or sufferer of those fruits. In some cultures the belief has taken root that he will be reborn to fulfil actions which did not run their full course in a previous incarnation. The notion that one is the *kartā* (doer of actions) is an aspect of man's ignorance of his true nature and the theory of *karma* and reincarnation, prevailing especially in Hinduism and Buddhism, is an offshoot of that ignorance (*avidyā*). Such a theory, arising from a field of ignorance, is one not accepted by a *jñānin* (man of wisdom). One who knows the Self, knows that all activities, internal and external, arising from him or from a source outside him, whether involving him or not, are part of the spontaneous self-expression of the One-Existent-Reality. Thus, even though man's intelligence and free will have roles to play in activity, he is not the real doer of any action whatsoever. In the sense that there is a real doer, it is the One-Existent-Reality which in its active state is called *prakṛti* (Nature). The functions of *prakṛti*, appearing to be actions, are called *vṛtti*s in Sanskrit.

Implying only the field of action, the word "Nature" does not have the sense of a doer of actions (*kartā*). Where there is no *kartā,* there is no *karma*. Seen as belonging to individual beings *karma* is unreal, but seen as belonging to *ātman* it is real. A knower of Reality is aware that what is seen as action is, in Reality, an illusion of action called *māyā*. The *Bhagavad-Gītā* says:

> What is action, what inaction?
> Even the wise are bewildered here.[3]

> He who in action sees inaction
> and in inaction sees action is
> wise among men. He is united, he
> has accomplished all action.[4]

The emergence from *ātman*'s *karma* of each specific form and its subsequent dissolution may be considered as a birth and a death of that form. If at all the notion of rebirth is to be admitted within the flow of these continuous creative expressions of *ātman*'s *karma,* it is in the sequential emergence of similar forms from the same flow. If *karma* is understood as the cause of birth, death and rebirth it should be understood to be the *karma* of *akṣaram* and not that of an individual being. In Vedāntic teaching there is no individual soul to be reincarnated in a new body, as soul, body and all other factors specifying an individual being are illusory configurations in Consciousness. They are merely different facets of the illusory appearance of an individual being.

Triguṇas

Each form emerging from the one Self has within it the creative urge, *karma,* that caused its emergence. It is the functioning of the three *guṇa*s (*triguṇa*s), the modalities inherent in *prakṛti* (Nature), which brings about the distinct qualities and

3. *Bhagavad-Gītā,* IV.16.

4. Ibid., IV-18.

characteristics differentiating one entity from another. The Sāṁkhya School of Indian philosophy teaches that the *guṇa*s do not remain in a state of equilibrium as, if they did, *prakṛti* would be changeless and inactive. The balance between them is constantly changing, increasing and decreasing in relation to one another. Thus there is movement in Nature, and in movement there is change.

Sāṁkhya propounds two fundamental categories of Reality, namely *puruṣa* (Person) and *prakṛti* (Nature), and the latter has the *guṇa*s (literally meaning "qualities" or "modalities") inherent in it. The *guṇa*s are *sattva, rajas,* and *tamas,* more generally known as *sattva-guṇa, rajo-guṇa* and *tamo-guṇa*. This concept was admitted by the other schools of Indian philosophical thought and interpreted by them in their respective ways. Advaita Vedānta, for example, considers the *guṇa*s to be inherent in *māyā*. The *Bhagavad-Gītā* devotes a whole chapter to them. It describes their functions and values in some detail and helps one to relate them to one's own personality and characteristics. The awareness that these are specific expressions of the Self in Nature's field helps one to better understand oneself (as a particular personality with particular characteristics) and live more peacefully and patiently with oneself.

These qualities of Nature (*guṇa*s) condition both the physical and mental aspects of everything in the world. *Sattva-guṇa* characterizes the pure, bright aspects of manifest existence. It can, however, exert a binding influence by causing an attachment to feelings of well-being and pleasurable aspects of life. *Rajo-guṇa,* the activating force in Nature, creates strong and intense desires in living beings, binding them to their actions. *Tamo-guṇa* is the dark and inert modality. It shrouds wisdom, causes delusion and lassitude, and creates bonds of illusion. The *guṇa*s are reflected in and give shape to life at every moment. They dictate one's character, values, interests and even preferences for food. The *Bhagavad-Gītā* tells us that a man of enlightened wisdom, a *yogī*, is one whose intellect, transcending the *guṇas*, is united with the Self. He sees the *guṇas* as having their source in the Self. Being attributes of the functional mode of the Self the *guṇas* are real, but as attributes, with no existence of their own, they are unreal. As both *sat* and *asat* they are the mechanism in Nature's field of action by which *māyā* produces the illusory appearance of the world.

Tripuṭi

Another set of triple factors emerging from the one reality of Pure-Consciousness is that of knower, known and knowledge (*jñātṛ*, *jñeya* and *jñāna*). These three are always linked together like a three-petalled flower and for that reason are known as *tripuṭi* (literally, that which consists of three petals). The division of these three arises in the context of a specific item of knowledge occurring in Consciousness. Later, it will be more fully elucidated how these three are mutually related and how they emerge as three from the one Consciousness which is their essence. For the present it suffices to say that the three, emerging from one Consciousness and being not apart from it, are *sat*, but in the sense of having no existence apart from it are *asat*.

The mind as subject perceives the world as object, but the perceiving mind is not different from the world perceived and is nothing other than a functional mode of Consciousness. However, in its erroneous view of itself as separate from the world, it is quite difficult for the observing mind to discern the *sat/asat* nature of its perceptions. All seem real. Behold what a great magic!

Other Worlds

In Consciousness, which is also *ānanda*, each specific perception is evaluated in terms of the extent to which it is helpful in actualizing the *ānanda* aspect of the Self — in simpler terms, to the extent to which it is helpful in actualizing happiness. So it is with man's perceptions, or concepts, of other worlds.

Religions conceive of higher and lower worlds, each a domain of different orders of beings; gods, angels, humans, demons and so forth. These are concepts entirely based upon mankind's notion of values. Some religions conceive of three worlds. These they name heaven, earth and hell, the first of which is considered to be the highest abode of God. In Sanskrit, these three notional worlds are called *svarga, bhūmi* and *pātāla*. The Vedas conceive of them as *bhūmi* (earth), *svarga* (heaven) and *antarikṣa* (the middle world, though the term is also used for atmosphere). Hindu mythology conceives of fourteen different worlds. They are called in Sanskrit *bhūloka, bhuvarloka, svarloka, maharloka, janaloka, tapoloka* and *satyaloka*, rising in order above the earth, and *atala, vitala, sutala, talātala, rasātala, mahātala* and *pātāla*, descending in order below the earth. Each of these worlds is considered to be the domain of a particular genus of living beings, as the earth is for humans. The criterion for this division is our value notion. Happiness, the state of life which humans aspire to and consider to be ideal, is supposed to be the condition prevailing in the higher worlds, with God seated in the highest of these. Misery is the supposed state of the Godless lower worlds. To prove or disprove the existence of other worlds than our own is a logical impossibility, so all that can be said of them is that these concepts too are *sat/asat*.

To assign a higher place in the scheme of things to that which is considered most valuable is natural to human beings. A guest of honour is given the most prominent seat. God, the most honoured and revered Being, is assigned the highest world as his abode. Misery and torment, the most unwanted of human experiences, are assigned the lowest world. All of these worlds have reality in human consciousness as different values. As such they are helpful to man in his moral evaluations, in his aspirations for the higher good and his desire to avoid the lower bad. It is the hope for a life hereafter in a world conceived as higher and better that, in the world here, helps man strive for the good in himself. The mythological worlds too are man's imaginative creations relating to his value-notions. To one who is Self-realized all worlds are simply diverse mental images superimposed on Consciousness.

The notional worlds and their mythological inhabitants, the *gandharvas*, *kinnaras*, gods and so on, are considered by rational and scientifically-biased minds to be religious superstitions. These worlds represent value gradations in the rational human mind. The same mind categorizes the beings of this world as animal, vegetable or mineral, man being considered as the highest creature in the animal kingdom. The entities in the mineral kingdom have no awareness of the vegetable kingdom. The living forms of the vegetable kingdom cannot be aware of the nature of the animal kingdom. The lower creatures of the animal kingdom cannot be cognizant of the nature and potentiality of human life. Similarly man is incapable of understanding the nature of beings who may, conceivably, inhabit dimensions beyond his perceptions. This limitation of the human mind is not in itself proof of the non-existence of other worlds and it is not a reason for denying the existence of higher beings. Seers, prophets, mystics and artists have visualized and portrayed these worlds and their mythical beings, creating images of a perfection beyond that experienced here on earth. It is man's aspirations and longings for that perfection which have led to the acceptance of those imaginative creations as real and substantial.

Logic and Reasoning

To subject the existence of notional other worlds to the test of logic and reasoning is meaningless. Logical thinking results from relating phenomena as cause and effect. To attempt to ascertain what is beyond the realm of human perceptions on the basis of logic is a pointless exercise. In the *Bṛhadāraṇyaka Upaniṣad* the limitations of logic and reasoning are illustrated in the following passage which quotes a dialogue between the sage Yājñavalkya and Gārgī Vācagnavī, an illustrious female character in the Upaniṣad:

> Yājñavalkya, since all this, here, is woven like warp and woof on water, on what is water woven, like warp and woof?
> On air, O Gārgī.
>
> On what then is air woven, like warp and woof?
> On the worlds of the sky, O Gārgī.
>
> On what then are the worlds of the sky woven, like warp and woof?
> On the worlds of the *Gandharva*s, O Gārgī.
>
> On what then are the worlds of the *Gandharva*s woven, like warp and woof?
> On the worlds of the sun, O Gārgī.
>
> On what then are the worlds of the sun woven, like warp and woof?
> On the worlds of the moon, O Gārgī.
>
> On what then are the worlds of the moon woven, like warp and woof?
> On the worlds of the stars, O Gārgī.
>
> On what then are the worlds of the stars woven, like warp and woof?
> On the worlds of the gods, O Gārgī.
>
> On what then are the worlds of the gods woven, like warp and woof?
> On the worlds of Indra, O Gārgī.
>
> On what then are the worlds of Indra woven, like warp and woof?
> On the worlds of Prajāpati (the Lord of Beings), O Gārgī.

> On what then are the worlds of Prajāpati woven, like warp and woof?
> On the worlds of Brahmā (the Creator), O Gārgī.
>
> On what then are the worlds of Brahmā woven, like warp and woof?
>
> Gārgī, do not ask questions too much about the beyond, lest your head should fall off. Verily, you are questioning too much about the divinity, about which we are not supposed to ask. Do not, O Gārgī, ask too much about the beyond.

Thereupon Gārgī kept silent.[5]

This section of the dialogue reveals the unknowability of Causal-Reality through the ordinary way of logical and analytical thought.

Reasoning is one of many functions of Consciousness in an individuated human mind. The mind has functions and areas apart from reasoning such as those of emotion, intuition and sensation. To attempt to measure and explain the whole range of mind's percepts with just one of those functions will not result in an understanding of them. The human mind is capable of perceiving the actual existence of this world; it is also capable of conceiving the existence of many other worlds. As all worlds, including our own, are value concepts, it is meaningless to either affirm or deny their existence on the basis of logic. Their existence, real or imagined, arising from one Reality, may also be considered as *sat* and *asat*. A close scrutiny of the concepts of *triguṇas*, *tripuṭi* and the three worlds reveals that the *guṇas* pertain to *sat*, *tripuṭi* to *cit* and the three worlds to *ānanda*. All of these arise as manifestations of one *saccidānanda*. Such is the great mysteriousness of *ātman*.

Names and Forms

All experiences in the human mind are in terms of name (*nāma*)

5. *Bṛhadāraṇyaka Upaniṣad*, III.6.1.

and form (*rūpa*). Each experience of form stimulates the memory with respect to the name, word, or linguistic symbol applied to that form. Conversely, hearing or reading the name arouses the memory of the form. Without name, form is unrecognizable and without form name is meaningless.

This nature of mind is an aspect of the self-manifestation of *ātman* protrayed in the *Bṛhadāraṇyaka Upaniṣad* as follows:

> At that time this world was unmanifested. "That" manifested itself as name and form. Thus it was said, one has such and such a name and such and such a form. Therefore, even today the world continues to be differentiated by name and form. He (the Self) entered therein to the nail tips, as a razor hidden in a razor-case, or as fire, the sustainer of the world, hidden in its receptacle. People perceive him, not complete indeed, when he is named *prāṇa* functioning as vitality, named speech when speaking, eyes when seeing, ears when hearing, mind when thinking. All these are names of his *karma* (creative self-expression). He who meditates on any of these names separately, as the Real, does not know Him, as each of these manifestations is not complete. Therefore Reality is to be meditated on as *ātman* for it is in *ātman* all of them become one . . .[6]

This Upaniṣadic passage first says names and forms had their origin in *ātman*, the source of the world, and then says that their emergence is an expression of the *karma* (action) principle inherent in *ātman*. Each expression is given a particular name, but the name does not express the pervasive reality of that expressed form. Its reality, *ātman*, remains unnamed as the inner content of all named forms. Therefore, the Upaniṣad urges seekers to meditate on *ātman* alone and not upon any names or forms arising from it. Names and forms are in fact the means by which the human mind conceives and

6. *Bṛhadāraṇyaka Upaniṣad*, I.4.7.

distinguishes the manifestations of *ātman*, albeit that the conceiving and distinguishing human mind itself is also named and formed as a distinct expression of *ātman*.

Names and words are oral and written symbols devised by human minds to signify particular things or ideas. Hearing a word or seeing it in writing causes a sudden explosion of meaning in the mind known as *sphoṭa* (literally, explosion) in Indian psychology. It is not possible to know whether the meaning "exploded" in the mind of one who hears a speaker is the same as the meaning in the mind of the speaker, as the perception of meaning is a purely personal experience. The mind of each individual is so conditioned that each of that individual's perceptions will have a particular colouration. For example, the individual members of an audience listening to the same speech by the same speaker may interpret what they are hearing in very different ways. The word "world," as a further example, has quite different meanings for a Vedāntin and a physicist. In the understanding of the Vedāntin it is an illusory appearance of a transcendent Reality. The physicist understands it as a substantial self-contained aggregate of particles, energies and forces. Yet both use the same word to communicate these very different perceptions. Similarly, the word "God" is perceived in many different ways and ascribed with many different values. Individuals exchanging words can never be sure that the words they are using are understood in the way in which they are meant. Thus the world understood through words may be very different for the different people using them and there is no way to know which words most aptly convey meaning. The meaning intended by a writer in writing some words may be quite different from the meaning created by those same words in the mind of a reader. Likewise, the world created in the mind of a thinker is a product only of his thought and not the reality of that which he thinks about.

Form, the object of experience, was defined by Kant as "that a priori element in experience by virtue of which the manifold of sense is synthesized and unified into meaningful perceptions and judgements." Form is that aspect of experience which makes it distinct. It is a configuration imprinted in mind simultaneously with a sense contact, but it cannot be known whether it corresponds exactly with the form it represents.

Senses have their own limitations and conditionings. For example, the same object may appear to be of different size to different people with differing eyesight. It may appear larger or smaller, taller or shorter, farther or nearer to long-sighted, short-sighted and normally-sighted observers. It may appear coloured to those who perceive colour and be colourless to the colour-blind. The same is true of the perceptions of all other senses. Therefore the aggregate of the sense experience of any individual is different from that of any other individual and one does not have the means to verify one's experience of the world with that of another. It may be thought that there is a common medium of measurement, determination and specification of objects. But as the instruments of determination are also inner perceptions, the objects examined remain personal inner experiences, not accessible to others.

The nature of a perception and the value assigned to it depends to a great extent upon the mental condition of the perceiver at the moment of its experience. One's mind may be fresh and clear or be dull and misty and the experience may accordingly be of this or that value. So perception of the world will be of this or that value to different people in different states of mind and it is not possible to determine its reality through one's personal experience of it.

The perception of the world is gained through the stimuli of all five senses, but they are so structured that when any single sense is concentrated on an object the other senses are dimmed or cease to function altogether. For example, one may be so lost in reading that words spoken to the reader may not be heard. All the senses do not function fully and together at any time and the picture of the world they build up is so variable that no one has ever perceived its real form. Which world then is *sat*? Is it the world of experience or the world which lies outside experience, or is it neither of these? The Vedāntin's solution to this paradox is that all perceived worlds result from the functional modes of *sat-cit-ānanda*, the Consciousness which alone really exists. The world can be considered as *sat* or as *asat* in the mind of the perceiver. But from any of these standpoints its appearance is undeniable. As was defined earlier in a verse quoted from the Guru's *Darśana-Mālā*, if considered to be real it is *sat*, if considered to be illusory it is *cit*.

In questioning whether the world of mental perception represents its actual form, Narayana Guru, in his *Advaita-Dīpikā*, considers it as having two aspects, the one subjective and the other objective. He calls them *pratibhā* (mental image, or idea) and *viṣaya* (object):

> Names in thousands, concepts in thousands and the corresponding objects, closely emerging, also in thousands. The world, being such, is true as long as not cogitated on. A dream is true until the dreamer wakes up and when awake all, without remainder, merges in the awakened.[7]

An object perceived as having external existence is merely a mental configuration. The real form and identity of the object remains veiled by, and confused with, the mind-made image. Its existence is perceived only as an image in mind; its real form remains unknown and unknowable. The external object called the world is such a mind-constructed-configuration, a conditioned mode of Consciousness. What really exists is Consciousness alone. The world and all its names and forms

7. *Advaita-Dīpikā*, v. 1.

are diverse images in that Consciousness. They are as the names and forms in dreams — existing nowhere but in the mind of the dreamer and disappearing when the dreamer awakes. Our dream-like experience of an external world, existing only in the sleep of human life, disappears when we are awakened by the wisdom of enlightenment. Only until awakened from the dream in our minds is the world perceived as an external reality.

Waking, Dreaming and Deep-Sleep (avasthā-traya)

One's self-existence and the existence of the world are experienced in the three alternating states of human consciousness (*avasthā-traya*) called *jāgrat* (waking state), *svapna* (dreaming-state) and *suṣupti* (deep-sleep state) respectively. This classification derives mainly from the *Māṇḍūkya Upaniṣad* and the commentary of Gauḍapāda called *Māṇḍūkya Kārikā* or *Gauḍapāda Kārikā.*

Jāgrat is the state of consciousness in which an external world is known and experienced through the senses. An individual's consciousness in that state is called *vaiśvānara*. Later Vedāntins have also used the word *viśvātmā* in referring to it. In the Śaṅkara school's introductory textbooks on Vedānta, the individual's body in the waking state is called *sthūla-śarīra* (gross-body). This term has no place in the *Māṇḍūkya Upaniṣad,* nor in any other major Upaniṣad, and nor do the terms, subtle-body and causal-body which are applied respectively to the other two states, mentioned in them. According to the Upaniṣad, *vaiśvānara,* which literally means "common to all," is characterized by knowledge of external objects (*bahiṣ-prajñā*) and by the enjoyment of gross objects (*sthūla-bhuk*).

Svapna means dream. In the *Māṇḍūkya Upaniṣad,* dreaming is qualified as *pravivikta-bhuk* (literally meaning, "that which knows and enjoys in solitary detachment"). It is a state of consciousness called *taijasa* (the bright one) in which the mind creates and enjoys objects within itself. This dream knowledge is called *antaḥ-prajña* (internal knowledge). Later Vedāntins added the concept of *sūkṣma-śarīra* (subtle body) to name and signify the physical correlation of this state of consciousness.

Suṣupti (deep-sleep) is the non-active state of consciousness called *prājña*, in which consciousness shrinks back into itself (as if a tree to its seed state) and in which there are no objects to be known and experienced. The *Māṇḍūkya Upaniṣad* says that the multiplicity of experiences is transformed into unity in this state. Waking from it, one feels some sense of enjoyment, summarized by its description as "sound sleep." This soundness, or happiness, was enjoyed without awareness whilst asleep and only after waking is the experience known. Therefore the Upaniṣad says this state is *ānanda-ghana* (the essence of happiness). It is supposed that this pure happiness is covered, in this state of consciousness, by a veil of ignorance. It is a state of consciousness considered in the Upaniṣad to be anterior to creation and posterior to dissolution of all beings and entities. The concept of causal body (*kāraṇa-śarīra*) was added to it by later Vedāntins.

Consciousness, which cycles through these constantly alternating states, cannot be compartmentalized into any one of them. Being life itself, it functions as a life-process and oscillates between extremes of fully-deep unaware sleep and fully-alert full wakefulness. In between are all the gradations of these two poles and the intermediate states. These are designated in such books as the *Yoga-Vāsiṣṭha*, for example, with names like *jāgrat, jāgrat-svapna, svapna, svapna-jāgrat* and so on.

Full wakefulness is a state which no one can claim to have experienced as what we call wakefulness always has in it an element of sleep. When awake, the mind is capable of being bright and thinking clearly or conversely may at times feel dull and be muddled. It can be seen therefore that some degree of sleepiness will always be present in the waking state. Becoming aware of some new fact, one may feel that until that moment one was "in the dark." So it can be seen that the awake mind is not always fully awake to all that it may know. If, as has been said, no one may claim to know full wakefulness, conversely, no one may claim to know the deepest sleep. Nothing known about, it too is a state which no one has experienced. Human awareness swings like a pendulum between these two poles of deepest-deep-sleep and most-awake-wakefulness reaching neither extreme at any time. The states experienced between them are as a dream, only known to be such on waking to the light of Self-realization. Until that awakening the dream of life and an external world is taken to be reality.

Narayana Guru, when referring to modes of human consciousness, mentions only the wakeful and sleeping states, considering individuated human life and all perceived externals to be dream-like. His vision accords with actual experience as life's flow, a flow of Consciousness, not compartmentalized. There is no place in the Guru's thinking (as there is not in the *Bhagavad-Gītā* or the major Upaniṣads) for the concepts of gross, subtle and causal bodies. Some post-Śaṅkara Vedāntins, holding on to these concepts, believe that the subtle body leaves the discarded gross body at the time of death to seek a new gross body in a world beyond. The Guru, however, considers gross, subtle and causal merely as different conditioned modes, or luminescences (*bhāna*) of the one Consciousness. He views gross body and all other gross objects to be illusory appearances of the functioning mode of *cit* which, because *cit* is also *sat*, seem real. In this view, the concept of a subtle body leaving the gross body at death simply does not arise. The Guru's vision is thus more in accord with Vedānta's fundamental teaching that one Reality alone exists. Even the fourth state (*turīya*), which is the transcendental non-dual consciousness attained in meditation, is, as a concept, considered by the Guru to be a *bhāna* (a conditioned, luminous state). The Guru's concepts of *sthūla-bhāna, sūkṣma-bhāna, kāraṇa-bhāna* and *turīya-bhāna* (gross, subtle, causal and transcendental conditioned luminescences of consciousness) may therefore be considered as a revision and revaluation of the Śaṅkara school's concepts of gross, subtle and causal bodies. It is a revision which revitalizes the concepts and makes them more true to the spirit of Vedānta.

Images seen in dreams are creations of the mind. The constantly alternating states of human consciousness and the worlds perceived in them are all mind-made-configurations, ever-changing modes of *cit*. As states of Consciousness they are real; as self-existent entities they are unreal. However, their distinctness is apparent and valid in *prakṛti*'s transactional field and so paradoxically it may be said of them that they are neither *sat* nor *asat* but are both at one and the same time.

We live in present time. No one can re-live the past, except in memory of past events, nor live in the future, except in expectation of future events. Both memory and expectation occur in the present, and so the present alone exists and is real. Past and future, non-existent, are unreal.

If at all time is real and measurable as past, present and future, then what is called present time is merely a point conceived to exist between a beginningless past and an endless future. The Real, *sat*, exists only at this present point as does *idam*, the world here. However *idam* is conceived, whether as the three worlds, the tripartite factors of knowledge (*tripuṭi*), the field of Nature's three modalities (*triguṇas*), or as names and forms or experienced in the three alternating states of consciousness (*avasthā-traya*), it is of the nature of a mental configuration in the present moment. The Sanskrit word for "the present" is *vartamāna,* meaning "that which exists as measurable" (either materially or mentally). Measurability is relevant only in the present as it is impossible to measure that which is past or that which has not yet come. The whole world with all the life and entities in it is a great enigma, being a measurable multi-dimensional, multi-directional expansion from a single point of Consciousness in present time. In the poetry of his hymn called "Nine-Gemmed Cluster of Blossoms" (*Jananī-Nava-Ratna-Mañjarī*) the Guru expresses this point of Consciousness as "the Mother:"

> O Mother, you become fish and deer, you are the snakes, the sky and birds. Even the earth, rivers, men and women, and the heaven and hell beyond are you. You are names and forms and even this "I" in it of multifarious functional nature, is also you. O thou of the essence of sound, Ah! Everything here is your drama indeed.[8]

The *Bṛhadāraṇyaka Upaniṣad,* in one of the *mahāvākyas* (great dicta), proclaims the non-duality of *ātman/Brahman* with the words *ayam ātmā brahma* (This Self is the Absolute). Giving emphasis to all the apparent dualities it goes on to say that the same non-dual Reality appears as everything in the world:

> This Self indeed is Brahman and exists here in the form of understanding, of mind, of *prāṇa* (vital breath), of eyes, of ears, of earth, of water, of air, of space, of *tejas* (fire or light) and the absence of *tejas,* of desire and the absence of desire, of anger and the absence of anger, of righteousness and the absence of righteousness, and of everything. That is why it is said "of the form of this" and "of the form of that." According to actions and according to behaviour so does one become. The doer of good actions becomes good, and the doer of evil actions becomes evil. One becomes virtuous by virtuous actions and bad by bad actions. Others however say, "The person is identified with desire alone." As is one's

8. *Jananī-Nava-Ratna-Mañjarī,* v. 6.

desire, so is one's resolve. As is one's resolve, so are one's deeds. As are one's deeds, so is the attainment.[9]

Good and Evil

All things arise from one Absolute Reality, *Brahman/ātman*. Therefore, the human concepts called sin and merit, good and evil also arise from that one Reality. The good and the evil of things and affairs are human perceptions based upon human values. Those values, varying from culture to culture, from one historical background to another and from one human being to another, have no absolute nor universal status. An exploding star in a far-off galaxy may be immensely catastrophic for planets and beings in its cosmic region. Viewed from here it is not seen to be a catastrophy nor the result of evil, but merely to be an interesting, common astronomical event. Good and evil, sin and merit, are linked dualities which are perceived values only in the small field of human experience and transactions. It is not possible in that field to eliminate all evil and establish a kingdom of all good. Only through the realization that the Self alone exists are both good and evil resolved in non-dual Reality. The Absolute Itself is neither good nor evil, or conversely, is both good and evil, according only to human points of view. Good and evil are real only when perceived as modes of Consciousness. Having no status apart from that, they are unreal. However, recognizing good and evil as actualities of human experience, Narayana Guru in his *Darśana-Mālā*, in a chapter in which the world is taken as real (*Adhyāropa-Darśana*), says:

> Terrible is this world, it is a void indeed, resembling an infernal city. Even as such did the all-pervading Lord create this world. A wonder indeed![10]

---

9. *Bṛhadāraṇyaka Upaniṣad*, IV.4.5.

10. *Darśana-Mālā*, I.8.

Vedānta's view that good and evil, sin and merit, are human perceptions with no substantial existence of their own, does not mean that it considers those perceptions invalid and valueless. To the contrary, it holds that in the field of life's actualities man's effort to raise himself towards good and away from evil is of the utmost value in his endeavour to fulfil his life's potential and realize his Eternal Divine Nature. The Creative-Intelligence, arising from *Brahman*, endowed him with a sense of right and wrong and with free will and choice. Seeing good and seeing evil, man is free to choose his path.

In the verse previous to that quoted above, Narayana Guru expresses the way in which negative energy may find a place in man's mind:

> When Self-knowledge declines then ignorance prevails, causing fear. Ghost-like it appears, assuming specific names and forms in the most terrible manner.[11]

It is *māyā* which in the absence of Self-knowledge causes non-dual Reality to appear as the pairs of opposites. It is therefore within *māyā*'s field of illusory identifications that man must make the effort to release himself from his own illusory identity. To gain that release he must realize the Self from which the illusion arises. If he earnestly desires it, Creative Intelligence may guide him to the inner awareness which brings that liberation.

---

11. *Darśana-Mālā*, I.7.

Sūtra 7

सच्छब्दादयो सदभावश्चेति ॥

sac chabdādayo sad abhāvaśceti ॥

sat śab-dādayaḥ	:	Such words as *sat*
sat abhā vaḥ ca iti	:	also imply their opposites

Such words as existence imply their opposites as well.

THE Guru in this seventh *sūtra* indicates the possibility of discerning an unmanifest, non-apparent or non-tangible value through the perception of its manifest, apparent or tangible counterpart. Thus the appearance of the world, with all its temporal multiplicity and tangibility, implies its non-apparent, non-tangible, eternal, unitive Reality. There is no duality in this nor in any other pair of opposites as all perceived dualities are the poles of progressive degrees of value/quality unitiveness.

The Great Illusion

The greatest difficulty human beings have in their perception of Reality is that human perception is always conditioned, so that the very act of perceiving causes the Real to appear unreal. Furthermore, one conditioned view of Reality may so differ from another that it becomes a matter of contention and conflict between persons. This illusory view of Reality, a universal error in human perception, is called *māyā* in Vedānta. It is in *māyā* (illusion) that contradictory views of Reality arise and so it is illusion which is the cause of human conflict and much unnecessary suffering. When viewed from different standpoints the world may seem to be a duality of its appearance and its non-apparent basis. But this illusion of duality in no way affects Reality. Of both manifest and transcendent aspects it remains One. The nature of the world will not be realized by those whose vision is obscured by conditioned modes of appearance. Only through the awareness that there is a reality behind all appearances may its realization be gained.

Unconditioned and without attributes, *sat* manifests itself as an illusory world. It is a great mystery and as such it is characterized as divine in the *Bhagavad-Gītā*, which says:

> Verily my divine illusion (*māyā*), of the essence of the *guṇas*, is hard to surmount. Those who attain Me, alone cross over this *māyā*.[1]

Māyā is the negative principle by which Reality becomes hidden within the apparent but illusory forms of *prakṛti*. *Māyā* and *prakṛti* are so closely linked that they are sometimes considered as synonyms. The *Śvetāśvatara Upaniṣad* is the only Upaniṣad in which the concept of *māyā* is propounded. It is this Upaniṣad which has been the basis of the conflicting theories of *māyā* of Śaṅkara and Rāmānuja. In it, *māyā* and *prakṛti* are interchangeable terms and *māyāvī*, the wielder of *māyā*, is the Great Lord (*maheśvara*) or *Brahman*. The Upaniṣad says:

> The Vedas, the sacrifices, the rituals, the religious observations, the past, the future and what the Vedas teach; all this is sent forth of this one by the wielder of *māyā*. The other is confined by *māyā* in this one. Know *māyā* as *prakṛti* and the wielder of *māyā* as the Great Lord. This whole world is spread out by beings; His own limbs.[2]

---

1. *Bhagavad-Gītā*, VII.14.

2. *Svetāśvatara Upaniṣad*, IV.9.10.

Narayana Guru also admits the idea of *Brahman* as the One God, the wielder of *māyā*, though he does not see *māyā* and God as separate. Addressing God, in his universal prayer called *Daivadaśakam*, he says:

> Are you not *māyā*, the wielder of *māyā* and also the enjoyer thereof? Are you not even the one who can remove *māyā* to grant the beatitude of supreme union with you?[3]

The word *māyāvī* (wielder of *māyā*) also means "magician" and thus *māyā* is a magic-like appearance. Narayana Guru sometimes considers *māyā* in this sense and in some of his works refers to God, or *Brahman*, as a supreme magician who projects the great illusion of the world from his own creative imagination.

It is through the *māyā* principle in *Brahman* that the perception of *sat-asat* appears in the relative field. It arises as if by magic from the undifferentiated Absolute. In saying "Such words as Existence also imply their opposites," the Guru, in this *sūtra*, is referring to the many pairs of linked opposites which emerge in the manifest world. All such dualities are expressions of values and qualities pertaining to the *sat, cit* or *ānanda* aspects of non-dual *ātman*.

Narayana Guru elucidates this vital aspect of *Brahman* in a chapter of his *Darśana-Mālā*, in which he views the Absolute from the point of view of *māyā*. The chapter, called *Māyā-Darśanam*, is quoted in its entirety here:

> That is *māyā* which by itself does not exist, but shines forth in various forms: as *vidyā* and *avidyā, parā* and *aparā, tamas, pradhāna* and *prakṛti*.
>
> Just as before the shaping of a pot, its prior potential is in the clay, so too before the origin of the world, that boundless potential in *Brahman*, which is not other than *Brahman*; it is *māyā*.

---

3. *Daivadaśakam*, Verse 6.

That means by which such knowledge arises as "the non-Self is unreal and the Self is real," as in the cognition of the truth of rope and the falsity of snake; it indeed is *vidyā*.

That means by which such knowledge arises as "the Self is unreal and the non-Self is real," as in the erroneous cognition of rope as snake, it indeed is *avidyā*.

The senses, mind, intellect, the five *prāṇa*s and the like constitute the subtle limbs of the Self's consciousness. That, because of which all these emanate, it is the *parā* (the transcendental).

Leaning on these limbs the conscious Self becomes deluded by its own *māyā*, as if it is happy and unhappy; but truly it is not so.

That by which this world appears as the object of the senses; it indeed is *aparā* (the non-transcendent), a concrete manifestation of the Self's creative imagination.

As the basis of the illusory appearance of silver in mother-of-pearl is ignorance of its nature, the basis of the illusory appearance of the world in the Self is known as *tamas* (darkness).

As a seed wonderfully contains a tree, so too that which wonderfully contains the whole world is, for this reason and by virtue of its importance, called *pradhāna* (that which is important).

This which through *māyā* marvellously projects and makes distinct all appearances; of the essence of threefold modalities (*guṇa*s), it is called *prakṛti* (Nature).[4]

Vidyā and Avidyā

All pairs of opposites arising from *māyā*, the great illusion, are themselves illusory. The duality of *vidyā* and *avidyā* is no exception. These opposing functional modes of *cit* are

4. *Darśana-Mālā*, IV.

conceived by Narayana Guru to be the twin aspects of *māyā*. In this he deviates somewhat from the Śaṅkara Advaita school according to which *māyā* and *avidyā* are synonymous, the former signifying universal illusion and the latter individual illusion. This difference, though slight, is one of the most important and unique aspects of Narayana Guru's philosophy. In Verse 72 of his *Ātmopadeśa-Śatakam* he says:

> On the one side there are activities pertaining to *avidyā*. On the other side is *vidyā* consisting of Pure Consciousness. Although, by virtue of *māyā*, these two stand apart, the awareness which transcends duality brings *turīya* (the fourth state).

In this view Narayana Guru relates to the *Īśa Upaniṣad* in which *vidyā* and *avidyā* are seen as inseparably linked opposites, though appearing, through *māyā*, to stand apart.

It is paradoxical that to transcend the realm of *māyā*, the seeker has by necessity to make use of the effects of *māyā*. This is accomplished in the dialectical approach of *yoga-buddhi* in which reasoning and meditative insight are united, each validating the other.

Narayana Guru defines *vidyā* as the function of consciousness by which one becomes aware of the reality of the Self and the unreality of the non-Self. As the Self is immortal those who follow the path of *vidyā*, (which does not exclude knowledge of *avidyā*'s role) come to realize their own immortality.

Avidyā is the function of consciousness by which the non-Self is mistaken for the real and the reality of the Self is not perceived. It is the realm of apparent forms in which activity also becomes apparent. All appearances arise and pass away as the endless creativity (*kriyā* or *karma*) of the Self. This rising and passing away is perceived as birth and death by living beings under the spell of *avidyā*. Death and the fear of death are thus the destiny of those who tread *avidyā*'s path. It is indeed a path of fear and darkness.

However, the view that *vidyā* alone leads to enlightenment and immortality is not correct nor complete. Those holding that view do not comprehend *avidyā* as an essential aspect of the Self's creativity. Without it there could be no actualities, no individual incarnate life and no thinking. Without activity (the realm of *avidyā*), corporeal existence would be impossible and unthinkable. Thinking, contemplating, meditating and all spiritual disciplines are of the nature of the world's actualities and no spiritual path which disregards actualities will succeed in attaining its goal. The non-dual Self will not be gained through a denial of the Self's dual aspects of Absolute-Eternal-Reality and Relative-Transient-Actualities. Without comprehending *avidyā*'s role in the realm of actualities the path of *vidyā* is incomplete. However, the aspirant on *vidyā*'s path, whilst admitting the actuality of the world, has to realize its ultimate non-existence and remain unaffected by its vagaries.

The *Īśa Upaniṣad* notes the following with respect to *vidyā* and *avidyā*:

> Into blinding darkness enter those who are engaged in *avidyā* and those who delight in *vidyā* enter still greater darkness as it were.
>
> Distinct indeed is the result of *vidyā* and distinct the result of *avidyā*. So we have heard from the sages of past times, who have explained such matters to us.[5]

Vidyā is the functional mode of consciousness of positive value, leading to the realization of immortality through a positive attitude. *Avidyā* is the functional mode of consciousness of negative value, leading to the negative and illusory view that death is real.

---

5. *Īśa Upaniṣad*, 9, 10.

The desire to gain immortality and the desire to avoid death are not essentially different, but the first is a positive view and the latter is negative. Both, however, signify the same meaning and the same goal, the neutral ground of which is realizable through inner awareness. Such is the nature of *yoga-buddhi*.

The *Īśa Upaniṣad* says that one who knows the nature of *vidyā* and *avidyā* together attains immortality through *vidyā* and crosses over death through *avidyā*.[6]

Vidyā and *avidyā* are the positive and negative conditioned aspects of non-dual *cit*. The knowledge of both together is to be grasped by the seeker and neutralized in meditation; in transcendental Consciousness there is no *vidyā* and no *avidyā*, but just pure Being.

To transcend dualities and gain awareness in the field of non-dual Being is the purpose of meditation. Whatever the technique practised, it is yogic meditation if it has that result. The word *yoga* derives from the root *yuj*, meaning, "to join together" and indicates a state of union in which opposites are reconciled in non-dual Consciousness. This yogic secret, embodied in the *Īśa Upaniṣad*, is not readily accessible. The Upaniṣad declares that it is like the secret and precious content of a golden casket, or as the face of truth covered by a golden veil. It says:

> The face of truth is covered with a golden casket. Unveil it O Pūṣan so that I who love truth and righteousness may see it.[7]

Having elucidated the concepts of *vidyā* and *avidyā*, the Upaniṣad applies the same dialectical consideration (*yoga-buddhi*) to the duality of creative becoming (*sambhūti*) and dissolution (*vināśa*).

---

6. *Īśa Upaniṣad*, 11.

7. Ibid., 15.

The *vidyā/avidyā* duality pertains to the realm of mental function whilst *sambhūti/vināśa* pertains to the realm of physical function. The one is meaningless without the other and what is called mental or physical are merely two functional facets of one Reality. This can be expressed graphically, as given below, where the vertical line represents mental function and the horizontal line, physical function. Non-dual Reality is represented by the zero point where the two meet.

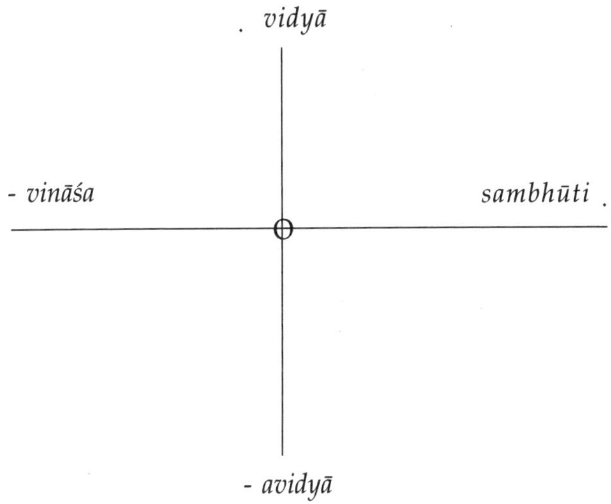

To realize the nature of these *māyā* dualities it is necessary to know them together; by doing so their secret nature is revealed. It is as if their nature is veiled by *māyā*'s wrappings. One may be so infatuated by the beauty of those wrappings as to all too easily mistake them for the content. They are like the golden casket of the *Īśa Upaniṣad* which the seeker (*satya-dharma*) must discriminate from the precious gem hidden within. It is as if by chance, or by the Grace of God, that this discrimination is accomplished.

The seeker here is given the epithet *satya-dharma* meaning one in whom truth (*satya*) and righteousness (*dharma*) meet and are unified.

Happiness and Suffering

The duality of happiness and suffering belongs to the *ānanda* content of the Self. The beatitude arising from the realization of non-dual *ātman* is not an experience of only sweetness and pleasure. It is a beatitude in which sweetness or bitterness, pleasure or pain are met with and experienced in peace and equanimity. It is the ideal of the *yogī* in the *Bhagavad-Gītā* where Śṛī Kṛṣṇa, addressing the warrior prince Arjuna, says:

> Having gained equanimity in pleasure and pain, in gain and loss, in victory and defeat, then come out to fight. Thus you will incur no sin.[8]

A little later Śṛī Kṛṣṇa says:

> Established in Yoga, O winner of wealth, perform actions having abandoned attachments and having become balanced in success and failure, for balance of mind is called Yoga.[9]

Such references to balance of mind, impartiality and non-attachment are frequent in the *Bhagavad-Gītā*.

The same views are implicitly expressed by Narayana Guru in many of his works. They are explicitly stated in his *Vāsudevāṣṭakam* (Eight Verses on *Vāsudeva-Viṣṇu*) in which *Viṣṇu* is praised as the Supreme Spiritually Exalted Personage (*rāja-haṁsaḥ*) who treats honour and dishonour equally (*mānāpamānā-sama-mānasaḥ*).

In Chapter 9 of the *Bhagavad-Gītā*, called *Rājavidyā-Rājaguhya-Yoga* (The Yoga of Kingly Wisdom and Kingly Secret), Śṛī Kṛṣṇa says:

> I am immortality and death; I am Being and non-Being, O Arjuna.[10]

---

8. *Bhagavad-Gītā*, II.38.
9. Ibid., II.48.
10. Ibid., IX.19.

Śrī Kṛṣṇa stands here as the personification of the Absolute, *sat-cit-ānanda*.

All dualities are implicit in the non-dual Absolute. They are the explicit expressions of the Absolute in its field of relativity. It is in this sense that Narayana Guru says that such words as *sat* also imply their opposites. The phrase "the words such as *sat*" of this *sūtra*, thus, signifies *sat-cit-ānanda* that define *Brahman*.

Sūtra 8

पूर्वं सदिदमनुसृत्य चक्षुरादयश्चैकं चेति ॥

pūrvaṁ sad idam anusṛtya cakṣurādayaś caikaṁ ceti ॥

pūrvam	:	in the beginning (First)
sat	:	Existence
idam	:	this world (appears as)
anusṛtya	:	followed by
cakṣuḥ ādayaḥ ca	:	eyes, etc. (senses also)
ekam ca	:	and one (and mind)
iti	:	thus

In the beginning this was Existence, followed by the apparent existence of senses and mind.

SOME of the Upaniṣads describe how the world emerged from the ground of undifferentiated Reality, but there are versions of this cosmic creation in some Upaniṣads which seem to contradict the versions in others. The *Chāndogya Upaniṣad,* for example, says: "In the beginning this world was *sat* alone, one without a second."[1] Stating what seems a contrary view the *Taittirīya Upaniṣad* says: "*Asat* verily was this world in the beginning."[2] This difference is no more, however, than views of Reality from different perspectives — from the standpoint

1. *Chāndogya Upaniṣad,* VI.2.1.
2. *Taittirīya Upaniṣad,* II.7.1.

of the causal substance of the world on the one hand and, on the other, from the standpoint of the non-existence of a manifest world apart from that as was stated earlier in *sūtra* 5. This and the following four *sūtra*s relate to the former view, whilst *sūtra*s from 13 onwards relate to the latter view.

The *Aitareya Upaniṣad* portrays the emanation of the world in a detailed manner with subjective and objective aspects, and shows how these two aspects are essentially of the same substance. The Upaniṣad begins with these words:

> The Self verily was all this world in the beginning. Nothing else whatsoever existed winking. He thought "Let me now create the worlds." He created these worlds constituted of the sky, light-rays, death and water. This sky is above the heaven; the heaven is its support. The light-rays are the atmosphere and death is the earth. Beneath them are the waters.[3]

The Upaniṣad then describes how the Self, having created the objective world from itself, imbues it with a subjective aspect of knower and preserver. This, on a universal level, is the Cosmic Person or God. On the individual level it is a human being.

The Upaniṣad goes on to provide a detailed allegorical description of the sequential emergence from a restless ocean of many subjective and objective aspects of the arising world. It describes the principles inhered in the Cosmic Person which are seen as distinct divinities. It speaks of the emergence of awareness, of mind and its functions, and of the senses, their instruments and their objects. It describes the emergence of vital breath, of the principles of urge in hunger and thirst and of the elements, earth, water, fire, air and space. It culminates with the emergence of human beings endowed with highly evolved functional attributes, born into a field of procreation and death. These functional attributes correspond to those of

3. *Aitareya Upaniṣad*, I.1.2.

the Cosmic Person and in this sense the Upaniṣad agrees with the Biblical concept that God created man in his own image. In another sense it may also be said that man conceives of God in his (man's) image. The Upaniṣad makes it clear that all these factors, principles, attributes and entities, emerging from *sat*, exist only as integral aspects of *sat*, the one Self.

The Principle of Urge

In the *Aitareya Upaniṣad* hunger and thirst represent an inner urge to partake of and enjoy the manifest world. All human functions have a specific physical abode, but the Upaniṣad declares that hunger and thirst have no abode. It says:

> Hunger and thirst said to Him (the Self): "for us two find an abode." He said to them: "I make you two partakers among these divinities." Therefore to whichever divinity an offering is made, hunger and thirst become partakers of it.[4]

The urge to partake of the world has no home. The functioning of one's faculties, at any moment, is directed by some inner need equatable to a hunger or thirst for something of the world. The contact of the subjective senses with their objects transforms the latter into the "enjoyables," the food (*annam*), with which to satisfy that hunger or thirst. With the emergence of the enjoyables and the desire for them, the creation of the world reaches its finality. Then, the Upaniṣad tells us, the Self looks at the world thus created and sees only Himself in it:

> He, being born thus, beheld the manifested beings; for what else was there perceivable, or what else here would one desire to speak of? He perceived this very person Brahman, all-pervading. He said to Himself: "Now I have directly seen it!"[5]

With this perception of the oneness of *sat* in everything, from

4. *Aitareya Upaniṣad*, I.2.5.

5. Ibid., I.3.13.

the Cosmic Person to the enjoyment of food by individual living beings, the picture is completed.

Senses, Mind and the Pramāṇas

The Guru in this *sūtra* says: "In the beginning this was Existence," and then says "followed by the apparent existence of senses and mind." The sequence, "In the beginning" followed by "followed by," implies the impossibility of there being existence without a means of knowing it. Existence without knowledge of it has no meaning. The senses, appearing with mind, are aspects of mind. Mind (*manas*) is reasoning, thinking, evaluating, deciding, sensing intelligence. It is a functional mode of Consciousness, the instrumentality of knowledge, the means of knowing anything at all.

Indian philosophers have always insisted on demarcating, right at the outset, the scope of their themes and the definition of the valid means of knowledge (*pramāṇas*) to be employed in that regard. This *sūtra* suggests that mind and senses are, therefore, the instruments of *pramāṇas* too.

Vedānta specifies six *pramāṇas* arising out of the functioning of the mind and senses. They are *pratyakṣa* (perception), *anumāna* (inference), *upamāna* (analogy), *śabda*, *āgama* or *śruti* (scriptural or verbal evidence), *arthāpatti* (presumption), and *anupalabdhi* (non-apprehension).

Narayana Guru in his *Darśana-Mālā* refers only to the first three of the six mentioned above, as means that help in acquiring conditioned knowledge (*sopādhika-jñāna*).[6]

Vedāntins accept that the *pramāṇas* are valid only until the final certitude of the Self is attained, as explicitly stated by Śaṅkara at the end of the "Introduction" to his commentaries on Bādarāyaṇa's *Brahma-Sūtras*. Narayana Guru defines this final certitude unattained by any *pramāṇa* as follows:

6. See Chapter VII of the *Darśana-Mālā*.

> That which is denoted by the words *aum tat sat* (*aum*, That Is The Existent) and the state of awareness of the oneness of *Brahman* and the Self; devoid of any conceptualization; it is said to be *para-jñāna* (transcendental awareness).[7]

This transcendental awareness is also known as *nirupādhika-jñāna* (unconditioned knowledge). The Guru affirms that the *pramāṇas*, being of the nature of conditioned perceptions, have validity only in the field of conditioned knowledge. He defines perceptual knowledge as:

> That knowledge by the presence of which alone all entities manifestly shine by themselves, it is indicated by the name *pratyakṣa-jñāna* (perceptual knowledge).[8]

The functions of mind and the contact of the senses with their objects are manifestations of *cit*. For that reason, the question of how mind and matter, which have unlike natures, become one in sense perception is not a problem in Vedānta. They are perceived in Vedānta only as two conditioned manifestations of unconditioned *cit* and not as two distinct and separate realities.

A popular standard reference book for students of Vedānta is a treatise written by Dharmarāja Adhvarīndra called the *Vedānta-Paribhāṣā*. It elucidates the *pramāṇas* and defines *pramāṇa* as that means by which one attains certainty (*pramā-karaṇam pramāṇam*).[9] When conditioned as specific objects, Dharmarāja Adhvarīndra refers to *caitanya* or *cit* (Unconditioned Consciousness) as *viṣaya caitanya* (Consciousness conditioned specifically as objects). Manifest as mental faculties he calls it *pramātṛ caitanya* (Consciousness conditioned as knower), and when conditioned as the active functioning of mental faculties

7. *Darśana-Mālā*, VII.10.

8. Ibid., VII.6.

9. *Vedānta Paribhāṣā*, p. 14.

he calls it *pramāṇa caitanya* (Consciousness conditioned as the valid means of knowledge).

The process by which an item of perceptual knowledge gets formulated is described in the *Vedānta-Paribhāṣā*. It is freely interpreted here as follows:

> As the water of a reservoir issuing through a hole assumes the form of a channel, then entering a paddy field assumes a rectangle, so also the luminous mental faculties gush forth through the eyes and other senses and assume the form of objects like "jar" and are modified into the form of the object. This very act is known as *vṛtti* (the function of acquiring perceptual knowledge). But in the case of the other *pramāṇas* such as inference as, for example, inferring fire on seeing smoke, the luminous mental faculties do not go forth to the space occupied by the object because these *pramāṇas* are not in direct contact with the objects.

Subject and object are conditioned aspects of *caitanya*. But in the instant of every specific cognition they forgo their conditioned states and are united and, thus, realized as one. Therefore non-duality is unconsciously experienced at every moment of cognition. That which differentiates perception from other *pramāṇas* (inference, for example) is whether this union of subject and object is of an external or internal cognition.

In every specific cognition, whether perceptual or inferential, subject and object are united in awareness. Narayana Guru defines inferential knowledge as:

> That form of knowledge by which something possible is ascertained (e.g. the presence of fire) as indicated by a sense contact (e.g. the sight of smoke) arising from incipient memory concerning the association of things; it is called *anumiti-jñāna* (inferential knowledge).[10]

10. *Darśana-Mālā*, VII. 7.

Some schools of thought consider *upamāna* (analogy), *arthāpatti* (presumption) and *anupalabdhi* (non-apprehension) as variants of inference and do not therefore think of them as distinct *pramāṇas*. Narayana Guru, however, does not define the latter two while considering *upamāna* as a distinct means of knowledge. He says:

> Nearing an object to be cognized knowledge of it is gained in the form of, for example, "this is the animal said to have such and such marks." This means by which knowledge of the object is ascertained is called *upamiti-jñāna* (knowledge by analogy).[11]

Narayana Guru does not mention scriptural evidence (*śabda*) as a valid means of acquiring knowledge, probably because its concepts have validity only through unconditioned transcendental awareness, where there is no discrimination of subject, object or *pramāṇa*.

Dharmarāja Adhvarīndra, however, defines *śabda* as follows:

> Such pronouncements whose relation to an intended meaning is not contradicted by any other means of knowledge, is called *āgama*.[12]

Āgama is another name for scriptures. Scriptures are valid only because no other means of acquiring theoretical knowledge of transcendent Reality can be availed of. Though derived from the intuitive perception of enlightened seers (*jñānins*), scriptural evidence too belongs to the field of conditioned knowledge. Its function is to formulate concepts of the Absolute. No matter what the many different scriptures purport, the unconditioned Reality of their matter is one and the same. It remains unaffected by any concepts of it.

---

11. *Darśana-Mālā*, VII. 8.

12. *Vedānta Paribhāṣā*, p. 86.

Arthāpatti and Anupalabdhi

It sometimes happens that an assumption is made about a perceived event which has no other obvious explanation. For example, a man is observed to grow fat although he is not seen to eat anything. It may then be assumed that he eats secretly. Such an explanation of an observed event which is otherwise inexplicable is called *arthāpatti* (presumption).

If a well-lit room is empty one may say that he does not see a jar in that room. Another, not apprehending its presence there, may say he sees the non-existence of a jar in the room. No perception is involved in either assertion, and were there a jar in the room it would have been seen. The valid means of knowledge by which the non-existence (*abhāva*) of something is ascertained, as in the latter case, is called *anupalabdhi* (non-apprehension).

The word *abhāva* means the absence of *bhāva* (manifest form) and in Indian thought it is a philosophical category. Whilst every *bhāva* is conditional appearance of unconditioned *sat*, every *abhāva* is the absence of anything manifestly perceived (needing a *pramāṇa* for its ascertainment) which has implied existence as non-apparent *sat*.

In this *sūtra* Narayana Guru asserts that senses and mind, the means of knowledge, are implicit in *sat*, for without means of knowledge there is no knowledge. Conversely, without knowledge there can be no *sat*, for how can there be existence without senses and mind to know it, and who is there with senses and mind who can deny existence?

Sūtra 9

ज्ञातृज्ञानयोरन्योन्यविषयविषयित्वान्मिथुनत्वमिति ॥

jñātṛ jñānayor anyonya viṣaya viṣayitvān mithunatvam iti ॥

jñātṛjñānayoḥ	:	regarding knower and knowledge
anyonya	:	mutually
viṣayaviṣayitvāt	:	because they are subject and object
mithunatvam-iti	:	thus they are paired

Knower and knowledge are paired, mutually subject and object.

THE triple factors (*tripuṭi*) of knower, knowledge and known, are involved in all human experience. They are the inseparably related aspects of the knowing function of consciousness, each meaningless without the others. This *sūtra* considers the mutuality of knower and knowledge as paired factors of the trinity. The mutuality and pairing of knowledge and known is considered in the next *sūtra*.

An individual being's knowledge is of a knowable perceived as having external or internal reality. The former is called objective knowledge and the latter is subjective knowledge. Knowledge requires a knower and in the concept of these as a pair each is able to occupy the seat of either subject or object. Looking outwards at an externally perceived knowable, oneself is the subject and the external knowable is the object. However, if one's attention is turned inwards, oneself becomes the object of one's own subjective awareness.

As subjective awareness in not other than oneself, subject and object are thus mutually paired. The "I" which is subject and the "I" which is object are not two, but in seeking to know the "I" of oneself they appear to occupy two seats. The one "I" sees itself as two in the apparent duality of erroneous perception. The same is true in the perception of an external world. The world and the "I" regarding it are not two but one Reality, one Self. In looking at the world as an external object an individual's perception of it is subjective; it is not the same as another individual's subjective perception. The subjective world of each is not that of another and in that sense each individual lives in his or her own isolated world.

Knower and knowledge are not two entities but two functional facets of one Consciousness. Unaware of his true nature, the individuated human being considers himself to be the knower of knowledge separate from himself. Narayana Guru says of this:

> Apart from Consciousness "I" does not exist. Consciousness does not exist apart from "I." Effulgence alone is all that is. Knowledge and knower when contemplated are inarguably one substance alone.
>
> Ignorant of the ultimate oneness of content
> Are those who treat knowledge as their own.
> Even when erroneously treated thus,
> Knowledge never really remains
> Distinct from the knower;
> Nor does the ultimate Reality.[1]

Consciousness, Knower, Knowledge and Transcendental Truth, are distinct and different only in the realm of words.

Many entities, having apparently separate existences, constitute the individual's knowledge of an external world. For example, a mosquito buzzes around "my ear." Responding

1. *Ātmopadeśa-Śatakam*, vv. 59-60.

to this stimulus "my hand" reaches up to brush it away. Still it persists in buzzing around and "I" am again incited to chase "it" away. In this example, the mosquito is perceived as a separate existence, my ear and my hand are seen as separate parts of "myself" and the situation is one in which "I myself" am annoyed by "it," the mosquito. It is a perception in which myself is the subject/knower of the mosquito as an external object. From its side the mosquito is the subject/knower of myself as object. Both myself and it respond instinctively to a threatening situation. But it is Knowledge Itself which incites an impulse of self-preservation in both and makes "myself" and "it" mutually subject and object.

It is *sat* expressed as myself and mosquito. It is *cit* in which each knows the other, and it is *ānanda* in which each has instinctive self-preserving responses. In this example, the one Self expresses its three aspects as myself/mosquito (Existence), awareness each of the other (Consciousness), and response each to the other (Evaluation).

The underlying truth of the "myself" and "mosquito" situation is the same truth of the mutuality between all sentient beings. The recent findings of modern science and the ancient knowledge of India's Upaniṣads accord in the view that nothing in this world is quite insentient; only the degree of sentiency differs in different entities. It is the mutuality of subject and object which indicates the non-dual Reality in both, of which all separate things are but more or less bright sparkings.

Knowledge, the Inciter to Action

Action (*karma*) is of two orders: the one is action performed by an individual being and the other is universal action. All action arises from some prior impulse of intelligence. Action follows action in an endless chain arising out of knowledge. A particular action is a subjective response to a particular object of perceptual knowledge. In the myself/mosquito example, myself's knowledge of the mosquito's annoying buzz provoked the instinctive action of myself's hand. In turn, the mosquito's knowledge of the threatening hand provoked its instinctive action to avoid the hand. It is the particular kinds of knowledge acquired by an individual from which particular kinds of individual actions arise and it is the particular knowledge content (Consciousness) of the universe from which universal action arises. In both, the triple factors of knowledge, knower and knowable are always there. The *Bhagavad-Gītā* says:

> Knowledge, the knowable and the knower are the threefold incentive to action.[2]

Each action performed by an individual brings a result which becomes the basis of further action. Action is movement, in movement there is change and through change life proceeds. Action following action continues even when it is autonomous and not in the individual's awareness as, for example, the heartbeat and breathing in deep-sleep. The *Bhagavad-Gītā* says:

> No one, indeed, can exist even for an instant without performing action, for everyone is helplessly driven to activity by the *guṇa*s born of Nature.[3]

The actions arising from natural forces also result in further action and nothing in the manifest world is completely devoid of activity. But only man, of this planet's beings, feels himself to be the doer of actions and burdens himself with the concept of being responsible for their fruits (*karma-phala*s). As long as he perceives himself to be the doer (*kartā*) he will indeed be bound by his actions and will continue in their bondage until he acquires knowledge of their Real Doer — that which in its active state (*kartṛtva*) is called Nature. Liberated then from their binding influence, his actions will quite naturally become

2. *Bhagavad-Gītā*, XVIII.18.
3. Ibid., III.5.

right actions bringing beneficial results. His ethical and moral sensibilities will assume universal dimensions and he will feel himself responsible only to Nature Itself. The actions which bring this liberation are called *karma-yoga*. The culmination of knowledge (Vedānta) is when knowledge, knower and knowable are merged in the effulgence of awareness called *nirupādhika-jñāna* (Unconditioned Knowledge). All other stages and kinds of knowledge are called *sopādhika-jñāna* (conditioned knowledge). Narayana Guru distinguishes these two in his *Darśana-Mālā* as follows:

> Knowledge is one and unconditioned indeed. Conditioned knowledge also is not different from it. That knowledge devoid of "I" consciousness and the like, is the Unconditioned One.
>
> That knowledge manifested as subject-consciousness within, and object-consciousness without, it is understood as conditioned knowledge.[4]

An experiential vision of this *nirupādhika-jñāna* is portrayed in the *Bhagavad-Gītā*, as if put in a nutshell, as follows:

> That in which all that has come into being is perceived in yourself, and then in Me. (IV.35)

"All that has come into being" signifies all the worlds and all the beings, living and non-living, in them put together. The core of Vedāntic wisdom thus consists in intuitively perceiving all the objects first in the consciousness of the perceiver or subject, and then that subject-consciousness in the Absolute or unconditioned Consciousness. In this state of experiential oneness, differentiating the knower and knowledge is impossible, and if at all such a differentiation is relevant, the two would be felt to be mutually subject and object.

---

4. *Darśana-Mālā*, VII.1.2.

The knowledge (*jñāna*) desired by a seeker of the Self is the "Unconditioned One" so defined. The way to it is indicated in these verses of the *Bhagavad-Gītā*:

> Freedom from conventional pride (*amānitvam*), unpretentiousness (*adaṁbhitvam*), non-hurting (*ahiṁsā*), forbearance (*kṣānti*), straightforwardness (*ārjavam*), loyal service to the teacher (*ācāryopāsanam*), purity (*śaucam*), steadfastness (*sthairyam*), and the state of self-restraint.
>
> Detachment from sense-interests (*indriyārtheṣu vairāgyam*), absence of egoism (*anahaṁkāra*), insight of the pain and evil of birth, death, old-age and sickness.
>
> Non-clinging (*asakti*) and absence of intense attachments to wife, children, home and such like and constant neutrality (*samacittatvam*) towards desirable and undesirable events.
>
> Unswerving, one-pointed, constant devotion to Me (the Absolute), a preference for secluded places and avoidance of crowds.
>
> Constant pursuit of Self-understanding, vision of the goal and meaning of knowledge (*tattva-jñānārtha-darśanam*). This is declared to be wisdom (*jñāna*). Whatever is other than this is ignorance (*ajñāna*).[5]

The path to Self-realization, indicated by these verses, is not to be undertaken without the determination to meet its requirements. The seeker may be helped to a better understanding of these requirements by some further definitions:

Amānitvam (freedom from conventional pride) is not a common social virtue. It indicates a complete lack of concern for one's standing in society or for the views of others regarding one's social status. It also indicates the values of a contemplative seeker whose moral norms are within the categorical imperatives of his own true nature. It will be his natural disposition, strengthened by its cultivation as a self-imposed discipline.

---

5. *Bhagavad-Gītā*, XIII.7-11.

Adambhitvam (unpretentiousness) is to be without false notions of oneself in the light of Self-knowledge. It is a positive virtue, its corollary being that one possessed of it will not claim superiority over others, nor will impose false and arrogant views on others, nor deride their views and convictions.

Ahiṁsā (non-hurting) is not merely a desire not to cause injury or pain to other beings, but is generous universal love for all beings and a positive desire for the happiness and welfare of others. The prevalent vegetarianism of Self-knowers is a natural outcome of this principle.

Kṣānti (forbearance) is the virtue of non-retaliation to the wrongs or hurts done to one. It is in "turning the other cheek" and not seeking "an eye for an eye and a tooth for a tooth." The latter is inherent in Nature's flow of action and reaction.

Ārjavam (straightforwardness) implies frankness and honesty in one's dealings with others and in speaking out and behaving in accordance with one's own moral integrity, without fear of disapproval or desire for approbation.

Ācāryopāsanam (loyal service to the teacher) is service to the teacher which is helpful and supportive of his work. The teacher implied in this context is a wisdom teacher, a *guru*. A true enlightened *guru* is able to remove the darkness of ignorance and bring the light of realization to those he instructs. Loyal supportive service is his due; it is freely rendered in love and gratitude for the great gift of the teaching he provides.

Śaucam (purity) means to be free of extraneous harmful substances. It implies the taking in only of that which is nourishing to body, mind and spirit and the avoidance of harmful matter. This does not apply only to such toxins as tobacco, alcohol and bad food and drink, but to the avoidance of all negative influences and associations which may obstruct or divert one from the path of wisdom seeking. It also implies cleanliness of body, mind, senses and habitation and purity in words and actions.

Sthairyam (steadfastness) implies the resolute nature of one's life and conduct on the path to Self-realization and the constancy of one who will not be swayed from that path.

Ātma-vinigrahaḥ (self-withdrawal) implies a withdrawal from sensory attachments and transitory values, and the drawing-out of Self-knowledge from the ignorance which veils it.

Indriyārtheṣu-vairāgyam (detachment from sense-interest) is the lessening of interest in sense-objects and sensory experience, resulting from a growing interest in that which transcends sense perception.

Anahaṁkāra (absense of egoism) implies the absence of erroneous identification with the concept of oneself as an incarnate personality of worldly status; it results from the realization of one's true identity. This makes one recognize the nature and impermanence of one's identity as a body and personality subject to the pains of birth, change, disease, old-age and death, and brings release from identification with it.

Asakti (non-clinging) is the lessening of attachments to worldly, transitory relationships as one's relationship with the unchanging Reality grows. The strongest of worldly relationships is with one's immediate family of parents, brothers, sisters, husband or wife and children. Non-clinging does not mean a lessening of love and concern for them; to the contrary, one's love for them grows and becomes less selfish. But knowledge of the true identity does mean less of anxiety for them and reduced dependence on them for one's fulfilment and happiness.

Samacittatvam (neutrality) is the ability to meet the different experiences of life without being overwhelmed by them. The events of life are a stream of changes and to live incarnate in the manifest world is to experience constant change. Sometimes life's events are pleasurable and one wishes to hold on to them but they pass away. At other times they are painful and tormenting, but these too pass. With growing knowledge of the unchanging Consciousness in which all events are structured, they come to be regarded as changing pictures flickering on Reality's screen of awareness. With inner stability established, an attitude of neutrality develops towards whatever life brings. Then without becoming indifferent to the many ups and downs of life, one becomes better able to weather them.

With requirements of the seeker in view, the *Bhagavad-Gītā* indicates that dwelling in a secluded place away from crowds is conducive to gaining wisdom. On one level that means keeping oneself away from the noise and bustle of crowded living. But on another level, it means dwelling in the peaceful seclusion of inner awareness. It declares the vision of the Absolute (*Brahman*) portrayed as quoted above to be wisdom (*tattva-jñānārtha-darśanam*), and all else to be ignorance.

Vedāntic wisdom is not mere theoretical understanding of Reality directed towards gaining intellectual satisfaction. Its acquisition, a vision of the Absolute, is Self-knowledge in which the Self-Reality alone is directly perceived in all that is manifest as all the fleeting phases of life. The attitudes and aspects of self-discipline detailed above, which the *Bhagavad-Gītā* enjoins on the seeker (*jñātṛ*), are to aid his or her attainment of that wisdom (*jñāna*). Practising them in faith and constancy the seeker will come to know that in which *jñātṛ* and *jñāna* are mutually subject and object.

One who treads the path to Self-knowledge, the realization of *Brahman*, is a *brahmacārin*. He himself is mutually subject and object, the mutual knower and knowledge of Himself, the prize sought for and its attainment.

Sūtra 10

एवं ज्ञानज्ञेयविभागे ॥

evam jñāna jñeya vibhāge ॥

evam	:	so too
jñāna	:	knowledge (and)
jñeya	:	known
vibhāge	:	in the division between

So too, with the division of knowledge and known.

IN the previous *sūtra* Narayana Guru coupled knower and knowledge in a mutually interchangeable relationship. Now in this *sūtra* he does the same with knowledge and known.

Knowledge in the Western World

As the three factors, the knower, knowledge and the known, are involved in **all** experiences, the pairing in both cases (knower and knowledge, and knowledge and known) is simply a means the Guru employs to express different aspects of the one phenomenon. Knowledge (*jñāna*) is the common factor in both these conceptual pairings. It is a word, however, which has a meaning in the "Western world" different from the meaning of the word in the context of Vedānta. In the former, the word is used to denote some specific content or contents of awareness. Even when it expresses a field of knowledge its use invariably indicates some particular content of the field as, for example, "the field of knowledge of botany."

In the Western world knowledge is always some perception possessed by mind. The word is never used to express knowledge itself as the knower of the field; it would never be said that knowledge is the **subject** of perception, but it is **about** or **of** a perceivable or conceptual entity, value, idea or abstraction. The terms "Unconditioned Knowledge" and "conditioned knowledge" which have been employed in these commentaries in translating the Vedāntic concepts, *nirupādhika-jñāna* and *sopādhika-jñāna,* would, in the West, elicit the question — "Unconditioned and conditioned knowledge of what?" To express the idea of the field in which knowledge is structured, either the word "consciousness" or the word "awareness" is used. These two words, understood to indicate a function of mind, are freely interchanged as synonyms. These words too, in the West, are always used in the objective sense of "one **having** consciousness or awareness" and never in the subjective sense of "one **being** consciousness or awareness." In Vedānta, the words consciousness, awareness, knower, knowledge, and known all denote the one *cit*, Consciousness Itself. Separable only in the field of word usage they are the known field, the knower of the field and the knowing of the field, together, one Indivisible Reality. Knowledge (*jñāna*) is the Knower (*jñātr̥*) of Itself, the Known (*jñeya*). It is not something from outside to be possessed. In his work entitled *Aṛivu,* Narayana Guru says:

> Knowledge is never known as an object.
>
> Once known, the two become one.[1]

In Western thought those states in which there is no objective awareness as, for example, in deep-sleep or under a general anaesthetic or in coma, are not considered to be states of consciousness at all. Rather, they are thought to be unconscious states: meaning, states of mind without awareness. They are thought to be states of mind caused by a resting or impaired

1. *Aṛivu,* v. 5.

brain, located nowhere but in the brain. As states of mind are certainly related to the workings of the brain this, in a certain mechanistic sense, may be a valid view. But the view of the brain as itself a somehow autonomously conscious physical organ, a consciousness-creating-master of an integrated organic system, is not valid. In truth the brain is an instrument of consciousness and not its master.

Jñāna, Jñeya and Kṣetra

The conceptual duality of knowledge and known is valid in the field of human communication when they are expressed as subject and object. In the absence of the need for such a communicable expression of duality the concept has no relevance. It is a dialectical expression which does not dim the luminosity of non-dual Knowledge, the Self, the one and the same Universal Intelligence which shines in and illuminates all entities. It is our species alone which makes of it a *jñeya* (an object of knowledge). The nature of this conceptual *jñeya* is described in the *Bhagavad-Gītā* in the following verses:

> I shall declare to you that which is to be known, by which, through being known, one gains immortality, the Supreme Absolute, beginningless and endless, neither Being nor non-Being.
>
> With hands and feet everywhere, eyes, head and mouth everywhere, ears everywhere in the world, enveloping all.
>
> Shining as the senses, their functions and their objects, but beyond them. Sustainer of all, without attributes, yet the enjoyer of attributes.
>
> Within and without all beings, animate and inanimate, too subtle to be discerned, it is the unknowable. Standing far off and near too is That.
>
> Indivisible, yet divided as it were in beings, the sustainer of beings. It is that, remaining back yet coming out, in endless transformations.

> The light even of lights it is said to be beyond darkness; knowledge, knowable and known, it dwells in the hearts of all beings.[2]

These verses speak of Knowledge Itself and not some specific knowledge objective to be gained and possessed as, for example, the knowledge of molecular matter gained by physical science. The very processes of logic and reason create the artificial divisions of knower, knowledge and known; divisions which do not occur in intuition and disappear altogether in the fourth state of consciousness.

Discriminating between the known and the knower of the field, the *Bhagavad-Gītā* says:

> The perishable (*śarīra*) is called "the field" (*kṣetra*) and the one who knows it is called, "the knower of the field" (*kṣetrajña*) by the knowing wise. Know Myself to be the *kṣetrajña* in all *kṣetras*.[3]

The word *śarīra* literally means "changeful and perishable" but in common usage it refers to the body. In describing the *kṣetra* as the perishable all its physical and mental aspects are included. The *Bhagavad-Gītā*, instead of following this with a description of "the knower of the field," *kṣetrajña*, as might be expected, goes on to a description of knowledge (*jñāna*) and the knowable (*jñeya*) and concludes by saying:

> Those who knowing this meditate on Me, attain My Being.[4]

The *Bhagavad Gītā* indicates here the *jñāna* and *jñeya* as awareness modes of the *kṣetrajña*. It reveals that they, mutually subject and object, are not other than the *kṣetrajña*, Itself the inconceivable and indescribable Knower of the field.

---

2. *Bhagavad-Gītā*, XIII.12-17.
3. Ibid., XIII.1.
4. Ibid., XIII.34.

Unity in Human Perceptions

The unity of knower, knowledge and known is understandable in terms of common human perceptions. For example, an object is recognized as being red in colour. The perception of colour is a result of light-waves reflected by the object passing through the eye lens and acting upon the retina, triggering off electrical impulses in the brain. The perception then depends not only upon the particular rays of light but upon the physical condition of the eyes, brain and so forth of the physical perceiver. The reactions to the same light-waves may not be exactly the same in different perceivers who have no way of comparing the colour red they see in their subjective experience. However the red they see is taken for granted to be the same. Similarly the world each perceives is a subjective experience about which there can be no absolute certainty, excepting the certain existence of a perceiver perceiving a perception. Knowledge or Consciousness, our own essential content, by functioning as the knower knowing the known, which essentially are not different, is the greatest of all mysteries.

It is the Vedānta secret expressed by Narayana Guru in these *sūtras*. The Guru reveals that all dualities are pairings of the two opposite poles of the same intrinsic field of value, just as magnetism is the intrinsic value of the field between the negative and positive poles of a magnet, and temperature is the field spanning the extremes of hot and cold. It is the inseparability of two poles which reveals that they share the same intrinsic nature as the field they link. The poles represented in the concepts of knower-knowledge and knowledge-known thus reveal their intrinsic nature to be Consciousness Itself.

Consciousness, not knowable as an object, is realized by the seeker to be himself. He finds his nature, with respect to the ocean of Infinite Eternal Consciousness, as a drop of the ocean's water, as it were, and knows that what is real in the ocean is also what is real in the drop. All other knowledge is based upon the erroneous perception of knowledge and oneself as separate subject and object. The Guru says of this:

> Apart from realizing Consciousness here as oneself, it is not to be known. One does not know it through habitual dependence on seeing "other." It is indeed the supreme mystery of the wise. Ah! who does see it?[5]

It is the impulse of Indivisible Creative Consciousness that assumes the forms of subject and object as *māyā* expressions of separate knowables. It is *ātman*, Consciousness, actualizing its *ānanda* in self-knowledge. This emanation of knowledge and knowable from an apparently separate knower is expressed by the Guru in his composition called *Aṛivu* as follows:

> That, Consciousness, is yourself. Investing it with your own knowledge it becomes the knowable.[6]

These words are in the context of instructions, directed to seekers, in which the Guru further reveals the knowable to be of aspects known or unknown and conceivable or inconceivable. As a conceivable known object it may be examined, analysed, classified and described by the five senses and comprehended through their perceptions. Even those concepts not subject to sense contact are based upon sense contact experiences. All percepts therefore are variants of sensual experience. But no sense contact is possible with an unknown object and it cannot be classified. It may be that there are unknown objects, but it cannot be said that they exist until they become, in some way, known. Even to conceive of an unknown is projecting it as known in imagination. The Real Unknown is One and Inconceivable. In the same verse, following the lines quoted above, the Guru, perhaps with some ironic humour, makes this enigmatic statement:

5. *Ātmopadeśa-Śatakam*, v. 63.

6. *Aṛivu*, v. 12 (first part).

> Such knowables are of two categories, one which is known and the other which is not known.[7]

The not known or the inconceivable here and the *jñeya* (what is to be ultimately known) alluded to in the *Bhagavad-Gītā* verses quoted earlier refer to one and the same *Brahman*, the unknowable yet realizable.

The knowable of the verse, which can be known, is always perceptible to the senses, the five instruments of an individual being's knowing mind. Narayana Guru continues from the above verse as follows:

> Likewise, knowledge fills the knower and subsequently one spark of it falls into the first category of knowables and splits into five.[8]

Categories of Knowledge

The five senses comprise five categories of knowledge; sight, sound, smell, taste and touch. A sixth category is in the knower's awareness of "I am knowledge"; a seventh is "I am the knower of knowledge" and an eighth category is in the knowledge of the One Unknowable. The Guru expresses this eightfold categorization of knowledge as follows:

> One knowing that knowledge is in his awareness knows also that he is the knower. There being six knowables, plus knowing and knower, knowledge is thus eightfold.[9]

The *Bhagavad-Gītā*, in the following verses, says that knowledge based upon the *guṇa*s has three distinct values:

> That knowledge by which One Being is seen in all separate entities, the Indivisible in the divided, it is *sāttvika*, pure knowledge.

---

7. *Aṛivu*, v. 12 (conclusion).
8. Ibid., v. 13.
9. Ibid., v. 14.

> That knowledge by which multiplicity of entities is seen as separate and distinct, it is *rājasa*, active and pragmatic knowledge.
>
> But that knowledge which attaches to one single effect as if it were the whole, without reason or meaning, based on no principle and insignificant, that is called *tāmasa*, inert, dark knowledge.[10]

This classification of knowledge is based upon its value in leading or deterring one's progress towards the realization that Knowledge Itself is its own final goal. Narayana Guru's ontological eightfold division and the threefold value division of the *Bhagavad-Gītā* is of knowledge as it pertains to individual beings. In the final verse of his *Aṛivu* the Guru says:

> In the field of the knowables Consciousness, being of the seven and oneself, becomes eight.

These categories are simply analytical mind-creations which in no way affect the unity and integrity of the one Consciousness being analysed. Such an analytical mind is able to see the many in the One and the One in the many, just as gold may be seen in many shapes and many shapes may be seen in gold. The Guru concludes the final verse of *Aṛivu* with these words:

> Knowledge thus is known divided only when analysed.[11]

Whether understood as the Guru's eightfold division, the threefold division of the *Bhagavad-Gītā* or the *tripuṭi* of knowledge, knower and known, Consciousness remains the One Indivisible Reality, *ātman*, the One Self expressed as the many. The seeker's goal is the realization of himself as That. The Guru says:

---

10. *Bhagavad-Gītā*, XVIII.20-22.

11. *Aṛivu*, v. 15.

Knowledge, the knower and the knowing are but one; the primeval Great One alone. By merging into that Indivisible, Supreme Consciousness shining forth, do become That alone.[12]

12. *Ātmopadeśa-Śatakam*, v. 4.

Sūtra 11

एकैकं रुद्रत्वमासीदिति ॥

ekaikaṁ rudratvam āsīd iti ॥

eka-ekam	:	each apart
rudratvam	:	cause of sorrow
āsīt	:	has been (always)
iti	:	thus

Each apart has always been a cause of sorrow.

In the Indian tradition human beings (*manuṣya*s) are the descendants of Manu, the one who thinks. It is apparent, however, that man's thinking does not bring him the understanding of the nature of his existence nor of the nature of the world he perceives as separate from himself. It is this understanding that would enable him to live in peace with himself and in harmony with the natural laws governing his life in the manifest world. The understanding he lacks is of himself — that the knower (*jñātā*) and his knowledge (*jñāna*) is one with the known (*jñeya*). He needs to realize that his nature and the nature of his perceptions are, in essence, pure Consciousness. In the absence of awareness of this One Reality, he sees a world of multiple and separately existing entities and lives in a world in which his own existence is separate from everything and everyone else. His erroneous understanding of the nature of perceived existence, an ignorance which in Vedānta is called *ajñāna*, is the cause of all his suffering. The realization of one's unity with the perceived world brings an automatic end to the sorrow and suffering inherent in the perception of separateness. Suffering is always seen as having an extraneous cause but both happiness and misery are inner states, the poles of the *ānanda* content of man's value sensing nature. Although suffering is a response to stimuli understood as external, the cause of suffering is within oneself, in the perception of oneself as a separate sufferer of sufferings.

In the unity of knower, knowledge and known there is nothing outside oneself to fear or to cause suffering. But perceived as existing apart, knower, knowledge and known will always be, as Narayana Guru asserts in this *sūtra*, a cause of sorrow. There are many separate situations which are seen, feared and experienced as causes of suffering. However, as long as life persists in them there can always be a glimmer of possibility, some little hope of recovery. Only in the finality of death is there no possibility of recovery and the death of a loved one or one's own death is greatly feared. But the Real in one is never born and never dies, and death is real only in the realm of born beings. One who realizes this truth transcends the realm of birth and death and is freed from the fear of death. But "one who sees multiplicity goes from death to death" as Narayana Guru says in the verse quoted earlier from his *Darśana-Mālā*.[1]

Rudratva

In Indian tradition suffering is conceived, in an allegorical sense, as being a state of *rudratva*. Rudra is an epithet of Śiva. Derived from the root *rud*, meaning, "to shed tears," its literal translation is "the one who makes others weep." In Hindu mythology Śiva is the Dissolver in the trinity of chief gods in which Brahmā is the Creator and Viṣṇu is the Preserver. It is

1. See p. 35.

paradoxical that his name means "the most auspicious" though he functions as the continual dissolver of manifestations. But it is only with the dissolution of old forms that new forms emerge and it is in this auspicious process that life and creation flow everlastingly new. That which is seen from a human perspective as destruction is an indispensable aspect of creation and so it is that Śiva is "the most auspicious." In ancient Indian scriptures Rudra has eleven forms, called *ekādaśa Rudra*s, suggesting the many forms of evil. Their function is the annihilation of evil-doing and, in this sense, Rudra is understood to be the one who makes evil-doers weep. The cause of man's suffering is his ignorance of Reality and therefore his perception of knower, knowledge and known as separate realities is an evil reducing him to *rudratva*, the state of being in sorrow.

The word *āsīt* used by Narayana Guru in this *sūtra* is a past tense meaning "that which was in the beginning." In scriptures and philosophical literature it refers to the origin of the world. Man's misconception of himself, as a knower separate from the known, is as old as his appearance on this planet and has always caused him sorrow.

Rudratva in Fear

Fear is the greatest of torments, the emotion that is most feared. But as "oneself" is the one percept which is not a separate other, one does not fear oneself. Fear is always of "other" and where no other is perceived there is nothing to fear. The state of fearlessness (*abhaya*) is, therefore, one of the definitions of the Absolute given in the *Bṛhadāraṇyaka Upaniṣad*.[2]

With the attainment of *abhaya* (fearlessness), *rudratva* (the state of being in sorrow) is transformed into *śivatva* (the state of being the most auspicious). *Śivatva* is a state of being without fear and suffering. It is attained in one's identification with a

2. *abhayam vai brahma* — *Bṛhadāraṇyaka Upaniṣad*, IV.4.25.

world no longer perceived as separate. The *Bhagavad-Gītā*, speaking of the union of knower and known, says:

> Even a little of this *dharma* (way) delivers from great fear.[3]

Rudratva in Changefulness

Indian tradition refers to the world as an ocean of suffering called *saṁsāra-sāgara* (literally, "an ocean of changefulness"). In his universal prayer called *Daivadaśakam* (which he wrote for simple devout supplicants for whom his philosophical teachings were inaccessible), Narayana Guru addresses God as the captain of a mighty ship. He prays for protection in crossing that fearful ocean, also called *bhava-sāgara*, "the ocean of becoming." In ten verses, the Guru prays to be carried across the ocean of change and sorrow, and prays to be immersed in the beatific ocean of God's everlasting glory. In this prayer Narayana Guru reveals that the world, appearing as an ocean of suffering when one is ignorant, becomes an ocean of God's glory when one awakens. It is not then the ocean which is transformed, but the voyager.

Rudratva in Ethics

The problem of setting an ethical norm for good and bad, right and wrong has beset man since he first "fell from grace," which means since his birth as a thinking animal in a world perceived as a separate jungle. Good and bad, right and wrong are relative terms and what seems good and right to one may seem bad and wrong to another. All ethical and moral norms are relative to the cultural, religious, philosophical and social context in which they are perceived and none gain absolute, fixed and universal status. It is a problem of ethics assuming the wretchedness of *rudratva*, a problem arising from the erroneous perception of separate existences. As all beings have their existence in *sat-cit-ānanda* the interest and happiness of

3. *Bhagavad-Gītā*, II.40.

one cannot be essentially different from that of another. Any perceived differences will be in the objects of interest and happiness and not in the interest and happiness aspired to. An absolute ethical norm is one in which activities bringing happiness to oneself also bring happiness to others. Activities causing suffering to oneself or others are unethical and should be avoided. Proclaiming a Vedāntic view of ethics as a basis for an absolute norm, Narayana Guru says:

> What is dear to another is dear to me, what is dear to me is dear to another too. Do keep to this norm and accordingly the action performed for the benefit of one will also ensure the benefit of others.[4]

Only actions benefiting oneself and others are ethical, and therefore even altruistic actions, performed for the benefit of others, are not ethical if they bring unhappiness to oneself. The basis of this view of ethics is the knowledge that what is real in one is real in all. It is a view the Guru expresses in the following verse:

> Whomsoever is understood as "he" or as "she," as "this one" or "that one," all when properly considered are but forms of the one Primordial Self. Therefore action performed for the sake of self-happiness should also ensure the happiness of others.[5]

In this way the *rudratva* prevailing in relativistic ethics dissolves in the absolute ethical dimension of *śivatva*.

Rudratva in Science

The separation of knower, knowledge and known in erroneous perception and the *rudratva* arising from it affects all areas of man's activities. This is nowhere more apparent than in the enquiries of modern physical sciences, the very starting point

4. *Ātmopadeśa-Śatakam*, v. 22.

5. Ibid., v. 24.

of which is the perception of a world separate from the enquirer. The scientist looks out on a matter/motion world of substances and energies and does not see himself in it. His attempts to define it in terms of its physical origins are only in terms of the transitory appearances emerging from its *sat* aspect. When he attempts to examine the contents of mind and feelings arising from *cit* and *ānanda,* these too are regarded as objective fields which the enquirer is thought to be able to examine with dispassionate objectivity. In its fields of communications, travel, medicine, agriculture and industry the achievements of modern science are immense. But so are its achievements in the production of weapons of mass destruction and in the technologies which denude the land and seas of their riches and threaten man's very existence on this planet Earth. Science which does not regard its purpose as being for the good of Earth's inhabitants is unethical. Sciences regarding a multiplicity of separate knowables in which the nature of the scientist himself is not the starting point, will fail to produce any lasting benefit for the world's beings. In this is the sorrow of science, its *rudratva.* To remove its *rudratva* and elevate it to the auspicious state of *śivatva,* a holistic science is required, a science of the Absolute which in Vedānta is called *brahmavidyā.*

Rudratva in Religion

Of all the areas of man's activities and concerns that of religion should be where most of care, love and harmony prevails between peoples. It quite apparently is not so, and that there is great conflict, hate and violence between peoples holding different religious beliefs is the shame and sorrow of religion. The very word "religion" derives from a sense of binding back to God or source — the same God and source common to all peoples everywhere. The purpose of religion should be to elevate man's consciousness so that he knows himself as one with his Source/God/Reality. It should bring man to celebrate that knowledge with joy, love and reverence for all beings and all creation. Instead, cleaving to scriptures, with dogma, rites and rituals evoking moods of devotion but devoid of spiritual light, religion separates man from man and man from God. Man is left godless on earth and God is exiled and consigned to a conceptual and inaccessible region called heaven. It is the greatest *rudratva*.

During Narayana Guru's lifetime, the separation of man from man through religion was most pronounced in the Hindu caste system, then so rigidly established in south India. The Guru vigorously opposed the caste system and through the example of his own life and teaching did much to loosen its oppressive hold on people. He proclaimed:

> One in kind, one in faith and one in God is man;
> of one source, of one form, difference therein none.[6]

He clarifies what he means by "one in faith" with these words from his *Ātmopadeśa-Śatakam*:

> Always and everywhere all make efforts to ensure self-happiness; understand this as the one faith in the whole world and, self-contained, be without sin.[7]

The Guru's view of different religions was expressed with these simple words:

> Whichever be the religion, it suffices if it makes man better.[8]

Believing that their creeds and dogmas provide the exclusive way to salvation and rejecting and deriding all other ways, conflicts erupt between different religions. Not expressions of God's glory which should come from religions, they are expressions of narrow vision, ignorant preachings and the

---

6. *Jāti-Nirṇayam* (Critique of Caste), v. 2.
7. *Ātmopadeśa-Śatakam*, v. 49.
8. *The Life and Teachings of Narayana Guru*, Nataraja Guru, Narayana Gurukula Foundation, Varkala, 1990, p. 72.

bigotry of fanatical followers. The Guru warns of this folly in the following verse from the *Ātmopadeśa-Śatakam*:

> All religions have but one essence. Like blind men describing an elephant, fools distress the world with their doctrines. Beholding this, be not disturbed, yourself be steady.[9]

Knowing the essential content of one's own religion means also knowing the same content in all religions. Religious conflict is then seen to be a disgraceful absurdity and in seeing thus, religious *rudratva* becomes religious *śivatva*.

Rudratva in Nationalism and Racialism

Nationalism is the drawing of quite imaginary boundary lines around cultural, linguistic and racially identified groupings. Those lines proclaim ownership of the land and resources within them and warn others to keep out. Nationalism and racialism compete closely with religion in separating man from man and as the principal causes of conflict between peoples. In defence of those imaginary lines and in attempts to expand their territories, men trundle out their war-machines and blood pours in torrents over the face of the beautiful Earth. It is the most wasteful expenditure of the Earth's resources and the most unnecessary self-inflicted suffering. The planet is rich and generous and if loved and cared for is well able to provide for all its beings. Only greed, fear and ignorance cause men to separate themselves on the basis of the quite superficial differences between them and violently compete for, rather than joyfully share, the gifts and bounty of this beautiful blue planet. Only through knowledge of its Reality and the realization of *ātman*, the planet's true owner, will the *rudratva* of narrow nationalism and racialism be transformed into universal *śivatva*.

In the fields of economics, society, relationships and so

9. *Ātmopadeśa-Śatakam*, v. 44.

forth, in all areas of man's life on earth, *rudratva* is the state of sorrow resulting from the quite spurious separation of knower, knowledge and known. It is through the realization of the unity of knower, knowledge and known that the *rudratva* of separately perceived fields can be transformed into the *śivatva* of the unified field of the Self.

Sūtra 12

ब्रह्मैवाहं तदिदं ब्रह्मैवाहमस्मि ॥

brahmaivāham tad idam brahmaivāham asmi ॥

brahma	:	*Brahman*
eva	:	indeed
aham	:	I (am)
tad	:	that (indeed is)
idam	:	this world
brahma	:	*Brahman*
eva	:	indeed
aham	:	I (am)
asmi	:	am (so)

Brahman indeed am I. "That" indeed is this world. *Brahman* indeed I am.

Ahanta and Idanta

At this half-way point in his *Vedānta-Sūtras*, Narayana Guru makes three succinct, concise statements. He reasserts *brahmaivāham* ("*Brahman* indeed am I"), mentioned in the first *sūtra*. He states *tad idam* ("That indeed is this world"). Then again he says *brahmaivāham*, adding the word *asmi* to slightly shift the emphasis. In this *sūtra* he summarizes the points made in *sūtra*s 5-11 and reaches a clear conclusion. It is an affirmation of his enlightened vision of Reality, the vision he has been revealing through perspectives of the undeniable fact of existence and the awareness that knows it to be. He pauses as it were to reassert the nature of the perceiver and the perceived. In this *sūtra*'s first *brahmaivāham* he is asserting the subjectivity of Reality and saying "I am That." With *tad idam* he is asserting the objectivity of Reality and saying of the world perceived as object, "that object too is 'That.'" Then he puts the two together and says "One Absolute Reality only am I." It is an assertion that the *ahanta-idanta* duality apparent in *Brahman* is to be transcended.

The word *ahanta* is derived from the word *aham* ("I"); by adding the suffix *ta*; it means "the state of being "I." Similarly, the word *idanta* is derived from *idam* ("this") and *ta* to mean "the state of being this." In a philosophical context the former word represents the subjective aspect of existence and the latter word the objective aspect of existence, both arising from the "One Unconditioned Existence" which Vedānta names as *ātman* or *Brahman*. Thus, with this *sūtra*, the Guru has revealed a further aspect of Vedānta's esoteric knowledge — the knowledge that the Self, one indivisible Reality, is both eternal and unbounded in its unmanifest transcendence, and temporal and finite in its manifestation as the world. The world, structured in One Eternal Consciousness, is continually appearing and continually passing away. The One thus becomes the many! The Indivisible thus becomes the separated out.

The Guru's assertions here relate to the previously quoted Upaniṣadic *mahāvākyas*,[1] which, in the context of this *sūtra*, may be repeated. They are: *tat tvam asi* (that thou art), *aham brahma asmi* (I am *Brahman*), *ayam ātmā brahma* (this Self is *Brahman*), and *prajñānam brahma* (*Brahman* is pure Consciousness).

"I" and "Brahman"

The oneness of *Brahman* and the multiplicity of "I"s may be likened to an ocean upon the surface of which countless waves

1. See p. 16.

appear. They rise and fall and are inseparable in the oneness of the ocean from which they ceaselessly emerge. Every individual "I" is as such a wave in the infinite ocean of *Brahman*'s Being.

Narayana Guru did not feel any further explanation was required of an individual's distinctness than that, but Śaṅkara, in his commentaries and introductory Vedānta textbooks, treats the separateness of "I" and *Brahman* as a semantic issue. In his view "I" denotes a minute, finite, transitory individual, knowing only very little, whilst *Brahman* is an omnipresent, omnipotent, omniscient and indivisible infinite Being and therefore, in Śaṅkara's view, it is not logically possible to equate them.

Literal and Indirect Meanings

To reconcile the disparate concepts conveyed by the two words, "I" and *Brahman*, Śaṅkara does not resort to their literal meanings (*vācyārtha*) but takes up their indirect suggested meanings (*lakṣaṇārtha*). But indirect suggested meanings too are of different kinds. There are indirect suggested meanings entirely devoid of literal meaning. For example, one may say "the red marches on," meaning "the red-army marches on." The literal sense is absent from the former statement as "red" being a colour cannot literally march. Nevertheless its implied sense is fully understood by the hearer. Such indirect suggested meanings are classified by Śaṅkara as *jahal-lakṣaṇā*, the word *jahal* meaning "given up."

Another kind of indirect meaning may be conveyed by this example: If one says "I live in such and such street of such and such town" it does not mean that one literally lives "in the street" but in a house with access through that street. In this case the literal meaning is not given up, but something more is implied to make its sense understandable. Indirect meanings of this kind are called *ajahal-lakṣaṇā*, *ajahal* meaning "not given up."

There is yet another kind of indirect meaning called *jahajahal-lakṣaṇā* in which the literal sense is partly given up and partly retained. For example, one may say, "This is that person." The pronouns "this" and "that" are mutually exclusive as, in literal terms, "this" can never be "that." Nevertheless, the statement may be taken as true as its contradiction is neutralized in its understood meaning. This type of indirect meaning is also called *bhāga-tyāga-lakṣaṇā*, the word *bhāga* meaning "part" and *tyāga* meaning "to give up." In Śaṅkara's view, the statement "I am *Brahman*" is to be understood in this sense with the disparity in the words "I" and *Brahman* being partly given up. In the notion of "I" it is such attributes as finite, minute, transitory, of little knowledge, etc. which are given up. In the concept *Brahman* it is such notions as omnipresent, omnipotent, omniscient, infinite, indivisible, etc. which are given up. In the meaning that remains, the two are identical.

Both are conditioned concepts. The conditioning of "I" is in its given attributes and the conditioning of *Brahman* is in its given definitions. In ineffable transcendental Consciousness these two dissolve in a oneness expressible as "*Brahman* indeed am I." The nature of this oneness is also expressed by the words *sat-cit-ānanda*. As *sat* it is imperishable unbounded existence. As *cit* it is self-effulgent self-aware Consciousness. As *ānanda* it is supreme ineffable Self-contentment unaffected by the vagaries of individuated life.

The goal of the seeker is the direct experience of that oneness. As a conscious experience of immortal *sat*, Vedānta calls it *amṛtatva* (immortality). As an experience of *cit* it is known as *parā-jñāna* (transcendental knowledge) and as an experience of *ānanda* it is called *paramānanda* (supreme transcendental Self-contentment).

The Meaning of AUṀ

In the realm of words this ineffable experience is represented by the monosyllable *auṁ* (more usually written as *ōṁ*). *Sat* blooms as all manifest forms, *cit* blooms as multiple states of consciousness, and *ānanda* blooms as all value feelings such as likes and dislikes: such is the experiential world. In the field of verbal communication everything perceived is designated by a word; so the experience of all-inclusive oneness is designated by the all-inclusive word *auṁ*. The *a* at the beginning of this word is pronounced with the opening of the mouth; the *u* in the middle is pronounced with the mouth half open, and *ṁ* at the end is pronounced with the closing of the mouth. Thus in the pronunciation of *auṁ* there is an emerging, a preservation and a dissolution and with this one word the creative processes of manifestation are communicated.

Indian psychology conceives experience as being of three distinct worlds. The first of these is the external world of gross objects. It is experienced by the fully open senses (in which functional mode consciousness is called *vaiśvānara*) in the wakeful state called *jāgrat*, signified by the syllable *a*. The second is the world of subtle objects. This is experienced (by the functional mode of consciousness called *taijasa*) with half open senses in the dream-sleep state called *svapna*, signified by the syllable *u*. The third is the non-objective world of the fully closed senses in the deep-sleep state called *suṣupti*; it is signified by the syllable *ṁ*. In this third state consciousness lies dormant, like a tree in a seed, and the world is born from it on waking. In this sense it is considered as the causal state of consciousness and the knower of everything; thus it is called *prājña* (the fully aware one). So it is that in the realm of words, all things subjective and objective are comprehended as the meaning content of *auṁ*, also known as *praṇava*, literally "the ever new." Nothing is excluded from it; it vibrates as everything.

The seeker has to experience it in the transcendental fourth state of consciousness called *turīya* and know it to be the meaning content of his own existence. It is a knowledge not derived from the direct perceptual experience of the senses called *pratyakṣa-jñāna*, nor is it an indirect knowledge like inference, called *parokṣa-jñāna*. It is therefore given the special name *aparokṣa-jñāna* or *aparokṣa-anubhūti*, meaning "non-direct intuitive experience." Realizing the meaning of *auṁ*, realizing one's self-reality, realizing Absolute-Reality, and realizing the oneness of all these is the essence of *aparokṣa-anubhūti*. Experiencing it, one then knows that those states of consciousness called *jāgrat*, *svapna* and *suṣupti*, are merely conditioned forms of the one unconditioned unmanifest Consciousness called *ātman* or *Brahman*.

In *turīya*, the transcendental fourth state, there is only self-effulgent awareness in which the worlds of multiplicity dissolve. Narayana Guru defines this state as "awareness of the beginningless and endless, from beginning to end."[2] It is a state which cannot be signified by any syllable but only by the silence which is the fourth quarter of *auṁ*.

The Meaning of "God"

In religious terminology experiencing the fourth state of Consciousness is called "God-Realization." However, the term "God-Realization" implies the duality of God and realizer and does not therefore signify the indivisibility of *Brahman*. Although the words "God" and *Brahman* are often used synonymously, God-Realization is still one degree away from non-dual, Absolute-Realization. In Vedānta, therefore, devotion to God has meaning only where the identity of God and worshipper is not fully realized as One.

The Sanskrit word for God is *īśa*, meaning the one who controls or rules. Adding the suffix *vara* (of the highest order)

2. *Ātmopadeśa-Śatakam*, v. 28.

we have the word *īśvara* for God conceived as the highest Being, the Creator, Preserver and Destroyer of the world. These functions of God, conceived in Indian mythology as the trinity of Brahmā, Viṣṇu and Śiva, are not Unconditioned Absolute Reality. They are the creating, preserving and destroying conditionings arising from It, having such attributes as omnipotence, omniscience, omnipresence and so forth. The Absolute, according to Śaṅkara, when conditioned by *māyā*, becomes *īśvara* and therefore, in that sense, God is an effect of *māyā*.

Devout feelings and the need for prayer arise from the duality of worshipper and worshipped. The most cogent prayer is for the resolution of that separation and for attainment of the supplicant's union with God. In *Daivadaśakam*, a prayer in ten verses composed by Narayana Guru in his native Malayalam language, the Guru concludes as follows:

> Let us be immersed in the deep ocean of Thy Glory; there to dwell for ever in the union of felicity supreme.[3]

In another composition, a hymn to Śiva, he prays:

> O God, this humble supplicant has no other wish than for the attainment, this very day, of that state in which Thou and I become one.[4]

All events arise from the Being of God, the Omniscient, Omnipotent Creator. So in a religious sense, all events and all that happens to one must ultimately be an expression of God's will. Therefore to pray for personal benefits, or for things to be other than they are, is contrary to the acceptance of God's will. Nevertheless it is common religious practice to pray for changes in the world, or for personal favours. Whatever we pray for, however, we are bound to accept God's will. God is

3. *Daivadaśakam*, v. 10.

4. *Sadāśivadarśanam*, v. 5.

not bound to accept our will. A good prayer is "Let thy will be done." God however does not require this permission and His will be done anyway. But if that prayer is offered in a true spirit of acquiescence then at least it is not contrary to the acceptance of God's will. To pray for a better understanding of one's nature and the nature of the world, is a good prayer. To pray for the happiness of all beings is also a good prayer as all beings and God are One.

Many of India's great poets/*guru*s have themselves been non-dualists but have, nevertheless, composed sublime poetical hymns addressed to various deities. In these they visualize the concerned deity as a particular personification of the Absolute, or as a particular proto-linguistic expression of the Absolute. Proto-language is the universally understood language of visual symbols which transverses the limitations of verbal communication. It may, with significant detailing, express verbally inexpressible values of non-dual Reality. Many forms of India's deities, for example, embody cosmic mysteries and convey a message of divine existence and beauty which is a visual expression of transcendental *ānanda.*

Bhakti

In Sanskrit the word *bhakti* means devotion, but it originally meant the state of constant contemplation (*bhaj*) of something of high value. Śaṅkara, in his *Vivekacūḍāmaṇi,* defines *bhakti* as unceasing contemplation of the Self. Narayana Guru also adopts that line of thought and devotes a whole chapter of his *Darśana-Mālā* to clarifying various aspects of *bhakti*. For example, one of its verses reads:

> All meditate for *ānanda* alone, none meditates for suffering. That meditation which has *ānanda* for its goal is *bhakti.* So it is instructed.[5]

5. *Darśana-Mālā*, VIII.3.

The Guru's definition of a *bhakta* (one who is devout) is of one who realizes that *ātmā, Brahman* and *ānanda* are merely different names for one and the same Reality. He says:

> '*Ānanda, ātmā* and *brahman* — these are said to be different names of the One Itself. He who has that conviction is known as a *bhakta*.[6]

In the first chapter of the same work, in which the phenomenal world is considered as the perspective from which Reality is discerned, God is alloted the major role as its Creator, Sustainer and Dissolver and is equated with the creative aspect of *Brahman*.

Feelings of joyful devotion to anything or anyone may, in a certain sense, be considered *bhakti*. The love one feels for the Self is considered as *parā-bhakti* (supreme or transcendental *bhakti*), and its benefit is the dissolution of suffering (*rudratva*) in the experience of *śivatva*, the auspiciousness of the Absolute.

Non-realization of oneness in no way affects the oneness of Reality, but it is as if, through non-realization, we make a *rudra* in life of *śiva*, the Auspicious Absolute. It is however only in erroneous perception that *śiva* and *rudra* are two; in Indian mythology they are epithets of the same One Being. The state of being auspicious in *śivatva* is the great benefit derived from realizing the oneness of "I" and *Brahman*.

---

6. *Darśana-Mālā*, VIII.5.

Sūtra 13

अतीतागामिनोरसत्त्वं यतः यदेतदन्विच्छत ॥

atītāgāminor asattvaṁ yataḥ yad etad anvicchata ॥

atīta-āgāminaḥ	:	of past and future
asattvam	:	state of being without substance (non-existent)
yataḥ	:	for that of which
etat	:	this (cause)
yat	:	that which is such
anvic chata	:	seek continuously

By which everything past and future is non-existent.

A NEW section begins with this *sūtra.* The search for the cause of appearances encompasses two contrary perspectives, which are of *sat,* the real, and *asat,* the unreal. In *sūtra*s 5-12 Narayana Guru visualized the Absolute from the point of view of *sat* and arrived at the conclusion which formed the text of *sūtra* 12. Now his visualization is from the point of view of *asat.*

Vedānta's definition of *sat* is of one Unbounded Existence; the one Reality which has always been, which is now, and which will everlastingly continue to be. Indestructible, without attributes, imperceptible, unthinkable and indescribable, it is the substratum from which all awareness of dualities arise and therefore it is *cit*, Consciousness Itself. It is the field from which all feelings arise and therefore it is also value-sensing *ānanda*. Itself indistinct, it is the ultimate substance of everything distinguishable. Itself uncaused, it is the cause of everything. Itself without abode, it is the habitation of all beings. Itself without form, it assumes the form of everything.

We human beings, seeking our source, do so in a field in which distinct, finite, multiple entities appear to our senses. We observe that in time they pass away. We observe that others appear, emerging and disappearing, always in time. All these appearances, being transitory existences in the observer's awareness, are not the *sat* defined above. Of course they have no other reality, no other substance and no other cause than the *sat* defined above. Still they are appearances which pass away and having no substantial existence in themselves are defined as *asat*. With this *sūtra* Narayana Guru begins the search for the cause of such appearances.

Appearances in Time

The appearance of anything at all presents to the perceiver only the most outward aspects of the perceived entity. For example, we perceive the light emitted by an electric light-bulb without being able to see the electricity flowing through it; we simply have to operate a switch to gain the benefit of electric light without perceiving the vast powerhouse providing it. We glance at the wristwatch we are wearing to read the time indicated by its face, without seeing its inner workings. The faces of other people may smile or frown, masking other inner emotions. We see only the external appearances of others; their inner reality is invisible to us. But whilst seeing only the external appearances of other beings we nevertheless discern that they have a non-apparent inner reality. So it is that in perceiving the external appearance of the world we are able to discern that it has a non-apparent Reality.

The Nature of Time

The observer of appearances, perceiving himself to be a time-bound individual, is no less an appearance, no less transitory, no less temporal. He observes that he emerged from a point in past time before which he apparently did not exist. He observes his existence to be now, in present time. He knows that he will apparently cease to exist beyond a point in future time. Always, the observer's experience of existence is in the present. The past is gone, a memory only in present time. The future, that has not yet come, is an anticipation only in present time. Neither past nor future can be reached except in memory or in expectation and so neither can be said to have existence; thus they are *asat*. Only the present exists, but it is a present which cannot be fixed in time; it is a mathematical point between a past without beginning and an endless future, a non-entity. No moment can be held and time is a continuous flow of transformations from a point of awareness in the observer. Thus the observer himself is the one fixed point in time.

The individual perceives himself to exist for an impermanent period in time which stretches back in eternal recession and forward in eternal progression. All events are perceived to occur and all entities and beings are perceived to exist at points in time discerned from the one fixed point of the perceiver's awareness in the present. It cannot be said of that point that it is *sat*, for *sat* is not time-bound; thus in Sanskrit it is said to be *trikālātīta* (that which transcends past, present and future). It is a point of perception of appearances, a birthplace of the illusion of dualities called *māyā* and, therefore, it is *asat*.

Though illusory, time is very real in human experience and conditions man's attitudes and activities. Time, for the time-bound human, is measurable backwards and forwards from a point called the present. His units of measure derive from the spinning of this tiny planet around its axis, flashing days and nights as it orbits its ever-shining star (which itself has no days and nights). Those successive spins and orbits have no absolute status as temporal events, and their temporality is conceived by man as relative to his own temporality. Each orbit he calls a year, which he divides into months and weeks, and each spin he calls a day, which he divides into hours, minutes and seconds. He evaluates these allotted time periods by the span of individual and historical human life on earth and by the pulsating of human heart and breath. Time in this sense is the span of life between the birth and death of an individual, in which he experiences night, day and seasons and in which he breathes and pulsates in a time-bound body. Time is conceived and evaluated in terms of the movement of bodies relative to one another; the measurable number of units of periodicity it takes for one entity to reach another and also the measurable number of units of periodicity between events. An ant may be stamped on in a moment but it takes many light years to even reach a star.

Time is a *sat-cit* perception, experienced in *ānanda.* If experienced with interest and enjoyment time flashes by but seems very full and rich and one wishes to hold on to it. If experienced with boredom and misery it seems interminable and empty and one wishes for its end. Narayana Guru says in his *Ātmopadeśa-Śatakam*:

> For those fortunates who relish the nectar of the transcendent, ten thousand years are but a moment; for those whose awareness is bound by immanent nature half a second is like a thousand years.[1]

Time is thus the perception and value experience of a flow of events during an individual's life on earth; it has no existence apart from that perception and value experience. In whatever way they are experienced and evaluated all events are *asat*

1. *Ātmopadeśa-Śatakam*, v. 15.

appearances flowing out of *sat*'s Reality, the one reality behind all things past, present and future. It is a reality which cannot be denied as it is the pervading substance of every conscious being's present awareness and to deny it would be to deny one's own present awareness.

So it is that the *Taittirīya Upaniṣad,* in a verse quoted earlier, says:

> Verily, one does become unreal if he considers Brahman as non-existent.[2]

Perceiving appearances to be transitory, the perceiver is brought to consider the timeless Reality from which they must arise. It is a consideration generated by the certain knowledge that neither time nor events nor awareness can appear from non-existent nothingness. Narayana Guru therefore urges the continual search for the cause and substance of all appearances, past, present and future.

The Search

The search for cause and substance of appearances is defined in the *Bṛhadāraṇyaka Upaniṣad* by the sage Yājñavalkya, in answer to a question asked by an illustrious scholar called Uddālaka Aruṇi at the court of King Janaka.

Uddālaka asks Yājñavalkya:

> Do you know that thread by which this world, the other world and all beings are held together? Do you know the inner controller from within who controls this world and the next and all things? He who knows that thread, that inner controller, indeed knows *Brahman*. He knows the worlds, he knows the gods, he knows the Vedas, he knows beings, he knows the Self, he knows everything.

2. *Taittirīya Upaniṣad*, II.6.

Yājñavalkya answers:

> Air verily is the thread. By air verily, as by a thread, this world, the other world and all beings are held together. Therefore, verily, they say of a person who dies that his limbs have been loosened, for they are held together by air as by a thread.

Uddālaka then asks Yājñavalkya to describe the inner controller.

Yājñavalkya answers:

> He who dwells in the earth, yet is within the earth whom the earth does not know, whose body is the earth, who controls the earth from within, he is yourself, the inner controller, the immortal.

He concludes his definition with the words:

> He is never seen but is the seer. He is never heard but is the hearer. He is never perceived but is the perceiver. He is never thought but is the thinker. There is no other seer but He, there is no other thinker but He. He is yourself, the inner controller, the immortal.[3]

The search for cause and substance, the Self, is conducted within the field of vibrating existence between the poles of *sat* and *asat*. It is the field of appearances, the field of all dualities and of the erroneous perception of knower and known as separable. Seeking the Self in it will not be successful if it is confined to the appearances presented by the outwardly directed senses. In order to succeed in this search, awareness must be turned away from the objects of sense experience to the inner controller, the perceiver of the apparent world. It is in the transcendent fourth state of Consciousness that the sought-for cause and substance of appearances is to be found.

3. *Bṛhadāraṇyaka Upaniṣad*, III.7.

Sūtra 14

परिमाणं ततः ॥

parimāṇaṁ tataḥ ॥

parimāṇam	:	measurement
tataḥ	:	because of "That"

There is measurement because of "That."

To measure anything at all means to ascertain the degree of some value it has in comparison with something else, and in that sense everything perceivable is to some extent measurable. In the realm of temporal physical existence, within three-dimensional space, many measurements may be made and things may be classified in terms of their relative length, width, height, volume, weight, hardness, durability, velocity and so forth. Such values as these are derived from universally established standard units of measurement. This method of comparing one object with another is known in the ancient Nyāya school of logic, as *aṇu-mahat* (minuteness/vastness) and *dīrgha-hrasva* (longness/shortness).

In earlier sciences only the more gross aspects of size, mass, content, time and motion were measurable. With the development of more and more sophisticated technology it became possible to measure all manner of non-tangibles. Energies too have become measurable in terms of their intensities, frequencies, motion and speed. But such values as beauty, desirability, love, happiness and awareness, which give meaning to human life, are not subject to any standards.

Beauty will remain measurable only in the eye of the beholder and love will remain quantifiable only in human hearts.

Now, with the use of electrocardiograms and the like, it is possible to detect, measure and quantify electrical activity and chemical changes in the physical organ called brain. As these measurable electro-chemical patterns and associated specific mental conditions arise together, and as the one does not occur without the other, it is not conclusively ascertainable that the one is cause and the other effect. The prevailing scientific view, that everything has a cause in matter, is no more valid than the religious view that everything is caused by God. Whilst different facets of phenomena are measurable the immeasurable Reality underlying them is the one unquantifiable substance because of which all measurements are possible. Therefore Narayana Guru says: "There is measurement because of 'That.'"

Bhāva and Abhāva

In a purely physical sense measurements arrive at the boundary separating the apparent existence of entities from their non-existence. Something extending endlessly cannot be measured and entities are measurable only till the point where their perceived existence terminates. Beyond their apparent boundaries, entities are thought to be non-existent and so, paradoxically, an object is seen and can be measured only when its non-existence is also perceived. Measurement, in this sense, means gaining some specific knowledge of an apparent existent entity by the circumscription of its own non-existence. In Indian thought the apparent existence of something is called *bhāva* and its non-existence *abhāva.*

Different classifications of *abhāva* are applied to different kinds of *bhāva*. These are *prāg-abhāva* (anterior non-existence), *pradhvaṁśa-abhāva* (posterior non-existence), *anyonya-abhāva* (mutual non-existence) and *atyanta-abhāva* (ultimate non-existence). For example, a lump of clay has in it the potential form of a pot, so it may be said that there is an anterior non-existence of a pot in the clay. If broken, a pot becomes shards, which, having once assumed the form of a pot, may be said to contain the posterior non-existence of a pot. Where there is only light there is no darkness and where there is only darkness there is no light; so each may be said to contain the mutual non-existence of the other. Ultimate non-existence has no potential — never has been and never could be. It has no location, contains nothing and nothing can arise from it. In the Vedāntic tradition it is likened to the non-existence of the horns of a horse, the child of a barren woman, or a flower growing in the sky. Specific knowledge involves perception of both an apparent existence and its non-existence where these are experienced in Consciousness as a mode of its own functioning.

All measuring requires means and accepted standards against which results may be compared in order to establish precise and definite knowledge. In Vedānta, such means are the *pramāṇa*s which were defined earlier in these commentaries. A *pramāṇa* defined as *pramā-kāraṇam* (that which enables one to arrive at a certitude) has validity only because it defines a *tripuṭi* perception (of knowledge, knower and known). Any final certitude concerning Ultimate Reality can only be in the knower's realization of his oneness with It. No external measuring rod or *pramāṇa* is helpful in gaining that awareness. Śaṅkara in his commentary on the fourth *sūtra* of Bādarāyaṇa's *Brahma-Sūtras* clarifies this as follows:

> Hence all injunctions and all other means of knowledge end with the cognition expressed in the words "I am Brahman"; for as soon as there is comprehension of the non-dual Self, which is not either something to be eschewed or something to be appropriated, all objects and knowing agents vanish, and hence there can no longer be means of proof.[1]

---

1. *The Vedānta-Sūtras of Bādarāyaṇa,* with commentary by Śaṅkara, I.1.4, p. 44, tr. by George Thibaut, New York: Dover Publications Inc.

Narayana Guru also confirms this and says:

> The substantial and the non-substantial exist united, which state indeed is a great logical contradiction. How can "That" which is beyond the bounds of words and mind, be known through any means of measuring or a *pramāṇa*?[2]

In the search for the ultimate building blocks of the universe, sense perception and inference are the *pramāṇa*s of scientific enquiry. They are aided by the measuring instruments of modern technology. But enquirer, enquiry and instruments exist together in one Reality only and the enquirer cannot step outside it and treat it as an external object. Objects are external only in a relative sense and, therefore, measuring done in the world of science has relative value only.

Absolute measuring is absolutely impossible, even in a physical sense.The scientist and his instruments function in accord with the very same law of relative existence governing his enquiry. One transcendent Absolute Existence alone appears as the measurer, the measured, the measuring instruments and the act of measuring. This one substance of everything is *Brahman*. The enquirer, the enquiry and the measuring instruments exist together in *māyā*'s field of seeming but illusory dimensions; they can never succeed in measuring the immeasurable substance of Reality Itself.

The impossibility of setting *Brahman* within the field of dimensions was known to the ancient *ṛṣi*s of the Upaniṣads. Guru Varuṇa, for example, in the *Taittirīya Upaniṣad*, whilst instructing his son and disciple Bhṛgu to realize *Brahman* through *tapas* repeatedly reminds him:

> The very *tapas* is *Brahman* indeed.[3]

How the immeasurable formless substance of Reality appears

---

2. *Ātmopadeśa-Śatakam*, v. 94.
3. *Taittirīya Upaniṣad*, III.5.1.

in the multiple forms of measurable non-substantialities is a great and impenetrable mystery. The Upaniṣads teach that the formless *Brahman* assumes forms to actualize, see and know Itself in endless transformations. In religious terminology these are considered to be the never-ending sport *(līlā)* of God.

In Advaita Vedānta, *Brahman* is considered to be neither subjective nor objective, neither physical nor mental, but as the Reality underlying all subjectivity, all objectivity and all physical and mental phenomena. Therefore, it is not merely an idealism as some would have it. The only means by which an enquiring mind, *mati*, can realize *Brahman* is through knowing itself as not different from the *Brahman* of its enquiry. Narayana Guru says:

> Meditation, by merging *mati* (the enquiring mind) into "That," is to be pursued without lapse, in order to clear the mind of *māyā*'s delusion.[4]

The Distinct and the Indistinct

The measuring of an apparent existence is possible only when it is seen as a distinct entity, its distinctness being dependent upon the situation in which it is perceived. For example, a blade of grass growing in a lawn may be seen as distinct only up to the point at which it becomes merged and lost in a view of the lawn. Similarly the distinctness of the lawn disappears in the view of a town seen when flying above it. Flying higher, the distinctness of the town is lost in a view of the countryside which, in turn, is lost in a view of the landmass and sea. Rising higher still, the landmass and the sea is lost in a view of the planet. Flying towards the outer limits of the distinct solar system, the planet recedes to become a mere dot and then, with further distance, disappears completely. The sun dwindles to become a minor star in one of countless galaxies

---

4. *Ātmopadeśa-Śatakam*, v. 53.

(cloud-like smudges of billions of stars, rushing away from each other in an expanding universe). The cosmic space in which they are perceived to exist is an indistinct and seemingly endless non-substantiality. In the field of relativity the distinctness of entities in the macrocosm is perceivable only within a very limited frame of reference. This applies equally to the entities perceived within the microcosm where the distinctness of sub-atomic matter disappears in indistinct energy.

Whatever the measurements of any perceived physical entity, it is negligible when compared to the immensity of the cosmic space beyond its boundaries, a space so immense that we refer to the distances between the dots of matter it contains in terms of the thousands or millions of years it takes light to travel between them. On our own tiny dot of matter we ourselves are tinier, imperceptible and indistinguishable dots at only very short distances apart. We are distinct only in our present state of existence. Our previous states are indistinct as are our future states. Yet we existed previously and will continue to exist in the future, for existence is not a temporary condition but is eternal. Measured with the measuring rod of our eternal existence our present life is merely a tiny, quite negligible, phase of an unending whole. Yet lacking an Absolutist norm, we are beset with problems and anxieties. With the attainment of knowledge of our true unbounded being those problems and anxieties diminish and fade into indistinctness, for only in the middle state, between the very large and the very small, the very far and the very near and our beginningless past and our unending future, are we distinct individuals. The *Bhagavad-Gītā* says of this:

> Creatures are of indistinct past, are distinct in the present state and are of indistinct future. O Arjuna! What grief is there in this?[5]

---

5. *Bhagavad-Gītā*, II.28.

Not perceiving our vast indistinct reality we believe ourselves to exist only in the distinct, minute, middle state. Yet each tiny individual, an indistinguishable dot in the spatial and temporal immensity of the cosmos, is large enough to contain the whole universe within his awareness. The measurer and the measured are distinct entities in the finite middle state of existence, beyond the boundaries of which immeasurable Reality stretches infinite and indistinct. With his measuring rod the measurer attempts to fix the distinct world as a known value. But he has no other world with which to compare it and no boundary in which to set it. The *Bhagavad-Gītā* therefore warns:

> Only the ignorant consider Me as the indistinct come to distinctness, not knowing my transcendental nature to be changeless and supreme.[6]

It is Pure Consciousness, the Absolute, that measures knower, knowable and knowledge. The threefold aspects of knowledge (*tripuṭi*) are a dream-like configuration in Pure Consciousness. Thus the dream-like vision of a measurable world does not exist outside the dreaming mind. Narayana Guru, in his work called *Aṛivu*, says:

> That which is known without any means of knowledge as a measure, It is indeed luminous Pure Consciousness. Even as a dream arising in mind is mind alone, so too is everything else.[7]

Being but dream-like configurations of Pure Consciousness, the one substance, entities are perceived to be distinct and measurable only because of "That."

Sin, Merit, Destiny and Free Will

Every perception has in it some element of measurement in that some evaluating response automatically arises in the

6. *Bhagavad-Gītā*, VII.24.

7. *Aṛivu*, v. 3.

perceiving mind. These responses, weak or strong, will have the perceiver's sense of values as their frame of reference. That is to say, his sense of what is right or wrong, good or bad, meritorious or sinful, helpful or harmful, desirable or repellent, beautiful or ugly and so forth. These value senses, whilst fundamentally arising from *ānanda,* are highly conditioned by prevailing social, cultural and religious precepts as well as by individual inclinations.

Sin and merit are valid and helpful concepts in the conduct of human life. Whatever is conducive to the attainment of Self-realization, and whatever is life supporting, elevating and beneficial to oneself and others, is naturally meritorious. Conversely, whatever is lowering, harmful to oneself and others or impedes progress to Self-realization is naturally sinful. The Guru says of this:

> Actions beneficial to oneself but harmful to others deny the basic oneness of the Self. Those who afflict misery on others will fall into the fiery sea of hell and burn.[8]

The hell meant here is the tormented state of individuated awareness resulting from an ignorant obstruction of Nature's creative flow. We have free will to act in accord with that natural movement or to impede it. In that sense we choose to move towards heaven or hell and in that sense too our actions are ethical or unethical.

Ethics is one of the main branches of philosophy. Its purpose is to measure the morality of human behaviour and provide guidelines for its conduct. A universal, non-relative criterion for such measurement and guidance has been lacking in the world of ethical thought. Narayana Guru, for the first time in the history of philosophy, provides an absolutist norm of ethics. According to the Guru actions which uphold the basic principle of the oneness of the Self are morally sound

8. *Ātmopadeśa-Śatakam,* v. 20.

whilst actions which violate this principle are immoral. One who becomes aware of such a principle, that everything is an expression of one Reality, transcends the bounds of morality and immorality in behaviour. Freed of such constraints and with a mind illumined by the light of Self-knowledge his actions will quite naturally be ethically sound and will benefit himself and others.

The sense of sin and merit is the natural corollary of one's sense of being the *kartā* (doer of actions). All actions, even those of free will, arise from Nature's flow of creative transformations. The actions of all beings, including man's so-called *karma*s, are as sparks of Nature's bonfire. Realizing this, that Nature is the true *kartā* and originator of all actions, releases one from attachment to the concepts of sin and merit and frees one from all *karma-bandha*s (bondage to actions). The *Bhagavad-Gītā* says:

> Thus you will be liberated from the bonds of action and its good and evil fruits. Self-steadfast in the yoga of renunciation, emancipated, you will attain union with Me.[9]

Man is a social animal and establishes laws governing social behaviour which if contravened incur penalties. These man-made laws define behaviour not acceptable in society, but they are not laws imposed by Nature. Riding on a train without buying a ticket, or parking one's car in a restricted area, for example, are misdemeanours which may entail a fine but contravene no natural law.

Religion imposes further behavioural laws, promulgated on the basis of what is thought to be God's will and teaches that if these are contravened sin will be incurred. It is pronounced to be sin, for example, to engage in a sexual relationship and engender offspring outside marriage, though mating, sexuality and parenting arise from natural law;

9. *Bhagavad-Gītā*, IX.28.

marriage is a purely man-made institution to regulate mating, sexual union and parenting within society.

Natural law upholds the elevation of man's consciousness to the status of Self-consciousness. In choosing to support or oppose it we choose our destiny. Man-made law in harmony with natural law is ethically correct.

Dharma

In addition to socio-religious constraints and compulsions man is impelled to act in accordance with the laws governing his incarnate nature. Natural law compels us to breathe air, to eat and drink, to defecate and urinate, to reproduce through the union of male and female and to live our earthly lives within a very small range of temperatures and pressures. Each man enters the world with a particular genetic inheritance. He is born into a particular family and is subject to particular social, cultural and religious or irreligious influences. All these provide the basis and conditions from which his personality, inner compulsions, desires and values develop. Such imperatives and urges are often in conflict within him, creating confusion, uncertainty and feelings of inadequacy, guilt or shame. This was much the condition in which Arjuna, the warrior hero of the *Bhagavad-Gītā,* found himself on a field where members of a family and their supporters were in conflict with other members of the same family and their supporters. The two sides into which the family had split were preparing to battle. Arjuna saw many dear friends, beloved kinsmen and venerated teachers who, fighting on the other side, had become his opponents and enemies. The situation rendered him incapable of acting in accordance with his role as a warrior-prince or of knowing right action from wrong. He threw down his bow and begged Kṛṣṇa, his charioteer, to instruct him. Kṛṣṇa's teaching, the theme of the *Bhagavad-Gītā,* begins at this point. Arjuna is taught to discriminate the real from the unreal, the eternal from the transitory and to know what action is and who its doer is. With this knowledge he gains free will. He is able then to perform right action, action incurring no sin and action in accordance with his *svadharma* (one's own *dharma*, or "that which is proper for one"). The word *dharma* means that which upholds and is in accord with Nature, the creative Self-expression of the Real.

In a religious context the word "sin" means any action which transgresses the will of God and, conversely, merit is action which is in accordance with and upholds the will of God. As to what God's will is, it is, to say the least, a contentious issue. To know the will of the Transcendent/Unknowable/Incomprehensible/Eternal/Infinite/Omniscient/Omnipresent/Supreme/Divine Creator, is not given to any man. Furthermore it is both paradoxical and contradictory to consider that He, from whom all actions arise, may be acted against and that His will may be transgressed. What blasphemy! As for merit, God requires no help and no favours! Vedānta's definition of merit is simply, that which upholds *dharma* and sin is that which obstructs it. They have relevance only in *māyā*'s field of dualistic perceptions and are valid only where there is free will to choose between them.

From *prakṛti* arise all action and all motivation, therefore free will too is a function of *prakṛti*. It is an individual's ability to exercise choice in *prakṛti*'s field of action, an ability which comes in greatest measure when the clouds of ignorance obscuring awareness of the Self are lifted. Then the conditionings and compulsions which impelled one's actions and robbed one of choice are neutralized. Released from attachment to action and its fruits, and with an ability to exercise choice in action, one may then fulfil one's destiny in freedom.

Siddhis

Natural laws are relative to particular species and particular beings. Obviously the laws which apply to mammals are different from the laws which govern the lives of fish, reptiles, birds, insects and plants. Within each genus different laws apply to different species and within each species different laws apply to different subdivisions, to different genders and even to different individuals possessing different physical or mental attributes. As well as governing the physical nature of beings natural law relates to the level of awareness in living things. The higher the level of awareness the greater is the field of possibilities in which the beings live and function. So it is that in the human species individuals who have realized their identity with the Absolute and stabilized it in their lives sometimes acquire uncommon abilities which in the Indian tradition are called *siddhi*s.

Every religion and tradition can claim its share of saints and prophets possessed of miraculous powers. These powers may be of divination or foresight, or an ability to effect miraculous cures or to levitate, manifest items out of the air, appear in several places at once and so on. Even relics of such saints, venerated items such as hairs, bones, bits of wood and cloth, etc., are sometimes attributed with miraculous powers.

There are those who totally discount the possibility of such uncommon attributes, holding the view that those who apparently perform miracles are invariably hypocritical tricksters. Such an assessment is based upon preconceived notions of what is natural, unnatural or supernatural. Yet it is impossible to know what unusual and inexplicable phenomena may appear in Nature's realm of manifestations and, indeed, what may appear miraculous to some may appear quite ordinary to others, and vice versa. All that can be said about this is that some phenomena are more common and more familiar than others and so are regarded as natural and therefore not remarkable. As all of Nature's processes are mysterious the word "natural" is the word we use to explain inexplicable common events. One may know how to plant an apple seed, how to tend the newly sprouted seedling and the growing tree, know how to care for it through its budding and fruiting stages until it is possible to pick and enjoy its harvest. But the processes of transformation from seed to fruit remain a mystery to even the most experienced and expert apple-farmer. The seed, tree and fruiting are no less miraculous than the less common phenomena which are dubbed miraculous, or regarded as supernatural or unnatural. The appearance of even one grain of sand, if it alone existed, would be an inexplicable miracle, for not even one grain of sand can come out of nothingness; and nor can an awareness to know it.

To explain anything means to describe it in terms of its cause and effect, but as cause is never known except as a previous effect nothing is ever really explicable. It is possible to explain the stages of growth of an apple tree whilst remaining quite ignorant of the nature by which it grows. The tree, inexplicable, is said to be natural as is everything else that ordinarily appears to the senses!

One phenomenon is no more natural or unnatural than another. In Nature everything is natural but things or phenomena vary in their occurrence. To those with enlightened vision everything is immeasurably miraculous whilst to those who cannot see the wonder of Existence everything measurable is just ordinary.

In Vedānta one of enlightened vision is called a *jñānin*. The natural state of functional existence of a *jñānin* always remains beyond the comprehension of the unenlightened, and therefore the latter treats the uncommon phenomena seen in the former's life as miraculous. Such uncommon gifts of some of these, seen by others as miraculous, are not considered so by *jñānin*s themselves. They are not thought to be spiritual attainments or goals to be desired and sought. Indeed it is thought that they may be a hindrance to the attainment of the aspirant's goal of merging his awareness in the Supreme Consciousness called *ātman*. None of India's basic scriptures proclaim *siddhi*s to be a spiritual goal nor consider them to be a measure of spiritual growth. The Yoga system alone refers to them, as an incidental attainment of some aspirants at an intensely concentrated stage in their spiritual development. It warns that assigning high value to *siddhi*s hinders the effort for attainment of *kaivalya*, Yoga's name for the final goal. Narayana Guru, too, in classifying the diffferent orders of that goal (also called *nirvāṇa*) considers the attainment of *siddhi*s to be *aśuddha-aśuddha-nirvāṇa* (impure-impure-*nirvāṇa*). Conditioned by the *guṇa*s they are the appropriate and generally inconsequential attainment of *siddhikāmī*s (those desirous of psychic powers). The unenlightened see uncommon phenomena as miracles and the beings from whom they emanate as divine, whilst common phenomena are simply regarded as ordinary and natural. The enlightened see everything as extraordinary and divine, and holding *Brahman* as the Absolute Measure of everything, see everything as miraculous.

Birth, Death and Reincarnation

A problem which exercises the human mind everywhere, in all cultures and in all times, is the question of continuance after death. A corollary of this is the question of whether there was existence before birth. Vedānta's perspective may be summarized as follows: Only one Reality, the Absolute, exists. Through its own *karma* it transforms itself in endless manifestations as forms which emerge, are sustained for a while and then sink back into the ocean of Being. The emergence of a new form we call birth and its reabsorption death. The imperishable substance, Being Itself, continues to exist in and through all these endless transformations, as gold continues to exist in the changing forms of ornaments. Those who know this Reality know that there is no birth and no death. The *Bhagavad-Gītā* says:

> He is never born, nor does He ever die;
> nor once having been, does He cease to be.
> Unborn, eternal, everlasting, ancient,
> He is not slain when the body is slain.[10]

The ignorant, not aware of their own imperishable beingness, are mystified by birth and fearful of death. They mistake the unreal for the real, the non-substantial apparent for the substantial non-apparent, and they worry about the continuance of what doesn't really exist at all.

Some of India's ancient sages provided an answer acceptable and comforting to simple, unenlightened people. They taught that after death, according to the *karma* of its present life, the soul will travel through ascending realms either to reach the world of *Brahman,* or to return to earth to enter a new body. This notion, valid only in the realm of measurable things, has taken a firm hold on the minds of the ignorant and burdened them with a false idea of the authorship of *karma* and a false sense of responsibility for it. The ancient masters reinforced this view by teaching that those who perform meritorious deeds in the present life will reap beneficial fruits in the next and may progress to final release.

In fact the reality of life is the same for the *jñānin* and the *ajñānin,* the only difference being that the *jñānin* knows it and lives in the joyful secure knowledge of immortality, whilst the *ajñānin* lives in the miserable insecurity of mortality. The *jñānin* sees one life only, but it is everlasting. The *ajñānin,* mistakenly foreseeing many lives, goes from birth to birth and death to death.

Birth, death and rebirth are problematic questions of life when appearances are the measure. When the Absolute is the measure, those problems and questions dissolve in immeasurable immortality.

---

10. *Bhagavad-Gītā*, II.20.

Sūtra 15

सदसतोरन्योन्यकार्यकारणत्वात् ॥

sad asator anyonya kārya kāraṇatvāt ॥

sat asatoḥ	:	of Existence and appearance
anyonya	:	mutually
kārya kāraṇatvāt	:	being cause and effect

Because Existence and appearance are mutually cause and effect.

THE incomplete statement above is the first part of a syllogism, the second part of which is given in *sūtra* 16.

In Vedānta *sat* means that which exists beyond all conditionings of time, space and appearances. That which is manifest and subject to those conditionings, which appears to exist but has no substantial separate existence, is called *asat*. Another word for *asat* is *bhāva* (becoming), meaning that which has come into being. Although opposite in nature and meaning, *sat* and *asat* are inseparably related to any understanding of human life on earth. In the *Bhagavad-Gītā* the word *sat* means ontological Reality, as well as indicates values of life and human conduct. The *Gītā* says:

Sat means Existence and likewise Goodness, O Arjuna.
To all laudable actions the word *sat* is applied.

> Steadfast loyalty to sacrifice, austerity and charity
> are also called *sat*, as is action so intended.[1]

The word *sat*, therefore, even while meaning Existence, indicates positive, life-supporting behaviour. Such behaviour, known as *sadācāra*, is the ethical expression of those who, with awareness of underlying Reality, are called *sat-puruṣa*s. Conversely the word *asat* means non-Existence and indicates negative, harmful, ignorant behaviour also.

Underlying apparent existences there is a non-apparent reality. That reality is conceived as the *sat* defined above. Every living thing and everything else in the world has emerged from that underlying reality and, in due course of time, will be reabsorbed by it. This evanescent aspect of existence is termed *asat*, and its insubstantial nature is indicated as transitory appearance. The non-apparent *sat* pervading all transitory appearances is eternal.

Still the two are inseparably linked, for without a basis in reality there would be no world and without a world there would be no expression of reality. Reality and the world may therefore be considered as counterparts of an ultimate dialectical situation in which Reality is conceived to be One Existence of two distinct and opposing aspects. It is as if the mutual opposition of "being" and "becoming" imbues everything with their contradictory nature and defines Existence. Everything manifest in the world is therefore both *sat* and *asat* together.

Cause and effect (*kāraṇa* and *kārya*) are similar counterparts of another frame of reference. In this *sūtra* Narayana Guru indicates that Existence and appearance are related as mutual cause and effect. This is the paradox at the root of the enquiry into the nature of *Brahman;* in terms of cause and effect, it is

---

1. *Bhagavad-Gītā*, XVII.26-27.

the enquiry into the nature of Reality, the perceived world and ourselves, its perceivers.

The Logic of Causality

It is through the perception of an existing world by an existing perceiver that the enquiry is provoked, as without that perception there would be no enquiry and no enquirer, and there would be nothing perceived and nothing to know it. In that sense it can be said that the appearance of the world is the cause of existence and that *sat* is, therefore, an effect of *asat*. Perceived and perception, however, have their basis in underlying Reality and in that sense *sat* is the cause and *asat,* the effect. In logic and reasoning cause and effect turn back upon themselves as it were, each effect becoming the cause of knowing the cause behind. Cause and effect relationships are simply a perceiver's discernment of linear progressions in *māyā*'s illusory field of manifest multiplicities (*bhāva*s). In Vedānta's theory of non-creation, called *ajāta-vāda*, non-dual Reality, transcending all relationships, is neither a cause nor an effect. Reality, in its spontaneous unfolding as the world, is not subject to any law of causality. Causality arises as a concept in human minds attempting to discern the genesis of appearances, but when the logical mind merges in transcendent Consciousness cause and effect disappear in the oneness of non-dual Being. Śaṅkara, in his famous Hymn to Śiva, the archetypal Guru, says:

> This world appears subject to causality because of the inseparability of cause and effect from their Master — The absolute.[2]

In Vedānta the concept of a causal law pertains to the realm of changefulness called *saṁsāra* (continuous phenomenal becoming). The purpose of Vedānta is to lead aspirants across

---

2. *Dakṣiṇāmūrti Stotra*, Śaṅkara, v. 8.

saṁsāra's sea of confusion and suffering to the ground of blissful Being in immortal and immutable Reality. Gauḍapāda, in his work called *Māṇḍūkya-Kārikā* (a versified elucidation of the *Māṇḍūkya Upaniṣad*) and Śaṅkara, in his commentary on the *Kārikā,* weigh the concept of causality and find it meaningless in regard to Ultimate Reality.

Scientific studies of apparent existences, both mental and physical, are based upon the concept of a causal law. This concept, central to the common understanding of life, is challenged by Vedānta's deeper view. Gauḍapāda, in his *Māṇḍūkya-Kārikā,* says:

> As long as mind is possessed by the idea of cause and effect, causality appears real. When the idea of cause and effect is dispelled causality is extinguished. As long as mind is possessed by the idea of cause and effect *samsāra* ensues. When the state of being resulting from the idea of cause and effect is dispelled, one does not enter *samsāra* or worldly life.[3]

When the law of causality is found to be baseless then the reasoning mind too becomes baseless, as reason would have it that when one event is seen to ensue from another the former is cause and the latter effect. But particular events ensue from prior events only as specificities in Nature's course of continuous transformations. When, in a reverse of causality's flow, knowledge of a prior event is gained from the perspective of a latter event, it is then inferential knowledge of a past cause derived from a present effect. In some of the schools of Indian philosophy, including Vedānta, seeking the underlying principle of causality is considered as a means of gaining some certitude in regard to Ultimate Reality. Although constituting an aspect of their methodology this principle has never been precisely defined in these schools. Vedānta does not purport to explain each and every phenomenon in Nature

3. *Māṇḍūkya-Kārikā*, Gauḍapāda, IV.55-56.

but indicates that Reality which, Itself uncaused, is the Ultimate Cause of all phenomena. Thus in Vedānta, causal law is regarded as a concept projected upon the matrix of Reality, to explain how manifestations are sequentially related. It is seen as a methodological device in the search for the Final Cause of everything, in relation to which the entire world is considered as an effect. The search terminates in the realization of that Uncaused Reality, where cause and effect are understood to be merely superimpositions created by the mind upon It and both are known to be *asat*.

Causality in Western Thought

Many eminent Western thinkers too have pondered upon the nature of causality. The empiricist David Hume, for example, noted certain constants in causal chains. He observed that related phenomena, following each other in time, are perceived as cause and effect simply because they are related and sequential; as heat, for example, follows ignition and cold comes with snow. Seeing that certain conjoined phenomena always arise, the one from the other in the same order, the mind assumes that an observed event is an effect of the preceding one which is thought to be the cause. Hume takes the view that such belief is based upon the experience of observing present events and relating them in sense and memory to previous events. But he says that as each event is distinct it cannot by its qualities or by reason be inferred to be either a cause or an effect. He concludes that it is meaningless to attempt to follow a causal chain to an incipient cause and thus the very foundation of both philosophy and science is unsound.[4]

Hume's proposition that both causality and time are

4. David Hume in *An Enquiry Concerning the Human Understanding in Perspectives in Philosophy*, Robert N. Beck, New York: Holt, Reinhart and Winston Inc., 1966, pp. 215-21.

nothing but human fantasies is in agreement with Vedānta's view of those concepts. Narayana Guru, in the *Ātmopadeśa-Śatakam,* states that inference is possible only on the basis of something previously experienced. He says:

> Without prior experience there can be no inference; this object of our enquiry, never previously perceived by the senses, cannot be known by inference.[5]

F.H. Bradley examines the logical dilemma implicit in the concept of causality and he too exposes it as meaningless. He argues that causation must be continuous or there would be a finite point at which there would be no conjunction with anything following. But causation cannot be continuous, he observes, for this would mean that cause was entirely without duration in time. His conclusion is that when changing states are perceived as sequential and related, then cause and effect become apparent in human understanding. He comes to the view that what really exists is one changeless Reality, which he calls "the Absolute" — the term understood as the translation of the Sanskrit word *Brahman.*[6]

Bertrand Russell says of causality:

> The strict, certain, universal law of causation which philosophers advocate is an ideal, possibly true, but not **known** to be true by virtue of any available evidence. What is actually known, as a matter of empirical science, is that certain constant relations are observed to hold between the members of a group of events at certain times. Any such constant relation between events of specified kinds with given intervals of time between them is a "causal law."[7]

5. *Ātmopadeśa-Śatakam,* v. 31.

6. *Appearance and Reality,* F.H. Bradley, New York: Macmillan and Co., 1897, pp. 60-61.

7. From "On the Notion of Cause, with Applications to the Free-will Problem", in *Philosophy in the Twentieth Century,* vol. 2, ed. by William Barret, New York: Random House, 1962, p. 693.

He defines cause thus:

> A cause is an event, or group of events, of some known general character and having a known relation to some other event called the effect; the relation being of such kind that only one event, or at any rate only one well defined sort of event, can have the relation to a given cause.[8]

Russell concedes that it is customary to give the name "effect" to an event which is subsequent to a "cause," but sees no inherent law in this. He admits that there is a sort of vagueness at the root of philosophical thinking which, of necessity, conceives of causal law and inference as methodological tools. He says:

> It will generally be found that all our initial data, all the facts that we seem to know to begin with, suffer from vagueness, confusion and complexity. Current philosophical ideas share these defects; it is therefore necessary to create an apparatus of precise conceptions as general and as free from complexity as possible, before the data can be analysed into the kind of premises which philosophy aims at discovering.[9]

He submits that the logical method which relies on causal laws does not finally provide an answer to the major and obvious problem of philosophy, but merely sets the stage for the philosophical vision of genius. In his words:

> When everything has been done that can be done by method, a stage is reached where only direct philosophical vision can carry matters further. Here only genius will avail.[10]

These three eminent Western philosophers seem to arrive at

8. "On the Notion of Cause, with Applications to the Free-will Problem", in *Philosophy in the Twentieth Century*, vol. 2, ed. by William Barret, New York: Random House, 1962, p. 692.
9. Ibid., p. 701.
10. Ibid.

the same conclusion that the law of causality is a human fantasy imbued with vagueness and confusion.

The work of other illustrious Western thinkers, perhaps most notably that of Newton and Darwin, has contributed to the causality concept without resolving its inherent uncertainty. The equivocal nature of the concept leads to the situation in which certain perceived phenomena, explainable in terms of cause and effect, are classified as natural, whilst phenomena not causally explicable are classified as unnatural or supernatural. Long before scientific theories came up and lines were drawn between natural and unnatural events, men thought that different phenomena were the provinces of different cosmic forces which, in India, were personified as *deva*s (gods) or *gandharva*s (demi-gods). When causality ceases to be the basis upon which explanations are founded everything is seen to be equally natural and mysterious. With its view of cosmic interconnections and causal relationships limited and confined within time/space boundaries, scientific explanations of events are shown to be no more valid than the observations of the ancients.

Causality and Non-duality

Causal law and human volition are not compatible. If it were accepted that everything happens in accordance with causal law it would also have to be accepted that everything is predetermined and that there is no free will and no choice in life's course. But predetermination and free will relate to levels of awareness in beings; the higher their level of awareness the greater is their free will and ability to choose.

Kṛti, meaning action, inheres in the Sanskrit word for Nature, *prakṛti*. That action is the unceasing flow of transformations which in *māyā*'s field of dualities is perceived as a stream of separate causes of separate effects. These are simply related states of transformations in Nature's non-dual, unchanging changefulness, but in so far as one event is a predictable outcome of another, as a bloom is the predictable outcome of a bud, it is convenient and useful to explain them within a conceived law of causality. Without such a concept there could be no science, no technology and no logically understood reasons for the events of life. It is not, however, incumbent on the seeker to disentangle the complexity, vagueness and confusion of causal law, but rather to know the non-dual Reality of causes and effects. The *Maitrī Upaniṣad* says of this:

> Where knowledge has attained non-duality, devoid of effect, cause and action; inexplicable, incomparable, indescribable; what is it? It is ineffable.[11]

Narayana Guru, referring to causality, says in his *Daivadaśakam* hymn:

> Thou art the Creator, the act of creation and the myriad, magic-like creations. O God, are you not the very stuff of creation?[12]

Causality is indeed an applicable concept in this world of illusory dualities but if traced to non-dual Being then, paradoxically, *sat* and *asat* mutually become the cause and effect of each other.

11. *Maitrī Upaniṣad*, VI.7.
12. *Daivadaśakam*, v. 5.

Sūtra 16

अहं ममेति विज्ञातो मत्तो नान्यः ॥

aham mameti vijñāto matto nānyaḥ ॥

aham	:	I
mama	:	mine
iti	:	thus (as)
vijñātaḥ	:	that which is known
mattaḥ	:	than Me (the Self)
na anyaḥ	:	is not other

that which is known as "I" and "mine" is not other than the Self.

THE above words conclude the statement begun in the previous *sūtra.*

Every individual is a subjective centre of awareness in which everything perceived as something other is known. In that sense there is nothing in the world, nothing anywhere existing, other than in each individual's knowledge of it. It is that subjective knower of a separate objective world which is the "I" of each individual. That subjective "I" is expressed by Narayana Guru with the *aham* of this *sūtra.* The superimpositions on the field of an individual's awareness constitute the *mama,* the "mine" of this *sūtra.*

The separation of "I" and "mine" is the separation of knower and knowledge perceived in the field of appearances, the illusory world which *māyā* presents through the senses. In this regard the following situation conceived by David Bohm demonstrates how a singularity can appear as a duality.

Bohm presents the idea of a glass fish-tank in which a single fish is swimming freely. Two television cameras are set up at right angles to it, projecting separate pictures onto two television screens in another room. The images seen on the screens are thus of the fish appearing at the same moment at different angles. Bohm then places a notional viewer before the screens who sees the two pictures simultaneously. The viewer is unaware of the source of the two pictures and has no way of knowing that they are not of two separate fish. When a fish on one screen makes a movement the fish on the other screen appears to make a different but simultaneous movement. On this basis, and ignorant of their being in one life process, the viewer may relate the two as cause and effect without being able to designate a specific role to either of the images. David Bohm calls the apparent phenomena seen on the screens the "explicate order" and the single reality of the fish, the "implicate order."

Similarly, different views of the One Reality, the "implicate order," are simultaneously projected onto the screen of individual awareness, as it were, and the One is seen as a multiplicity of forms and events (the "explicate order") which the viewer attempts to relate as causes and effects. Once the implicate order is known the problem of causality vanishes. Bohm's implicate order is not different in meaning from the *ātman* of Vedānta and his explicate order is not different from the world.

In such a vision the entire cosmic system is the effect of one cosmic memory. This vision cannot be dismissed as the mere intellectual play of philosophical thought. Even such eminent physicists as Fritjof Capra and David Bohm, in their search for a new dimension in physics, acknowledge the veracity of such a vision. In support of his own stand on the matter, Fritjof quotes the following words of John Jeans:

> . . . the universe begins to look more like a great thought than like a great machine.[1]

"I" Sense

Individual life is a continuity of "I" sense through constantly changing experiences which attach to the "I" with a sense of "mine." In Sanskrit the "I sense" is called *aham-kāra* or *aham-ta* and the "mine sense" is called *mama-kāra* or *mama-ta*. The enduring sense of an individual's "I" is both his present awareness and the accretion of his memories of past experiences. These past experiences become "mine" in relationship to the "I" sense and are evaluated in terms of the "I's interest." Thus "I" and "mine" occupy equal places in the experience of one's own being.

The sense of "I" continues through the waking, sleeping and deep-sleep states of an individual's consciousness and identifies itself with the individual's body and bodily states. So that, for example, he says "I am tired," or says "I (*aham-kāra*) have (*mama-kāra*) a headache." Or he says "I was sleeping," or says something that means "my sense of "I" will now go to bed and so will "my" body." These two, "I" sense and "my" body, are unified in the individual's perception of a self-identity separate from externals.

Intellect is the reasoning faculty by which an individual's perceptions are evaluated. It is one of the many faculties of individuated consciousness; it is the logic mechanism by which experiences are assessed and classified before being stored away in the individual's memory faculty. It is intellect that classifies the body as matter, separate from the non-matter of

1. *The Turning Point*, Fritjof Capra, Flamingo, Glasgow, 1988, p. 76.

mind. Although mind and matter have never existed as separate entities they are seen, like Bohm's fish, as two. To understand one's enduring nature (the "I" which endures through all the experiences of changing mind and changing body) it is necessary to know the nature of one's being which transcends the mind/body duality. In India that unitive vision of "I" is known as *yoga-buddhi.*

The view of "I" as bodily existence is called *dehoham-buddhi* and the concept of "I" as a continuous flow of personal consciousness is called *jīvoham-buddhi* (the concept of "I" as individual personal consciousness or soul). In the former, "I" sense identifies with the body. Whatever then pertains to the body, or is considered as belonging to it, is thought of as "mine." In the latter view "I" is conceived to be an individual, personal consciousness; a soul whose memory or knowledge is considered as "mine." Both these concepts are formulated by the mode of consciousness called intellect and have no existence outside it.

Memory plays a crucial role in the enduring sense of "I" and "mine." All knowledge one acquires, all one's inherited and acquired personal characteristics, all cultural peculiarities of both individuals and peoples are, in one form or another, manifestations of the faculty of memory. All the libraries of the world are treasure-houses of human memories. Human existence is meaningless without memory. Yet elucidation of how that faculty functions has eluded all efforts of the physiological and psychological sciences and certainly no theorizing about memory would be possible without memory. From a Vedāntic perspective memory is one of numerous functions of *cit*, its assumed storehouse of memories being known as *citta*. Unconditioned Consciousness, for the very reason that it is conscious, does not remain inert and inactive. It knows Itself and knows the happenings within Itself. What we call memory is simply the knowledge Consciousness has of its own assumed modes of expression. The functioning of memory in *cit* has a manifest counterpart in the physical and chemical changes which take place in the brain, another of its expressions. What we experience as memory and its corresponding neural changes are two facets of the "explicate order," whilst the "implicate order" is *cit* in its naturally functioning modes. The cosmic system has an integrity which is unaffected by all the transformations within it. The seed of a particular tree reproduces the same kind of tree. The human sperm and ovum reproduce a human being only. All such events as these are ordered and made possible through the cosmic memory which Indian mythology calls Viṣṇu, the Preserver. Cosmic memory is an aspect of *cit*'s awareness of the creative Self-expressions taking place within Itself.

The "I" as body (dehoham-buddhi)

The science of biology has made enormous advances in the areas of the physical, chemical and genetic nature of living organisms. With the knowledge of the DNA molecule the whole life of an organism may be known, from its embryonic inception through all its changing forms and states to its final disintegration in death. It is known that the cells constituting human bodies have lifespans varying between forty-five days and one-and-a-half years. Even a human infant above one-and-a-half years of age has no surviving cell of the body it was born with, whilst full grown adults have changed their bodies many times. Yet the sense of "I" which dawned in the new infant's awareness continues through all its organic life into senile old age. With the developing sense of itself as "I" the newly aware infant perceives a world it evaluates with a developing sense of "mine."

As a physical organism the human being is subject to injury, pain and disease. The organism may lose a limb, an eye, its teeth, its hair, or even internal organs, a kidney or lung, for example. Yet it will not feel its sense of "I" diminished in the slightest degree. It may live a full span of years but finally is subject to old age, weakness, death and disintegration. It may, when confronting that inevitability, ponder over the question of post-mortem continuance. Apart from perceiving itself as an objective physical existence capable of experiencing a range of physical sensations (from intensely pleasurable to intensely painful), it also experiences itself as a range of mental processes (of thinking, considering, evaluating, memorizing and anticipating). It also knows that it is subjected to changing moods (of happiness, joy, elation, love, compassion, boredom, misery, despair, anger, hate and the like). Biological studies reveal that these are accompanied by chemical changes in the central nervous system, and medical knowledge has been gained which enables both the physical and mental states of the human organism to be changed or modified by the administration of chemistry-affecting drugs. With this ability scientists may assert that chemistry is the cause of specific organic states and consider these to be mere effects of chemical changes in an organism. Science indeed has made very great progress in understanding the functioning of organic systems. It has contributed very much to the alleviation of physical and mental pain and disorder, but still it is unable to explain the nature of subjective awareness or reveal the nature of the aware subject. The "I" sense identified as the existence of a physical body is a mere, though highly complex, organic mechanism animated and informed by a completely inexplicable principle called life.

The "I" as Soul (jīvoham-buddhi)

A basic imperative of Vedānta is its discrimination between the Self and the non-Self (*ātma-anātma-viveka*) by which the realization "I am not this body" is attained. Śaṅkara, in his *Vivekacūḍāmaṇi* (Crest-Jewel of Discrimination) expounds this matter at some length. The Śaṅkara school, as has been said, classifies the body as gross, subtle or causal, relative to the waking, dreaming or deep-sleep states of consciousness. In discriminating the body to be non-Self, what remains is an indeterminate animating principle and sense of "I" in a field of witnessing awareness. It is this which in the English language is called "soul" and in Sanskrit is called *jīva*.

The idea became established that this soul was an individual self, a *jīva*. This term is not commonly used in Vedāntic literature. The names *jīvātma-buddhi* (the idea of soul as self) or *jīvātma-bhāva* (the state in which the soul is considered as self) are more usually employed. Śaṅkara's *jīvātman* concept, misunderstood as an idea of a multiplicity of souls, is contrary to the Advaita view of one Self which Śaṅkara himself expounded. In Advaita Vedānta the soul is not considered to be a self-existent entity. As a multiplicity of bodies is seen to be an illusion arising out of *māyā*, so too is a multiplicity of souls regarded. In this, Advaita Vedānta stands apart from other Indian schools of thought in which the identification of *jīva* with *ātman* took a firm hold. The Vedānta view of one *ātmā* and many souls can be illustrated by the following analogy:

Space is infinitely extensive (*mahākāśa*). A building standing in endless space encloses some part of it within its walls. The space enclosed by the building is called *maṭhākāśa* but it is not different from the space extending beyond the building. Within the building a pot encloses and shapes some of the space (then called *ghaṭākāśa*) within its confines. When the conditioning factors of pot and building are removed the spaces within them become one with the infinite space from which only illusion separated them.

It is in a like way that *Brahman* is conceived of in Vedānta. The conditioning factors of physical body, senses and mind make it appear that there are many individual selves, but when these conditioning factors are dispelled in *yoga-buddhi*, it is known that the many apparent selves and *Brahman* are one indivisible Reality. The veiling of *ātman* by such conditioning factors can be compared to the situation where a piece of rope appears as a snake in dim light. It is a superimposition of an erroneous identity on what is Real arising out of *avidyā* (ignorance). Through ignorance, erroneous identification of percepts is mistaken for their Reality.

In Advaita Vedānta, *avidyā* is known to be a negative functional mode of *cit* and ignorance and its effects are understood to arise from the very Reality they veil. Latter-day Vedānta schools sometimes lose sight of that important fact, especially when relating the concept of *jīvātman* (individual soul) to that of *paramātman* (Supreme Soul). Regarding the body as non-Self, they make the mistake of conceiving *jīvātman* as that which has an individual existence separate from the body. Advaita Vedānta's clear stand is that both bodies and souls are erroneously perceived as separate individual existences through the *māyā* principle inherent in the one *ātman*. As the word *jīva*, in its etymological sense, only means that which survives by breathing, it includes both the body and its animating principle. It should, therefore, be understood in that way.

"Mine" Sense

Through the dualism of knower and known all that is perceived as object becomes "mine" in the perceiver's knowledge. The sense of "I" attaches a sense of possession to knowledge of anything regarded as other. The immediate knowledge which arises, for example, with the first sip of coffee becomes "my taste of coffee" which in turn becomes "it is my coffee I am tasting." This sense of possessing knowledge as "mine" (called *mama-kāra or mama-ta*) is indicated in this *sūtra* by the Guru's use of the composite word *mameti* (*mama* + *iti*, thus mine).

Man, having this sense of "mine" in regard to sensory objects, becomes attached to them and identifies himself with them. So much so that if possessions or attachments he regards as precious are lost, he himself may feel lost and so bereft of all he values, that his life ceases to have meaning.

The sense itself of possession of objects, is called *eṣaṇā*. The dearest of possessions and strongest of attachments is one's spouse, children and wealth. The sense of possession of a spouse is called *dāreṣaṇā*, of children *putṛeṣaṇā*, of wealth *vitteṣaṇā* and of all three together *eṣaṇā-traya*. Such strong identifications and attachments obstruct one's progress towards Self-identification and it is necessary to free oneself from attachments to possessions if one is to gain Self-possession.

The bonds of attachment extend to all things with which one is identified: ideas and ideals, preferences, race, religion, caste, nation and all other externalizations. Yet releasing oneself from attachment to externals as separate entities, paradoxically, imbues them with greater value as they are then seen in the light of their true identity as expressions of the Self. Identification with externals then becomes identification with the Self in all its wondrous aspects. In this identification the whole cosmos, the whole of creation, becomes "mine," and the "I" sense becomes one with it. Such self-identification with the all of existence is the realization of the oneness of Existence, the oneness of the Self. It is the attainment of non-duality which is the goal of Vedānta. Narayana Guru says:

> The embodied being, losing body-sense, identifies with objects as "That is mine" and "This is mine." Anyone becoming aware of this as an inner experience, attains Realization.[2]

---

2. *Ātmopadeśa-Śatakam*, v. 48.

The sense of possession, *mamata,* can therefore be the Absolute unconditioned value of Self-possession or the relative, conditioned value of an individual possessed by his perceived possessions. Simply understanding this helps to free one from an identification with possessions and their three domains of knower (*jñātā*), doer (*kartā*) and enjoyer (*bhoktā*). Thus it helps release one from the bondage of "my knowledge," "my actions" and "my fruits."

The "mine" sense of knowledge, the "mine" sense of actions, the "mine" sense of fruits and the "mine" sense of everything else perceived as other, together with "I" sense, are dualities. They are as veils of ignorance concealing the identity of the one Real Knower, Real Doer and Real Enjoyer. With the lifting of those veils the ignorance of "I" and "mine" is dispelled and "I" and "mine" are revealed as not other than the Self.

Sūtra 17

तद्वत्तस्मात् ॥

tadvat tasmāt ॥

tadvat	:	likewise
tasmāt	:	than That (not other)

Likewise not other than "That."

IN the previous two *sūtras* and with this one, Narayana Guru states, "Because Existence and appearance are mutually cause and effect, that which is known as "I" and "mine" is not other than the Self. Likewise not other than That." With this sequence he reiterates that "Me," the Self, or *Brahman* is one and indivisible, and that all appearances, either individual or universal, have being only in that absolute Reality.

In Sanskrit literature the world is often referred to as *idam,* a word meaning "this/here." It implies the "this/here" of perception, i.e., the apparent world of "I" and "mine." Conversely the world's underlying non-apparent Reality is often referred to as That (*tat*). In emphasizing the non-difference of *idam* and *tat,* the Guru is emphasizing the non-difference of "I" and "mine" from *Brahman,* Reality. "This," not other than "That," is likewise not other than anything at all conceivable or inconceivable. Narayana Guru is reminding us that in Reality there is only undifferentiated *saccidānanda.* In his *Daivadaśakam* hymn he says:

> Counting one by one, when everything perceivable has converged in the knower's awareness, then, with steadied vision, let the inner being attain its rest in Thee.[1]

The knower's awareness is an infinitely small point of individuated consciousness in which the innumerable forms of an infinitely large manifest world converge. This pulsating point of "I"-consciousness realizes itself as Cosmic Consciousness and knows itself as the substance of all manifest forms. It is this which in the above verse the Guru addresses as "Thee." It is the never-ending stream of Creative Consciousness from Itself, within Itself, back to Itself, analogous to the curving space concept of modern physics. Consciousness, *Brahman*, God, creates the world from Him/Her/Itself and is located in it; the world, in turn, rests in that Absolute. It is not one finite world of one individual's awareness but the innumerable worlds of innumerable individuals, converging and known in the oneness of infinite Being, in That, the Absolute Reality. The "I" and "mine" of innumerable individuals therefore are not other than "That."

Vedānta and Modern Physics

The science of modern physics and Vedānta are sister disciplines in that both seek to reveal the nature and origin of the world. Both have discerned the existence of one ultimate substance of everything, which Vedānta calls *Brahman* and science calls "energy." These are merely the technical terms, each respectively applies to the same Reality, conceived differently in their different disciplines. Physics and Vedānta employ diverse and radically different methodologies in their investigations and explanations of existence. Nevertheless they meet at a point at which their objective is not discernible to the senses (even when these are greatly extended by the instruments of advanced technology). Physics declares that all matter is a form of energy and Vedānta has no quarrel

1. *Daivadaśakam*, v. 2.

with this assertion. But from that point of agreement they part company, taking their different directions, with physics looking outwards to objective existence and Vedānta looking inwards to subjective existence.

Physics confines its study to the material existence of the world and aims to explain the world's being in terms of the fundamental nature of matter. Understanding existence only in terms of matter, however, has an inherent limitation in the preconception that matter is the causal substance of existence. It is the paradoxical view that matter, born out of a pre-matter state in a "big-bang," begets matter and causes material changes. Confronted with the phenomenon of consciousness, physical science considers this to be an effect arising from and located in the material brain. It would reject or be confounded by the contrary view that the brain arises from and is located in consciousness.

Vedānta is not confined by the self-imposed limits of physical science. Its holistic approach to the question of the nature of the world does not differentiate matter and mind as separate realities, the one arising from the other. It sees mind and matter as distinct aspects of Reality only in the field of perceived dualities.

DIFFERENT GOALS

The goal of physical science is the acquisition of detailed, demonstrably accurate knowledge of the material world. The purpose of that aim is to add to the sum total of man's knowledge of the many manifest aspects of the world hopefully to gain benefit from some sought-for or incidental discoveries of new knowledge. Indeed, many and great have been the benefits derived from science and technology in many of the fields of man's interest, but still man continues to be beset by endless problems. His dilemma is that he resolves problems only to see new problems arise. It is neither realistic nor feasible to hope for the end of humanity's vexations and conflicts on the basis of increasing scientific revelations of the infinite details of the external world. Physical science trembles on the brink of acknowledging that there is a field of being beyond the bounds of sense discernment, and hesitates as that admission would not be "scientific."

Vedānta has quite another goal. It is to enable the seeker to realize that the fundamental nature of his being and the fundamental nature of the perceived world are one and the same Reality. This aim is not directed to the mere satisfaction of intellectual curiosity about the nature of existence, for Vedānta's goal is fully realizable in direct experience (Transcendental Consciousness) and in the great *mukti* (Freedom) it brings. As a knowledge system with a well-defined methodology, Vedānta may properly be called a science and, therefore, the name *brahmavidyā* (science of the Absolute) is associated to it.

The two disciplines, Vedānta and physical science, view the psycho-physical aspects of the world from very different standpoints. Physics, in its preconception of the physical nature of the world, conceives matter to be the basis from which the psyche emerges. It discerns fundamental matter to be wave/particle vibrations of energy and knows that all physical matter is, fundamentally, vibrating energy, but it cannot say what it is that is energetically vibrating.

There are and have been scientists with mystic vision and intuition (the great Albert Einstein was one such) who, confronting that impenetrable mystery, can only shake their heads in wonder and say of it, "It is God!"

Physics and Vedānta can shake hands at this point and share joy in the wondrous knowledge that "It/He/She" exists. Perceived as *Īśa,* the Cosmic Person, the Creative Intelligence from which the world arises, God is adored and worshipped in Vedānta as the Creator. He is the vibrating energy of everything, in everything, which everything is in. There is nothing else, nowhere else; only effulgent vibrating Consciousness, only God, only *ātman* the Self, the One Reality, the energy of physics and everything else. It is a paradoxical absurdity that people worry about an "energy shortage" in the physical world of science in which nothing exists but energy!

There can be no complete science in which the enquirer is separate from the enquiry. In the science of biology, the study of life-forms, life (bios) is studied as separate from the biologist but the biologist does not know what bios is. In the science of psychology, the study of the psyche (self), the psyche is studied as separate from the psychologist but the psychologist does not know what the psyche is. In the study of physics, the study of matter/energy, the physical is studied as separate from the physicist but the physicist does not know what the physical is. Only in the science of Vedānta, the study of Reality, is the object not separate from the subject of study.

Vedānta in its enquiry encompasses *sat* (Existence), *cit* (Consciousness) and *ānanda* (Value), and is therefore a holistic science. The preoccupations of the physical sciences (physics, astronomy, chemistry, engineering, geology, metallurgy and the like) are with the physical aspects alone of Existence (*sat*); as if it is devoid of Consciousness (*cit*) and devoid of Value (*ānanda*). The physical sciences are, therefore, incomplete. What they have in common with Vedānta is the impossibility of describing the object of their enquiries within any finality of definition. By whatever name it is called — Existence, Consciousness, Value, the Self, God or Energy — the one Absolute Reality is ultimately indefinable.

Indefinable One, Definable Many

The One Absolute Reality is imperceptible and inconceivable.

Infinite and impalpable, it cannot be perceived by the senses. Formless and without any confining boundaries, it cannot be conceived by the mind. The One cannot be defined. The Sanskrit word *saccidānanda* comes as close to a verbal definition as is possible in the discernment of its threesome nature — the trinity of Existence, Consciousness and Value. But even this does not define its One Identity and words can go no further than to say of it *auṁ tat sat* (*auṁ*, That is Existence).

Other than words, there are symbols and images owing their origin to the vision of rare mystic seers that communicate their realizations and perceptions on various aspects of the Absolute.

Judaism's fundamental proclamation, "the Lord thy God the Lord is One" is symbolized with a six-pointed star. A structure of two inverted triangles, it portrays the inseparability of the manifest and unmanifest realms of existence and the equilibrium of the trinity principles in each.

The cross of Christianity may be understood as more than just a symbol of Christ's execution. Its horizontal axis communicates the positive and negative poles of the earth's manifest actualities, and its vertical axis communicates transcendental realms called heaven and hell. A mystic vision of Divine Glory has inspired Christian artists in many centuries to produce a great wealth of wonderful works in paintings, sculptures, buildings, music, poetry and literature.

The art of Islam is rich in works of unsurpassed beauty for which, in India, one has to look no further than that exquisite jewel of architecture called the Taj Mahal, an expression of Allah's wondrous creativity in cool white marble. Islam's crescent symbol of a new moon suggests the rising of new revelation, the rising of Consciousness in the manifest world.

The Chinese symbol of the *Tao,* with its S divided circle of tadpole-like dark and light forms, each containing a germ of the other, is a tremendously powerful symbol. It suggests the twin aspects of non-dual Reality, eternally chasing each other in their mutual contradictions of being/non-being.

Buddhism and Hinduism, each has its deeply significant symbols. Each has inspired a fantastic treasury of art in paintings, sculptures and temple buildings, especially in the powerful images of their gods and demons. Hinduism's portrayal of Śiva as the divine dancer, Naṭarāja, in the Chidambaram Temple in south India is surely one of the world's most famous, wonderful, expressive and profound sculptures. Naṭarāja dances in *cidambaram* (the void of *cit*). He is dancing the universe into creation on the back of a crouching dwarf representing human ego in the manifest world. The dwarf serves as a footstool or dance-ground of the Absolute. Naṭarāja is shown with four hands, one of which gestures wisdom and another grace. In a third hand he holds aloft a bowl of fire, sparking and flaming the life and activities of the world in the heat of transformations. In the fourth he holds a small drum which resonates the primal sound giving rise to all the music and languages of creation. The Hindu god Gaṇeśa, Śiva's son, is the Lord of Hosts, the Auspicious One, the god of wisdom and the remover of obstacles. He is represented as a pot-bellied human torso with four arms and an elephant's head. He too carries powerful symbols in each of his four hands. The symbolism of his imagery is deeply significant in Hinduism, depicting as they do different aspects of divinity and supreme wisdom. But on the obvious level of his appearance he is an improbable and unlikely figure. What could be more improbable than a divine being in the form of a pot-bellied human with the head of an elephant? Yet, in Indian mythology, he is the first-born and dear child of the Divine Parents. Hinduism is also telling us through this depiction that there is nothing so impossible to conceive or so wonderfully wrought that the Infinite Absolute Creator cannot bring it into being.

Numerous other mystic symbols and images exist in man's treasure-house, which are of great value in informing us of a Reality far beyond the range of human sensory perceptions. Yet none can define and communicate the incommunicable, indefinable Absolute. What can be defined are its many manifestations as finite, perceptible and conceivable forms, of which it is possible to say, for example, "it is a star," "it is a bird," "it is a human being." All percepts, taking shape as individual entities and individual phenomena, are structured in knowing Consciousness as "I" and "mine." They are composite appearances, accretions of many things appearing as one. All are particle/wave motions. Some have tangible molecular constructions and some have subjective awareness of sensation, and some of these have an "I" sense also.

What seems to the senses to be the most substantial reality of entities is their outward, gross appearance. It is yet another paradox that their most apparent and, seemingly, most substantial aspect is the least real aspect of them and, conversely, what is the least apparent and, seemingly, the most insubstantial aspect of them is also the most real. The human entity is recognized by many outward aspects of appearance: by the attire with which it modestly covers itself and with which it helps to identify itself; by the shape of its body, its features and voice which proclaim it to be male or female; by the colour of its skin, its hair type and the features which proclaim it to be of this or that race and culture; by its ornament and other things which proclaim its status, and so forth. All such differences, though surface superficialities, contribute a wonderful richness and diversity to human life (how much less interesting the species would be if we were all tall, white, blond and blue-eyed, or all short and dark with curly black hair). But looking for the true identity of a being is to discern of each of its outward aspects that it is not this, not this (*neti, neti*). The One Reality, *ātman,* cannot be found in the many outer aspects which constitute and define individual entities and so it cannot be found in the outer aspects which constitute and define an individual human being.

Vedānta's definition of human nature is that it is not other than a specific expression of *ātman*. Humanity, as an aspect of an illusory world, is viewed as a dream-like Self-illusion. In this context, the words of the sixteenth-century great English poet and playwright, William Shakespeare, come to mind; he defined human nature with these words:

> We are such stuff as dreams are made on, and our little life is rounded with a sleep.[2]

The human being is a sum total of many objective/subjective aspects, which define a psycho-physical personality and constitute an individual, transient, empirical self, an "I." It is a manifestation of the unmanifest Self appearing as one form of a composite many. Each human being is one specific expression of the Self's infinite expressions. Each is a unique definable manifestation, a unique composite appearance of a unique indivisible Reality. Each is one of many unique definable human forms of one unique formless indefinable Being — "That," the ultimate definition of everything.

The Value of Science

Science has value only when its findings contribute to the enlightenment, dignity and well-being of mankind. Therefore, the science of Vedānta has as its goal the raising of man's awareness to that height where his true identity is known and his fulfilment in life is attained. It is knowledge of the whole not concerned with the acquisition of knowledge of infinite parts. It is the knowledge that all parts are not other than the whole; likewise not other than "That."

---

2. *The Tempest,* Act 4, Sc. 1., William Shakespeare.

Sūtra 18

दृग्दृश्ययोः समानकालीनत्वात् ॥

dṛg dṛśyayoḥ samāna kālīnatvāt ॥

dṛg dṛśya yoḥ	:	of subject and object
samāna kālīnatvāt	:	because of the simultaneity

Because of the simultaneity of subject and object.

THE seven *sūtras* of this work beginning with *sūtra* 18 together comprise a syllogism. The first five of them are premises, the steps of reason leading to the concluding statements Narayana Guru makes in the final two.

There are many precedents in Vedānta's literature for this means of coming to a deduced conclusion through one or more irrefutable premises. Sometimes there is an inversion of the limbs in a syllogistic statement. The *Brahma-Sūtras* of Bādarāyaṇa, for example, open with the following lines (*sūtras*) where the conclusion is made in *sūtra* 2 and the premises are stated in the following two *sūtras*:

1. Now then (*atha*) let us have the desire to know *Brahman*.
2. *Brahman* is that from which the origin, subsistence and dissolution of the world proceed.
3. Because scripture is the source of knowledge of *Brahman*.

4. Because *Brahman* is to be known from scripture by reason of that connection.[1]

Narayana Guru, in this *sūtra,* the first of five premises, points to the simultaneity of subject and object.

The perceiver, i.e., the subject of perception, becomes so only in the instant of perceiving an object. The object likewise becomes so only in the instant in which it is perceived. The existence of anything at all has no meaning if it is not **perceived** as existing. Once observed, either as an external object or internal percept, its continuance is assumed on the basis of this initial perception. When not held as an object in awareness its continuance is thought (according to the point of view) to be located in an individual's memory, or in the Omnipresent Consciousness of God.

When the perceiver and perceived, subject and object, simultaneously arise, it cannot be said that one is a cause and the other an effect unless in the sense of their mutuality. Neither can it be said that they have separate existences. This simultaneity of subject and object indicates a non-dual Reality from which they emerge as knower and known. The knowledge of knower and known can only be structured in an underlying field of Consciousness which is that non-dual Reality. Consciousness Itself, therefore, is the one substance of mutual perceiver and perceived, subject and object, knower and known.

Whether it is thought that the awareness of an individual entity is the perceiving subject of an objective world, or that a Universal Consciousness is the substance, subject and object called world, both views indicate the non-duality of awareness.

Dṛk and Dṛśya

The Sanskrit word *dṛk* means "the perceiver" (the subject of

---

1. *athāto brahma jijñāsā, janmādy asya yataḥ, śāstra yonitvāt, tat tu samanvayāt* — *The Brahma-Sūtras,* I.1-4, Bādarāyaṇa.

perception). The word *dṛśya* means "the perceived" (the physical or mental object perceived).

The nature of subject and object has always been a speculative theme in philosophy, both in the East and West. Narayana Guru has given the theme a great deal of attention and in his lengthier works considered it from different perspectives. Śaṅkara devoted a whole work, called *Dṛg-dṛśya-viveka* (Discrimination of Subject and Object) to this problem alone. He develops the theme in such a way that reason is led from objective perception to *pratyag-ātmā-darśana* (vision of the innermost Self) and the logical conclusion that Self and the world are not separate. His argument, freely interpreted, is as follows:

> We see the world with our eyes. In this the eye is the *dṛk* and the world the *dṛśya*. Eye is not capable of seeing by itself. Mind is there to oversee the function of eye. Mind (*manas*) then becomes the *dṛk* and eye the *dṛśya*. Mind functions with intellect to control it. Here mind is the *dṛśya* and intelligence the *dṛk*. Intelligence is a function of the witnessing Self. The Self then is the *dṛk* and intelligence the *dṛśya*. But there is nothing behind the Self that witnesses and controls its function. Thus, in the case of Self-perception, the Self is both *dṛk* and *dṛśya*. In other words, *dṛk* and *dṛśya* become interchangeable or non-dual in the case of Self-perception. It is a perceptual experience in which there is no separate, determinable subject and object. Our discriminating search for subject and object cannot be extended back beyond this limit. For this reason the Self, in this context, is referred to as *pratyag-ātmā* (the innermost Self), as it is attained at the terminal point in our backward journey where subject becomes object and vice versa. The prefix *pratyak* means "in the interior," "inwardly," or "in the backward direction." The compound word *pratyag-ātmā* used in reference to the Self does not mean that the Self is located somewhere in the innermost aspect of vision. They

have relevance only as an indication of the direction of the search which enables the Self to be realized. The interiority is thus merely of methodological significance and has no ontological relevance.

Narayana Guru depicts this search and the attainment of *pratyag-ātmā* in the following words in his *Svānubhava Gīti* (Lyric of Ecstatic Self-Experience):

> Do we not always perceive that everything seen merges in the seeing eye? Likewise sound becomes merged in the ear and touch is lost and disappears in the skin.
>
> Similarly, taste disappears merged in the palate. These in like manner disappear merged in and becoming one with the senses like the mouth which, in turn, emerges as real.
>
> No sooner do the senses emerge as existing than they too vanish; then utter darkness alone prevails. It is as if a rope-walker falls to the ground when the rope is broken and balance lost.
>
> If, on losing everything, one could see the Dearest One as abiding in that darkness; lo! one is free of sufferings. How can there be darkness to loom around one who sheds bright rays?[2]

Sense Subjects and Objects

As the sense-organs respond only to the stimuli of sight, sound, touch, taste and smell, these stimuli are considered in Indian thought to be objects and, in this context, the sense-organs are thought to be subjects. The perceived qualities of sense objects are dependent upon the abilities of their related sense-organs to define them so that, for example, the fragrance of a rose is defined and exists only through the ability of the nose to smell it. In this example, the nose is subject to the rose-fragrance object.

---

2. *Svānubhava Gīti*, v. 2-5.

In another example, a sound is heard and experienced in awareness. The sound is of a particular frequency, a vibration resonating in the air waves, but it is the ability of the ear which defines the sound and transmits it to awareness. The sound therefore is not something existing, arriving from outside and heard inside, but is frequency and hearing merged in instant non-dual sound awareness. It is because of this simultaneity of subject and object that Narayana Guru says taste and the like merge and disappear in their respective sense-organs. In a prose work called *Cijjada-Cintakam* (Reflections on Mind and Matter), he explains how sense objects exist only in their related senses:

> From a microbe to an elephant everything animal moves. From a simple blade of grass to a huge tree everything vegetable stands rooted. Even thus, our sense perceptions such as those of ear and eye, all, constitute *cit* (mind), *Brahman*. From earth up to the primeval veil, the visibles constitute the *jaḍa* (the inert, or matter). Everything exists here as belonging to one or other of these two categories, like beads strung in a rosary. On the one side there are distinct names, which come into being to enable us to know everything that belongs to these two categories. On the other side there are the distinct mental or physical sounds of the names of each of these entities. It is evident that each of these two, names and sounds, are known by us as inhering in our ears. Likewise, the distinct touches indicating the nature of the objects from which they originate, are known by us as inhering in our skin. Similarly, the distinct colours by which the luminaries such as sun, moon, fire and all things illumined by them are distinctive, are known by us as inhering in our eyes. In the same way the distinct flavours of tasty things, such as grapes and the like, are known by us as inhering in the palate. As also the smells by which we recognize as distinct the things from which they emanate, are known by us as inhering in our noses.[3]

3. *Cijjaḍa-Cintakam,* Paragraph 1, our translation from the original Malayalam prose.

Objects of sensory perceptions are defined by the abilities of the sense-organs to receive and transmit information of them to the mechanisms of awareness in which they are identified and evaluated as specific externalizations. Seeking beyond the senses locates and identifies objects as awareness perceptions, but seeking beyond that is like coming to a wall of darkness where the backward direction of seeking terminates. Nothing beyond it is distinct and there is no firm ground for further progress. Narayana Guru likens this to a rope-walker whose rope is cut and whose balance is lost. Yet that silent darkness, devoid of anything other to be aware of, is not devoid of awareness. Self-effulgent, non-dual awareness knows Itself by its own light. Nothing else is there to know it. It is Self-knowledge of the Self, the seeker's self and the self of all. Knowing it, there is nothing else to be known. It is the Absolute searched for and discovered through mystic vision to be the searcher.

Sūtra writing is a literature by which incommunicable mystic experience is indicated through progressive steps of logic and reason. There is nothing in the common experience of dualistic perceptions with which the uncommon experience of non-dual mystic vision can be equated. Narayana Guru, therefore, rather than attempting to describe an indescribable experience, indicates it in terms understandable to those who seek it but have not attained it.

Living and Lifeless

From earliest times, man has discerned the perceptual world in terms of living beings and lifeless stuff. These live and lifeless entities are classified as organic or inorganic and as animal, vegetable or mineral. An obvious definition of living things is that they are endowed with various functions, have more or less ability to respond to stimuli, are able to reproduce their kind from themselves and are subject to death and decomposition. Substances thought to be inorganic lifeless matter are classified as minerals and as solids, liquids, or gases. Of the same underlying molecular constitution as living things, these too change in time. Minerals crystallize and grow and therefore in a sense reproduce themselves. Rocks disintegrate and therefore in a sense die. With changing temperature water undergoes transformations, as ice, liquid and vapour and therefore in a sense responds to an outside stimulus. Air moves, smoke billows and disperses, and so forth. Apart from the entities defined as live or lifeless there are also some rudimentary molecular structures not easily determined as organic or inorganic, living or not living. The essential difference between the world's entities is only in the degree to which they reflect the *sat-cit-ānanda* aspects of their mutual underlying substance; all are equally specific expressions of that pervasive Reality of everything.

When living entities of the animal and vegetable realms are seen to die it is thought that a mysterious principle called life, soul, spirit, energy or individual consciousness, which had inhabited and animated them, has departed and they, left behind, have become lifeless. However, when ripe fruits are seen to fall from a tree and rot on the ground it is not thought that the living tree has departed and left dead fruit behind. When any fruit (animal or vegetable) falls from the tree of life the tree continues to stand unchanged where it was, in the everywhere of Being. From their seed state, through sprouting or embryonic stages, bodies change, ingesting, metabolizing and excreting matter, growing, maturing, reproducing, fading, then falling back into the ground from which they arose. Their continuous transformations have taken place in life; with their disappearance life remains. Their identity has been in that whole cycle and not just in any particular stage of it.

All these entities and the endless transformations of what

is perceived as living or non-living matter is called Nature. This, in the West, is conceived to be a sort of mechanical creation of a separate Creator/Controller called God.

In India the whole field of action, physical and mental, in everything from microbes to elephants and from microcosmic substance to stellar galaxies, is known as *prakṛti,* the manifest active mode of Universal Consciousness. That, when conceived as the Creative Cosmic Intelligence from which manifestations and activities emanate, is called *puruṣa*. This word literally translates as "person" and in the above context means the Cosmic Person, God. It can also, in a different context, indicate the individuated consciousness of a person. Nature therefore, in the Indian view, is not a separate creation of God but is God Himself appearing as the world.

Mind and Matter in the Six Schools

The six philosophical schools which developed in post-Upaniṣadic India each have their particular view of mind and matter (*cit* and *jaḍa*). The Nyāya and Vaiśeṣika schools conceive them to be constituted of substances of particular characteristics called *dravya*s. Soul (which these schools call *ātmā*) is considered to be one such substance, the chief characteristic of which is awareness.

The Sāṁkhya school endorses a modified version of the *puruṣa-prakṛti* division of the Vedas, in which *puruṣa* is not conceived to be God, the Cosmic Person, but is thought of as a witnessing principle of consciousness functioning on the level of manifest individuated awareness. In Sāṁkhya, therefore, there are as many *puruṣa*s as there are living beings. The Yoga system, however, which is an offshoot of Sāṁkhya, does admit of a universal *puruṣa*, God, called *īśvara*.

The Pūrva-Mīmāṁsā school does not concern itself with fine philosophical and ontological problems. Its attention is directed more to the interpretation of Vedic instructions, signs and rituals. It does distinguish two aspects of Vedic rituals which are similar to a philosophical mind-matter concept; these are *gauṇa* and *apūrva*. The former, *gauṇa*, is the act of performing rituals and the latter, *apūrva*, is the unknown factor by which rituals bring the intended results. Vedānta's view is that mind/matter duality is an effect of *māyā*, the universal possibility of error in human understanding.

The Western View

The view of the separate nature of mind and matter, generally held in the West, has evolved over many centuries of philosophic and scientific thought. It has its roots in pre-Socratic Greek philosophy. The penetrating vision of thinkers of that time discerned an underlying substance of nature which they called "physis." Modified and changed by the thoughts of later Greek philosophers, the pristine mystic insight of those early thinkers was lost. In its place the science of physics developed in which the "physis" came to be seen as inert matter of infinitely small indivisible particles called "atoms."

Later, in renaissance Europe, experimentation, observation and calculation became the accepted basis of philosophic and scientific enquiry into the atomic order of the world.

Descartes, sometimes called the "father of modern thinking," tracing back from thinking to being, declared *cogito ergo sum* ("I think, therefore I am"). Had he immersed his wonderful thinking mind in the silent, still ocean of transcendental Consciousness from which thinking arises, he might have said conversely "I am, therefore I think." He viewed mind and body as a duality, calling mind *res-cogitans* and body *res-extensa*. He saw the world as if it were a great windmill activated by an outside force — blown on by the breath of God, as it were.

The Cartesian view of a world machine and mind-matter duality was reinforced by the Newtonian law of mechanics which declares that "every action has an equal and opposite reaction." Later the view of a mechanistic world, evolving from causes to effects, was further reinforced by the work of Charles Darwin and his theory of the struggle for existence and the survival of the fittest.

Mind and body as an autonomous, self-correcting system in which the one affects the other, is not explicable in terms of the modern sciences of psychology, biology and physics. Harold J. Morowitz summarizes that situation as follows:

> First, the human mind, including consciousness and reflective thought, can be explained by activities of the central nervous system, which, in turn, can be reduced to the biological structure and function of that physiological system. Second, biological phenomena at all levels can be totally understood in terms of atomic physics, that is, through the action and interaction of the component atoms of carbon, nitrogen, oxygen and so forth. Third and last, atomic physics, which is now understood most fully by means of quantum mechanics, must be formulated with the mind as a primitive component of the system.[4]

Mind and Matter in the Bhagavad-Gītā

The *Bhagavad-Gītā* devotes the whole of its thirteenth chapter to the question of mind and matter. Kṛṣṇa, the incarnate Lord, tells Arjuna:

> This body O Kaunteya (Arjuna) is called the field (*kṣetra*) and he who knows this is thus called the knower of the field (*kṣetrajña*).[5]

---

4. "Rediscovering the Mind," Harold J. Morowitz, article in *The Mind's I*, ed. by Douglas R. Hofstadter, New York: Bantam Books, 1981.

5. *Bhagavad-Gītā*, XIII.1.

Śrī Kṛṣṇa clarifies that *kṣetra,* the field, includes all physical and mental phenomena (everything given to change) and that *kṣetrajña* is the unchanging knower of the field. Thus, they equate to *prakṛti* and *puruṣa;* the former is the field of Nature's multiplicities, and the latter its underlying, witnessing Self. He further teaches that these are not separable, but two aspects of One Indivisible Absolute Reality. To know it as such requires a special eye of wisdom (*jñāna-cakṣus*). The chapter concludes with these words:

> Those who by the eye of wisdom perceive the difference between the field and the knower of the field, effectively liberated from Nature's elements, they go to the Supreme.[6]

The Upaniṣadic View

The question of mind-matter duality is examined in the final chapter of the *Aitareya Upaniṣad,* in which a questioner asks:

> Of the two, who is he whom we contemplate as the Self? He by whom one sees, by whom one hears, by whom one smells odours, by whom one articulates speech, by whom one discriminates the sweet and the bitter.[7]

In transcendental consciousness devoid of any object of perception, there is still a glow of awareness. The questioner is asking, "Is that awareness the seer or the seen, and which of the two is the Self?"

The *ṛṣi* of the Upaniṣad leads the questioner to understand that the awareness of Self-perception is not a seer and a separate seen, but is one non-dual simultaneity of seen and seeing Self.

The question of mind-matter primacy is a controversy that continues among thinkers of both scientific and spiritual

---

6. *Bhagavad-Gītā,* XIII.34.
7. *Aitareya Upaniṣad,* III.1.1.

inclination, but mind-matter will remain an indivisible, indefinable mystic entity.

Sūtra 19

सुखैकत्वात् ॥

sukhaikatvāt ॥

sukhasya	:	of happiness
ekatvāt	:	because of the unity

Because of the unity of happiness.

THE word *sukha* (*sukhasya*) used here is a synonym for *ānanda*. It indicates the ultimate happiness value of Self-Conscious Existence in which nothing other is desired.

Definitions of Happiness

There have been many attempts to define happiness, both in the East and the West.

Aristotle said "it is that which is aimed at for the sake of nothing else" — a statement which does not actually define it, however.

Professor Mary Warnac, writing on the subject in the *Encyclopedic Dictionary of Psychology*, says:

> It seems natural, but not very illuminating, to say that it is "a feeling" — we feel pleased, we feel pleasure. But what sort of feeling? It is surely not a sensation that we feel on some part, or even diffused throughout our body. That is why it is not really the "opposite" of pain, which literally is felt as a sensation. But if it is a feeling more as emotions are feelings, is it one emotion? Is the pleasure of, say, listening

> to music the same as that of, say, playing football? We enjoy many different things and the enjoyment of one is not in general the same as (identically substitutable for) that of another; it seems, similarly, that a wide variety of "states of feeling" may be brought under the heading of "pleasure." But if pleasure is not one thing — one sensation, one feeling — it must clearly be doubtful whether "it" could, even in principle, be deployed in the reductive, simplifying role which some philosophers have cut out for it, either in the theory of action or the theory of value.[1]

Gary Zukhav, in his book *The Dancing Wu Li Masters*, says:

> It is a common misconception (literally) to take the description of a state of being for the state itself. For example, try to describe happiness. It is impossible. We can talk around it, we can describe the perspectives and actions that usually accompany a state of happiness, but we cannot describe happiness itself. Happiness and the description of happiness are two different things. Happiness is a state of being. That means it exists in the realm of direct experience. It is the intimate perception of emotions and sensations which, indescribable in themselves, constitute the state of happiness. The word "happiness" is a label, or symbol, which we pin on this indescribable state. "Happiness" belongs to the realm of abstractions, or concepts. A state of being is an experience. A description of a state of being is a symbol. Symbols and experiences do not follow the same rules.[2]

Pleasure and Pain

Sigmund Freud, the father of modern psychoanalysis,

---

1. Professor Mary Warnac, in *The Encyclopedic Dictionary of Psychology*, ed. by Ram Harré and Roger Lamb, Oxford, England: Blackwell, 1983, p. 483.
2. *The Dancing Wu Li Masters*, Gary Zukhav, Fontana Paperbacks, Glasgow, 1989.

introduced the concept of a "pleasure principle" in psychology. He conceded that this principle was not based on any prevailing systems of thought as these did not provide satisfactory explanations of the matter, but was discerned on the basis of undeniable facts. He says:

> . . . On the other hand we should willingly acknowledge our indebtedness to any philosophical or psychological theory that could tell us the meaning of these feelings of pleasure and pain which affect us so powerfully. Unfortunately, no theory of any value is forthcoming. It is the obscurest and least penetrable region of psychic life, and, while it is impossible for us to avoid touching on it, the most elastic hypothesis will be, to my mind, the best.[3]

The pleasure principle conceived by Freud supposes that all human beings are subject to various tensions. He propounds that every human function has its origin in some tension or other, felt as a restlessness. That particular function or activity is directed to gaining relief from the tension which is its basis. To be rid of that tension is to be released from its suffering, which is not other than the attainment of happiness. To quote his words:

> . . . We believe that any given process originates in an unpleasant state of tension and thereupon determines for itself such a path that its ultimate issue coincides with a relaxation of this tension, i.e., with avoidance of pain or with production of pleasure.[4]

Freud's pleasure principle developed against a background of the psychological tensions of the age in which he lived, whereas in Indian philosophy *sukha* is the natural state of Existence with no such tensions as its basis.

---

3. *Beyond the Pleasure Principle,* Sigmund Freud, Britannica Great Books, 1952, vol. 54, p. 639.

4. Ibid.

Happiness as Defined in Indian Thought

The six schools of Indian philosophy have a common objective in the attainment of Supreme Happiness, and each provides its particular definition of "happiness."

The Praśastapāda commentary on the *Vaiśeṣika-Sūtras* defines it as that feeling for which one has an inner urge to continue in, or possess.[5] In the Vaiśeṣika school, happiness is not thought to be mere absence of suffering nor considered to be the opposite of suffering. The *Vaiśeṣika-Sūtras* of Kaṇāda state:

> Happiness and suffering mutually differ in content, since they arise from the cognition of desirable objects and undesirable objects respectively and are mutually contradictory.[6]

Thus happiness and suffering, in the concepts of Vaiśeṣika, have different sources and in their experiential content and the ways in which they are derived are, respectively, of a different order of feelings. The Vaiśeṣika school attaches the following six conditions to the experience of happiness:

1. the proximity of the desirable object,
2. the contact of the object with the related sense-organ,
3. the conjunction of *ātmā* (the underlying knowing substance, or *dravya*) and *manas* (the mind),
4. the actual perception of the desirable object (*īṣṭopalabdhi*),
5. merit (*dharma*), and
6. the prevailing state of the perceiver (*svasthatā*).

According to this concept, sensory pleasure is aroused by

5. *Praśastapāda Bhāṣya*, Vijayanagaram Sanskrit Series, Benares, p. 259.
6. *Vaiśeṣika-Sūtras*, Kaṇāda, X.1.1.

a desirable object (*īṣṭaviṣaya*) only when certain conditions prevail. The desirable object must exist in the proximity of the perceiver or within a perceptible distance. The mere presence of the object does not excite pleasure; it must first stimulate the relevant sense-organ and produce a perception of its desirability in the individual's mind. The mind's attention to the object is required because if the mind is preoccupied with something other than the object, its presence, or even sense contact with it, does not arouse feeling. Happiness arises when the object is perceived as conducive to the perceiver's good. Happiness is experienced relative to the perceiver's inherent or acquired merit. A favourable subjective predisposition of the perceiver to enjoy the object must prevail as, for example, an object enjoyed by a perceiver at one time may not be enjoyed by him at another time. Bodily and mental states are always changing and one's likes and dislikes, as well as the experience of happiness, depend upon such states. The word *svasthatā* (well-being) is indicative of the favourable condition of an individual to enjoy a particular object at a particular time.

The experience of happiness is expressed through the brightness of the eyes (*nayana-prasāda*), beaming of the face (*mukha-prasāda*) and other such definite signs. The *Praśastapāda-Bhāṣya* divides pleasure into four categories of *sukha*. These are: *indriya-janya* (sensuous pleasure), *smṛtija* (retrospective pleasure), *saṁkalpaja* (prospective pleasure) and *ānanda* (happiness). Sensuous pleasures arise from the enjoyment of desirable objects. Retrospective pleasure is the result of recollection of past enjoyment. Prospective pleasure results when we anticipate future enjoyment. These three categories are relative to present, past and future objects respectively. The fourth category, *ānanda*, is the supreme happiness experienced by *jñānin*s. It arises from *vidyā* (wisdom), *śama* (tranquillity), *santoṣa* (contentment) and a specific merit called *dharma-viśeṣa*. In this context, wisdom means self-knowledge, tranquillity is perfect self-control, contentment is the absence of desire and the specific merit is the highest value of virtue bringing independence from objects of enjoyment. The happiness of the first three types is of the transitory nature of sense experience whilst the fourth type of happiness transcends time and senses. The first three types of happiness are experienced in the fulfilment of desires; the fourth type in the absence of desire. This last is considered the ultimate goal of life.

The Nyāya school differs somewhat from the Vaiśeṣika view. It holds that pain is a necessary element of pleasure and that the one invariably accompanies the other. It considers too that, sometimes, relief from pain is experienced as pleasure. Gautama, the author of the *Nyāya-Sūtras*, holds that pleasure, in a metaphysical sense, is not different from pain, yet he does not deny pleasure as a positive experience. The Nyāya school holds that attachments to some objects and aversions to others are caused by false knowledge; happiness is simply defined as "that which is felt agreeable." Pleasure and pain are not states of the absence of each other and they are inseparably linked. Four explanations are given for this inseparability by the Nyāya school:

1. Wherever there is pleasure there is also pain and where there is pain there also is pleasure.
2. The means of pleasure is also a means of pain.
3. The substrate of pleasure is also the substrate of pain.
4. The same agent is the perceiver of both pleasure and pain.[7]

The Sāṁkhya and Yoga systems consider *puruṣa* (Person) and *prakṛti* (Nature) to be the fundamental existent realities.

7. *Nyāya-Bhāṣya*, Vātsyāyana, IV.1.53-57.

In this, *puruṣa* equates to the "soul" of theological understanding and *prakṛti* to the "physical reality" of modern science. Happiness (*prīti* or *sukha*) is a functional mode of internal mental faculties, called *antaḥkaraṇa*, which in turn is a mode of *prakṛti*. In these schools, happiness is not a characteristic of *puruṣa* but belongs to *prakṛti*.

Patañjali, in his *Yoga-Sūtras*, claims that experiences of pleasures and pains are related to one's merits (*puṇya*) and demerits (*pāpa*). But he does not refute the Sāṁkhya view of pleasure and pain as evolved characteristics of *antaḥkaraṇa*.

According to the Sāṁkhyas, sufferings as well as pleasures are attributed to a lack of discriminative knowledge (*viveka*) of the *puruṣa*. Three kinds of sufferings are identified. These are: *ādhyātmika* (self-originated), *ādhibhautika* (caused by others) and *ādhidaivika* (caused by fate or supernatural powers). All these three types of suffering are dispelled by discriminative knowledge that can identify the transcendent *puruṣa* and its non-subjection to *prakṛti*'s transformations.

The Yoga system adopts three rather different classifications of sufferings. According to Patañjali these are: *pariṇāma-duḥkha* (consequential suffering), *tāpa-duḥkha* (moral suffering), and *saṁskāra-duḥkha* (suffering caused by the affective disposition of the sufferer).

Vedānta's view of Supreme Happiness, as *ānanda*, has already been expounded in these commentaries.

Śaṅkara defines worldly pleasures in his *Vivekacūḍāmaṇi*, equating them with *āhlāda* (delight — an experience which is favourable, pleasant and of the essence of pure existence). He does not regard pleasure to be an innate quality of the Self but a mode of *sattva-guṇa* experienced in individual minds. Pain and pleasure are both seen as belonging to the ego part of *antaḥkaraṇa* and not, as is sometimes conceived, to the Self proper.

In the *Bhagavad-Gītā* pleasure and pain are seen as a linked pair of opposites belonging to Nature's field of dualities and actions, the field of the *guṇa*s. Lord Kṛṣṇa teaches Arjuna that true happiness is gained only when the *guṇa*s are transcended and the Real is known. The inevitable pleasures and pains of life are then met with equanimity. Seeking happiness, man is given free will to choose his path and to choose his goals. Many, not knowing where happiness resides, choose wrong goals and paths leading to pain, unhappiness and despair. Knowing this confusion Arjuna asks:

> What is it that impels a man to commit
> sin, even involuntarily, as if driven by
> force, O Vārṣneya (Kṛṣṇa)?

Kṛṣṇa replies:

> It is desire, it is anger, born of
> *rajo-guṇa,* all-consuming and most evil.
> Know this to be the enemy here on earth.[8]

Desire and anger are together indicated as "the enemy here on earth" because they constitute the most powerful attachments of mind to the field of the *guṇa*s, the field of erroneous perceptions, binding it to seek worldly pleasures and find inevitable pains.

The *Gītā* teaches that one's self-contentment is dependent upon the extent to which one understands the particular characteristics of the functioning of *prakṛti* in oneself, as oneself. It depends too upon setting oneself on proper paths and involving oneself in proper activities; that is to say, the paths and activities in harmony with one's particular nature. This harmonizing of one's inner nature with external life activities is called *svadharma* in the *Gītā*. It says:

---

8. *Bhagavad-Gītā*, III.36-37.

> Activity appropriate to one's own nature (*svadharma*) is felicitous, even if performed badly, rather than the activity of another, even if performed well. Even if one were to die in its performance one's own *svadharma* is felicitous. Activity alien to one's nature is fraught with peril.[9]

Activities which are appropriate to one's particular nature may be identified as those which may be performed without strain, bring contentment and satisfaction and are life supporting. Whatever these activities may be and whatever one's particular nature, the happiness resulting from their harmonization is always the same recognizable and desirable experience. So it is that Narayana Guru refers in this *sūtra* to the unity of happiness.

The Upaniṣadic view of happiness is expressed in the *Chāndogya Upaniṣad*, where it is simply identified as the state for which effort is made.

The concluding view is that happiness is not something to be defined or described. It is simply a particular experiential state of being. Indefinable in reason and only to be experienced, it evades all philosophizing and attempts to define it.

The effort is made so that the reward may be gained and human life progresses through striving to attain goals of satisfaction. It is the nature of human beings to want more in life — more pleasure, more satisfaction, more happiness. It is the wish for greater satisfaction and more happiness that incites the action needed to bring a desired result. Indeed, the absence of a quest for happiness or zest for life is considered to be a major psychological disaster known as *āratī* in Sanskrit. The mind is a restless seeker and even when one is happy and satisfied in life there is always some appetite for more, always room for something to be added. The

9. *Bhagavad-Gītā*, III.35.

"something more" may be only the smile of a child or the fragrance of a flower. Whatever it is, there will always be room for it. No one turns away from more happiness and mind will continue to seek until it finds rest in Happiness Itself.

Happiness Itself is the state which all normally functioning human beings, knowingly or unknowingly, aspire to. It is the underlying hunger for its attainment which motivates human beings in their endeavours. Man strives to achieve goals, even wrongly chosen goals, in order to bring satisfaction and alleviate the hunger for satisfaction. Those goals are seen in externalized things of life as the desirables allaying the hunger and bringing the sought-for happiness. But happiness does not repose in external objects, nor in possessions, nor in other people, nor any other beings, but in oneself. Whatever the object or perceived cause, happiness is known as an upsurge of joyful or pleasurable feelings in oneself. It is always the same mood of an individual's awareness in which only its intensity, duration and preceived objects of desire change. The desired objects are not repositories of one's happiness but are the instruments of its awakening from within oneself. The sight of a good dinner or the smile of a child may provoke feelings of pleasure or joy. But those feelings are within oneself and are not in the dinner or the child's smile. It is one happiness in one Self, not many different happinesses in many different things. Narayana Guru, visualizing Happiness as related to an imaginative contemplative, says:

> One having such continuous feelings as "I am Happiness, I am the Absolute, I am the Self," is known as a *bhakta* (devout contemplative).[10]

It is latent happiness in oneself which spurs endeavour and

10. *Darśana-Mālā*, VIII.6.

gives zest to life. It is the prize of oneself, to be won by oneself. It is *ānanda* spurring all beings forward and upward in its manifest blossomings. It is the unstoppable expansion of Happiness in the world to its full realization.

Sūtra 20

व्यापकतया दिशामस्तित्वात् ॥

vyāpakatayā diśām astitvāt ॥

vyāpakatayā astitvāt	:	because of the extensive existence
diśām	:	of directions

Because of the extensive existence of directions.

SPACE, in Western cosmology, means the unlimited three-dimensional region beyond the earth's atmosphere containing all the other planets, stars, galaxies, dust and debris of the universe. It is space in which these material entities have their existence and through which they, and radiations from them, may pass. Space itself is generally considered to be a sort of endlessly extending three-dimensional nothingness, although formerly it was thought to be filled with a vague, non-specific substance called "ether." The picture then is of a void of non-being giving birth to and containing the entities which comprise the universe. It is a picture of getting something out of nothing in which the nature of neither the something nor the nothing is explicable.

The Sanskrit word *diś* (*diśām*), used by the Guru in this *sūtra,* or *dik*, its more usual form, literally means "that which points outwards and gives room for anything to exist." The word *dik*, therefore, implies direction as well as space. The word *ākāśa*, which translates "space" in English, also means "that which gives room for anything to exist."

There is a further essential difference in the meanings of the words *dik* and *ākāśa,* and that of "space." Space is thought of only as the environment in which physical entities and all else are located and through which passage can be made, whilst *dik* and *ākāśa* imply both physical and mental space.

The Upaniṣads sometimes equate *ākāśa* with *Brahman.* The *Chāndogya Upaniṣad* says:

> Verily, what is called *Brahman,* that is what the space outside a person (*puruṣa*) is. That is what the space within a person is. That is what the space here, within the heart, is. That is the full, the non-active. He who knows it thus obtains full, non-active prosperity.[1]

Space, in the view of modern cosmology, expands in all directions from the one fixed point at which it is thought to have begun in a big-bang. In that scientific view it stretches out, extending endlessly, or is expanding to a point at which it will stop, reverse directions and contract to where all entities in it will meet in a big crunch. Everything is located in it, but it is not known where, or in what, space itself is located. Neither is it known where its centre is. Its expansion radiates outwards in all directions from any point at which it is observed and so, paradoxically, it seems to have as many centres as there are observers and places from which to observe it. Science may finally concede that it has no other location than in a centre of perception and be compelled to conclude that perception is located in Consciousness Itself.

In the Upaniṣadic concept, *dik* too extends endlessly: above and below, in all sides, backwards and forwards, in all directions, outwards from one still, unmoving point of Consciousness which perceives it, in which it is located and which it is. It is the endless extensiveness of Infinite Being.

---

1. *Chāndogya Upaniṣad,* III.12.7-9.

The *Atharvaveda,* one of the four Vedas, has this to say:

> That receptacle indeed supports heaven and earth.
> That receptacle indeed supports atmosphere.
> This receptacle indeed pervades the six directions
> and the entire world.[2]

"This receptacle," supporting space and directions and pervading all the worlds, is *ātman,* the centre, substance and location of everything.

There is a well-known hymn, called *Puruṣa Sūkta,* which finds a place in all the Vedas and also in some of the Upaniṣads. Its first stanza is as follows:

> The *puruṣa* has a thousand heads, a thousand eyes, a thousand feet. He surrounds the earth on all sides and stands ten fingers breadth beyond.[3]

The thousand heads, thousand eyes and thousand feet signify the countless facets of Reality. The rest of the hymn comprehends all possible dimensions and all possible ways by which they are conceived.

The theme of directions and extension in space is examined in the *Bṛhadāraṇyaka Upaniṣad.* The sage Yājñavalkya is questioned by scholars at the court of King Janaka and one of the questioners is Śākalya. In the dialogue that ensues, the still point from which directions and space radiate is called "the heart," which, in this context, is a synonym for Consciousness, the Self.

Śākalya : Is it because you know *Brahman* that

---

2. *Atharvaveda,* X.7.35.

3. *sahasra-śīrṣaḥ puruṣaḥ*
sahasrākṣaḥ sahasrapāt
sa bhūmiṁ viśvato vṛtvā
aty atiṣṭhad daśā 'ngulam — The Ṛgveda, X.90.1.

		you have defied these brāhmaṇas of the Kuru-Pañcāla?
Yājñavalkya	:	I know the quarters, with their deities and supports!
Śākalya	:	If you know the quarters with their deities and supports, what deity have you in the eastern quarter?
Yājñavalkya	:	The deity Sun (light)!
Śākalya	:	That Sun, on what is it supported?
Yājñavalkya	:	On the eye!
Śākalya	:	On what is the eye supported?
Yājñavalkya	:	On forms, for one sees forms with the eye!
Śākalya	:	On what are forms supported?
Yājñavalkya	:	On the heart, for one knows forms through the heart; on heart only are the forms supported!
Śākalya	:	Even so Yājñavalkya! What deity have you in the southern quarter?
Yājñavalkya	:	The deity Yama (death)!
Śākalya	:	That Yama, on what is he supported?
Yājñavalkya	:	On the sacrifice!
Śākalya	:	On what is the sacrifice supported?
Yājñavalkya	:	On the offerings to the priests!
Śākalya	:	And on what are the offerings to the priests supported?
Yājñavalkya	:	On faith, for when one has faith he gives offerings to the priests. Therfore

		it is on faith that the offerings to the priests are supported!
Śākalya	:	On what is faith supported?
Yājñavalkya	:	On the heart, for through the heart one knows faith; verily on the heart alone is faith supported!
Śākalya	:	Even so Yājñavalkya! What deity have you in the western quarter?
Yājñavalkya	:	The deity Varuṇa (ocean)!
Śākalya	:	That Varuṇa, on what is he supported?
Yājñavalkya	:	On water!
Śākalya	:	On what is water supported?
Yājñavalkya	:	On semen!
Śākalya	:	On what is semen supported?
Yājñavalkya	:	On the heart. Therefore they say of a new-born who resembles (the father) that he seems as if he slipped out of his heart, he is built out of his heart; for on the heart alone is semen supported!
Śākalya	:	Even so Yājñavalkya! What deity have you in the northern quarter?
Yājñavalkya	:	The deity Soma (moon)!
Śākalya	:	That Soma, on what is he supported?
Yājñavalkya	:	On the initiatory ritual!
Śākalya	:	On what is initiation supported?
Yājñavalkya	:	On truth, therefore they say to one who is initiated, "Speak the truth." For

		on truth alone is the initiation supported!
Śākalya	:	On what is truth supported?
Yājñavalkya	:	On the heart, for through the heart one knows truth, therefore it is on the heart that the truth is supported!
Śākalya	:	Even so Yājñavalkya! What deity have you in this fixed quarter (zenith)?
Yājñavalkya	:	The deity fire!
Śākalya	:	On what is fire supported?
Yājñavalkya	:	On speech!
Śākalya	:	On what is speech supported?
Yājñavalkya	:	On the heart!
Śākalya	:	On what is the heart supported?
Yājñavalkya	:	You ghost, that you think the heart could be elsewhere than in ourserlves! For if it were anywhere else than in ourselves the dogs might eat it, or the birds tear it up to pieces![4]

Continuing, Yājñavalkya tells Śākalya that this heart, the Self, is "not this," "not this" (*neti, neti*). For whatever can be referred to as "this" is comprehensible, destructible and measurable and not the incomprehensible, indestructible and immeasurable Self.

The lesson of this dialogue between Yājñavalkya and Śākalya is that whatever is perceived, in whatever direction, in whatever region of existence and whatever its immediate basis is seen to be, its ultimate basis, source and location is "the heart," the Self, the ground of all being. It is Infinite

4. *Bṛhadāraṇyaka Upaniṣad*, III.9.19-25.

Consciousness from which all directions extend and to which they lead.

In *dik* there is room for everything to exist. East, south, west and north are its four quarters; all intermediate directions and upwards and downwards are in it too. At its centre the Creator looks out and sees it everywhere; He sees Himself in it and it in Himself.

The image of Śiva who sits quietly absorbing the torrential flow of the River Ganges into his matted hair, in its mythological passage from heaven to earth, is a powerful visual representation of this concept. So too is the image of Śiva as Naṭarāja dancing in the space or void of Consciousness (*cidambaram*) in the famous temple at Chidambaram in Tamil Nadu. These concepts of Śiva the contemplative, and Śiva the cosmic dancer, were very dear to Narayana Guru who wrote the following lines:

> Millions of billowing waves arrive and are worn on Thy thus constantly enriched head; the One who ever remains in unwavering stability in the abode of *cidambaram*. Obeisance to Thee![5]

What we perceive in all directions as cosmic space is not an emptiness containing a scattering of distant stellar particles, but is the fullness of Infinite Being.

Infinity is a difficult concept for time-bound finite human minds to grasp, perceiving as they do a temporal finite world of passing, finite events and finite entities. In cosmological science, time and space are conceived as extending backwards to a finite starting point, but science has no theories for time and space beyond that point. Infinity has no fixed points of time and space, no boundaries, no beginning and no end. It is the eternal present, eternally here. There has never been a

5. *Śiva-Śatakam*, v. 84.

time when "here, in the present" did not exist; there will never be a time when "here, in the present" shall cease to be. In the *Bhagavad-Gītā*, Kṛṣṇa, *ātman* incarnate, indicating the Eternal-Reality underlying all beings and all things, tells Arjuna:

> There never was a time when I was not,
> nor you, nor these rulers of men. Nor
> will there ever be a time when all of
> us shall cease to be.[6]

In a famous Vedic Peace Invocation, Infinity is expressed as that quantity of which, even when all is taken away, as much remains as before.

> *ōṁ pūrṇam adaḥ pūrṇam idam*
> *pūrṇāt pūrṇam udacyate*
> *pūrṇasya pūrṇam ādāya*
> *pūrṇam evāvaśiṣyate*
> *ōṁ śāntiḥ śāntiḥ śāntiḥ*

> *auṁ* That is plenum, This is plenum.
> From the plenum, plenum arises.
> When plenum is deducted from plenum
> then also plenum remains.
> *auṁ* Peace, Peace, Peace!

Plenum is the opposite of vacuum (empty, non-extensive nothingness). It means the fullness of Infinitely Extensive Being.

6. *Bhagavad-Gītā*, II.12.

Sūtra 21

अणुमहदवयवतारतम्यस्याभावात् ॥

aṇu-mahad-avayava-tāratamyasyābhāvāt ॥

aṇu	:	atomicity
mahat	:	immensity
avayava	:	limbs (physical form)
tāratamy-asya	:	of comparability
abhāvāt	:	the absence (because of)

Because of the absence of physically comparable atomicity and immensity.

THE Sanskrit word *aṇu* means that which is indivisibly small; it equates to the word "atom." Of opposite meaning is the word *mahat* that is indicative of the immeasurable immensity.

Smallness and largeness pertain to apparent physical forms which the Guru indicates, in this *sūtra*, by using the word *avayava*. This word literally means "physical limbs" but is applicable to any part of any physical body.

As physical attributes relevant only in relation to other things, smallness and largeness have no meaning in themselves. Nothing is large or small by itself; it is only in the comparison of one thing to another that entities acquire the attribute of relative size. A mouse, for example, is large when compared to a flea but is dwarfed when compared to an elephant.

All entities in the relative world are comparable and are known by their distinctness from one another. In a certain sense, it may be said that each entity is made distinct and is known by all the things that it is not. Describing a particular entity it may be said, for example, "it is not this form, it is not this size, it is not this colour," "it is not this, it is not this" (*neti neti*)! Each thing, in comparison with everything else, is seen then to be a distinct singularity separate from every other singularity. It is in these perceived differences, in comparing one thing to another in *māyā*'s field of illusion, that entities are erroneously identified as having separate existences.

Only the Absolute is incomparable as nothing other exists with which it may be compared. In Itself there is neither largeness nor smallness, but yet it is the pervading Reality of the smallest part of the smallest particle and the largest part of the greatest immensity.

Itself without size, without weight, without any such attributes whatsoever, it is that by which all entities have size, weight and all other comparable attributes. Therefore the *Śvetāśvatara Upaniṣad* says that it is:

> Smaller than the smallest and larger than the largest.[1]

Narayana Guru considers large, small and middle as merely comparable waves of expression arising from the infinite waveless space of Consciousness (*cidambaram*). In his work called *Cijjaḍa-Cintanam* (Reflections on Mind and Matter) he addresses God as that same *cidambaram*. Praying for stability and to be saved from sinking into *māyā*'s dross and confusion, he writes:

> As the great, the small and the middling too, steady and waveless you arise O *Cidambaram*. Save us from

1. *Śvetāśvatara Upaniṣad*, III.20.

> unsteadiness and from sinking into the confusion of *māyā*'s dross; grant us the grace of thy stability.[2]

Incomparable *cidambaram* is located nowhere but in Itself; yet it is everywhere and in everything. It is invisible, but can be seen as all forms. It cannot be touched and yet is the texture and feel of all touchables. It is without flavour but is the taste of all tastables. It is without odour but is the fragrance of all fragrant things and the smell of all smellables. It is silence but is the sound of everything heard. Formless, it is seen and is the seer. Untouchable, it is felt and is the feeler. Flavourless, it is tasted and is the taster. Odourless, it is smelled and is the smeller. Silent, it is heard and is the hearer. Motionless, it moves and is the mover. Inactive, it acts and is the actor. Unthinkable, it is thought and is the thinker. Unknowable, it is knowledge, knower and known. Incomparable, it is thus compared, by Itself, within Itself, through all its magical manifestations from Itself.

2. *Cijjaḍa-Cintanam*, v. 6.

Sūtra 22

असतोऽव्यापकत्वात् ॥

asato 'vyāpakatvāt ॥

asataḥ	:	of non-existence
avyāpakatvāt	:	because of non-pervasiveness

Because non-existence cannot be pervasive.

IN this, the last of the five premises, Narayana Guru considers the pervasive nature of existence.

All that is seen to exist in any way, for any short or long period of time, must have a basis in being. Even such insubstantialities as shadows or rainbows have a substantial basis for their appearances; there can be no shadow without a form to cast it, and no rainbow without light rays to pass through water-droplets and a seer to see it. Everything is permeated by Being, has its existence in Being and is perceived in and by Being. From non-existence nothing can arise; it casts no shadows and from it no rainbows appear. Nothing can come from nothingness and non-existence cannot permeate nor be the basis of anything at all, not even a shadow!

In the preceding *sūtras* the Guru indicated the pervasiveness of *sat-cit-ānanda* in all perceptions — in the simultaneity of subject and object, in the value experiences of pleasure and pain, hot and cold, etc., and in the perception of entities relative in space and time. All such dualities of seer and seen are structured in a matrix of underlying Being which permeates everything with its tripartite nature as Existence, Consciousness and Value (*sat-cit-ānanda*).

Ontology is the branch of philosophy which concerns itself with the nature of Being. The world as a space-time continuum is the physical expression of the Self. As such the pervasiveness of the Self, in the physical and mental forms of the world, is the world's ontological or *sat* content.

Every perception involves a subject and an object. These two arise as a functional mode of Consciousness in the acquisition of any knowledge. In philosophy the study of the knowing function is called epistemology. The existence pervading subject and object which enables them to interact, constitutes the epistemological or *cit* content of knower and known.

The word "teleology" indicates the theory that life and the world are purposeful. *Ānanda* is the aspect of the Self by which it knows Itself in eternal Self-contentment. In Vedānta the purpose of life is understood to be the experience of the expansion of *ānanda* through its manifest forms. Action involves movement and all action in Nature is, in a teleological sense, the movement of *ānanda* unfolding Itself as the world — as if it were a flower opening to reveal its full beauty. That movement is on the immeasurable timescale of "pure duration." Thus the pervasiveness of *ānanda* in the world equates to the world's teleological content. In this may be seen the purpose of life and the world's creation.

The Self, *ātman*, is the pervasive reality of all that exists. In the *Bhagavad-Gītā*, Arjuna, seeking greater understanding of *ātman*'s multiple expressions, asks this question of Lord Kṛṣṇa:

> . . . ; and in what particular forms of existence, O Mystic Yogi, art Thou to be cognized by me?[1]

1. *Bhagavad-Gītā*, X.17.

Lord Kṛṣṇa, *ātman* incarnate, answers:

> Yes, I will tell you of My divine manifestations, best of Kurus, but only the chief of them, for there is no limit to My fullness.
>
> O Guḍākeśa (conqueror of sleep) I am the very Self dwelling in the heart of all beings; the beginning, and the middle, and the end of all beings am I.
>
> Of the Ādityas (gods) I am Viṣṇu, of luminaries the radiant Sun; of the Maruts I am Marīci (the destroyer of darkness) among the heavenly bodies I am the Moon.
>
> Of the Vedas I am *Sāmaveda,* of divinities I am Indra, of the senses I am Mind and of beings I am Intelligence.
>
> Of the Rudras I am Śaṅkara (Śiva), of the Yakṣas and Rākṣasas (goblins and demons) the Lord of Wealth, of the elements I am Fire and of mountains I am Meru.
>
> Of priests, O Pārtha, know me to be Bṛhaspati (priest of the gods). Of generals I am Skanda (the god of war, Subrahmaṇya). Of waters I am the ocean.
>
> Of the great sages I am Bhṛgu, of words I am the syllable *om,* of sacrifices I am *japa* (silently repeated *mantras*), of immovables I am the Himalaya.
>
> Of trees I am Aśvattha (the Sacred Fig-Tree), of divine sages Nārada, of Gandharvas (celestial musicians) I am Chitraratha and of perfected ones I am silent recluse Kapila.
>
> Of horses know me to be Uchchaiśravas (Indra's horse, the long-eared) born of the nectar of immortality, of noble elephants Airāvata (Indra's elephant, the ocean born), and of men the King.
>
> Of weapons I am the thunderbolt, of cows Kāmadhenu (the heavenly milk-yielder), of progenitors I am Kandarpa (god of erotic love), of the serpents Vāsuki (their Chief) am I.
>
> Of Nāgas (snakes) I am Ananta (the endless), of dwellers of the deep I am Varuṇa (god of water), of the ancestors I am Aryamān, of chastisers I am Yama (god of death).

Of the Daityas (enemies of the gods) I am Prahlāda, of measurables I am Time, of beasts the lion, and of birds Garuḍa (Viṣṇu's eagle).

Of purifiers I am the wind, of bowmen I am Rāma, of fishes the Makara (a mythological voracious shark), and of rivers the holy Ganges.

Of chapters I am the beginning, the end and also the middle, O Arjuna. Of sciences I am the Science of the Self, of speech the words of the pre-eminent speaker.

Of letters I am the letter A, of grammatical compounds the paired-compound. I am unexpended time and the sustainer of all, facing all directions.

I am all-consuming Death, the source of all yet to arise. Of womanly values I am fame, grace, speech, memory, constancy, patience and endurance.

Likewise, of hymns I am Bṛhat-Sāma, of metres the Gayatri, of months I am Mārgaśīrṣa (December-January, lit. a path's destination) and of seasons the abundant flowering.

I am the chance of gamblers, the brilliance of the brilliant, I am victory, resolution and the goodness of the good.

Of the Vṛṣṇis (Kṛṣṇa's clan) I am Vāsudeva (Kṛṣṇa), of the Pāṇḍavas (sons of Pāṇḍu) Dhanañjaya (Arjuna). I am Vyāsa of reclusive seers, and of poets I am the poet Uśanā.

Of those who rule I am the sceptre, of those who seek victory I am the strategy. Of mystic secrets I am silence, and of knowers I am Knowledge.

That which is the seed of all beings am I, O Arjuna, nor is there anything moving or unmoving that can exist without Me.

There is no end to My divine forms O frightener of the foe; only in part have I declared to you the fullness of my unique aspects.

Whatever is glorious, graceful or of great strength, know that to spring from a fraction of My splendour.

> But of what use is there for you, Arjuna, in knowing these pluralities? Supporting this whole world with a fraction of My Being, yet do I remain unchanged, as ever.[2]

The lesson is that while *ātman* is known to be the pervading Reality in everything, the greatest of the great and the Self of all beings, yet He/She/It remains for ever beyond all forms, unchanged in incomprehensible and unknowable Infinite Fullness.

In the Indian tradition a logical conclusion must be based upon two aspects of reasoning — one positive and the other negative. The former indicates the presence of some causal pervasion in a phenomenon, whilst the latter indicates that in the absence of that causal pervasion the phenomenon cannot exist. For example, the appearance of smoke is indicative of the presence of fire; conversely, in the absence of fire there can be no smoke. The positive aspect of reasoning is called *anvaya*; the negative aspect is called *vyatireka*. A final conclusion can be reached only when tested by both these logical means. Narayana Guru has employed *anvaya* and *vyatireka* in these five premises (*anvaya* in the first four and *vyatireka* in the fifth) which have led to the conclusions he states in the final two *sūtra*s. These are not, in fact, two separate conclusions but expressions of a single ineffable non-dual experience.

---

2. *Bhagavad-Gītā*, X.19-42.

Sūtra 23

आत्मान्यत्किञ्चिन्नास्ति ॥

ātmānyat kiñcinnāsti ॥

ātmā anyat	:	other than *ātman*
kiñcit na asti	:	nothing exists

Other than *ātman* nothing exists.

NARAYANA Guru's conclusion is not stated merely on the basis of reason, logic or belief. As a relatively young man he gained the enlightenment of *paramārtha-jñāna* (direct knowledge of the transcendent Absolute), knowledge of *Brahman* which he presents in these twenty-four aphoristic *sūtra*s.

Having stated earlier that *Brahman* is incomprehensible and unknowable, it may seem paradoxical and contradictory to say that it is possible to know *Brahman* directly. But one may know the light and warmth of the sun without knowing its composition and all of its heat and one may bathe in the ocean without plumbing all of its depth or swimming to its farthest shore.

The knowledge that can be attained by the seeker of the Self is like that.

Vedānta is not a belief system. It is not a religion; it has no priests and no temples. It propounds neither dogma nor creed and prescribes no special rituals, no dietary restrictions nor codes of behaviour. But neither, in its universality, does it spurn these. Although coming from an ancient Indian Hindu tradition it is of universal application; just as atomic energy, discovered, quantified and harnessed in the West, is of universal application. It is the culmination of knowledge; the knowledge of Knowledge Itself. As such it is valid for all people everywhere, of all nationalities, races and religions.

It is knowledge of the nature of life, manifestation and Reality, which is as ancient as the Vedas. It is a teaching derived from the Upaniṣads, guarded and handed down through many centuries by a line of enlightened seers. The great Śaṅkara, and later Rāmānuja and Madhva, were such illustrious seers. These brilliant masters contributed to Vedāntic teaching and formulated it as the Vedānta philosophy, albeit each from his own particular standpoint and perspective. In their written works and in their teachings they have showed the way to the attainment of that ultimate Self-knowledge, the knowledge of *ātman*. Narayana Guru is in that line of enlightened masters; he is the one nearest to us in time. His revaluation of Vedānta has blown away the dust of time from the teaching and restored the Absolutist view of non-dual reality of the Upaniṣadic *ṛṣis*. It is the priceless gift of a rare and precious *guru*.

It has been given as a gift of his great love for all people seeking to understand what their life is and what it indicates. His love is not for the shadows of empirical transient egos, but is a deep compassionate love for life's children and a desire to help raise them from the inevitable sufferings of their unenlightened state. It is love and compassion for all people and especially for those struggling to lift their heads from the trough of gross materialism to seek finer nourishment; it is love for the Real in them raising to be known.

In this penultimate *sūtra* Narayana Guru states "other than *ātman* nothing exists." All and everything are expressions of the Self and therefore, the love of anyone for anything at all is an expression of Self-love. To love anything is to love the Self. "I" am that Self, that Self is "Myself" and so all love is "My" love for "Myself" and "Myself" is all and everything. How then can "I" despise or reject anything at all? One of enlightened awareness reaches out to all beings and all things. The happiness of such a *jñānin* is in the happiness of others and the suffering of others is his suffering. He loves not with a desire for any selfish return, nor for the love of anything or anyone external but for the love of the Self. In the *Bṛhadāraṇyaka Upaniṣad* the sage Yājñavalkya tells his wife Maitreyi:

> O my dear, not for the love of the husband is the husband dear but for the love of the Self is the husband dear. Not for the love of the wife is the wife dear but for the love of the Self is the wife dear. . . . Verily, not for the love of all is all dear but for the love of the Self all is dear. Verily Maitreyi, when the Self is known then all this is known.[1]

Narayana Guru expresses a view of love with these words:

> He who loves is he who really lives.[2]

He wants this to be considered as a modern nine-syllable *mantra*.

Love is the most noble expression of *ānanda*. In human beings it manifests through a wide arc of values. It may, in stressed and ignorant people, be distorted as consuming greed and lust, grabbing, trampling and hurting in an insatiable desire to gain and possess. In others it may flow so clear and strong that they want only to give and to serve, even to the point where they will be prepared to lay down their lives for the good of those they hold more dear than themselves.

In the parlance of religious teaching love at its highest is the all-embracing love of the Creator for His/Her/Its creation. It is His/Her/Its love for the wonder of the manifest world and for all its beings. Vedānta's view is that God's love for

1. *Bṛhadāraṇyaka-Upaniṣad*, IV.5.6.
2. *Anukampā-Daśakam*, v. 3.

the world and its beings is His love for the Self in the form of the world. The *jñānin* knows that Love is God and that God is Love and knows that God or Love infuses the world with Its Being and shines most brilliantly where it is most realized as Being Itself.

Vedānta teaches that in yogic meditation, when the *guṇa*s have been transcended, the experience of thc fourth state of Consciousness (*turīya*) is like bathing in the ocean of Being. It is an ineffable experience of a blissful, silent, self-luminous state of non-dual awareness, known to be oneself, one's essence, substance and life. It is known to be one's own pervasive Reality and known to be the same Reality pervading everything. Then one is filled with the wonder of Existence and the heart brims with the waves of Its love.

Sūtra 24

तस्मात् तस्य सत्वाच्च ॥

tasmāt tasya sattvāc ca ॥

tasmāt	:	Therefore
tasya	:	of "That" (of *Brahman*)
sattvāt	:	other than the being
ca	:	also

Therefore other than the Existence of "That" nothing.

With this concluding *sūtra* Narayana Guru completes a journey taken in steps of reason and logic around a circle of enquiry into the nature of Existence. He has returned to the point at which he began with the statement "*Brahman* indeed am I." Now closing the circle he concludes by stating that "Other than the Existence of 'That' nothing."

The overwhelming implication of those combined statements is that "I" alone am existent and all those seen as others are merely figments of "My" imagination as "I" dream my *māyā* dream.

That is indeed what is to be understood. The correctness of that understanding, however, is dependent upon the meaning given to the words "I" and "My" in this context. When the Guru says "*Brahman* indeed am I" and "Other than the Existence of 'That' nothing," he does not mean the temporary composite of body, ego and personality which mistakenly identifies itself as "I" and mistakenly identifies the world as not "I" but "other" and "mine." He does not mean the "I" of relative, temporal, incarnate actuality. The "I" of his meaning is the "I" of Absolute Existence, the "I" of Pure Unconditioned Consciousness. He means "I" without form, without location, without any attributes whatsoever, yet which is Self-Effulgent Awareness Itself. He means the one and only Reality; he means *Brahman*, the one and only Absolute, the one and only Indivisible, Eternal, Infinite Being. That is *ātman* the Self. Nothing other than that Self exists; therefore nothing other than that "I" exists.

His words, his teaching and his meaning are the words, teaching and meaning of an enlightened seer, an Absolutist; one who has perceived the non-dual status of Ultimate Existence. Narayana Guru was an Absolutist indeed, but one whose great, mystic vision did not exclude the relative from the Absolute. Narayana Guru's comprehensive vision does not exclude anything at all. It is inclusive of everything, everything of "This" and "That" together, in one non-dual Reality. It is a vision of Absolute Reality which is not devoid of relative actuality! Hence, knowing himself as a particular expression of that Reality, he also knows himself as a specific actuality. He knows his being to be none other than God and knows God to be an Unknowable, Infinite, Eternal Wonder. Therefore he bows to That with awe, and in reverence offers That his most devout prayers and submission. There is no contradiction in this, no compromise with the views of this or that school of Vedānta. His vision is Vedānta's culmination of knowledge. It is the comprehensive all-embracing vision of an enlightened knower of Ultimate Reality, a knower of the Self. One who was a *maharṣi*, an *advaitin* and an Absolutist.

Reality and Actuality

Reality is not devoid of actuality. The suffix "-ity" means the state or condition of what is indicated, and so the word "actuality" indicates the state or condition in which action takes place, i.e., the world. It is a state and condition in which innumerable forms, qualities, identifications, values, actions, moods, sensations, thoughts, memories and anticipations and all other relative, manifest things are perceived in individuated awareness. It is the actual world of innumerable aspects in which the aware individual is himself a specific aspect. The "actual world" is a canvas of Creative Consciousness upon which the Creator paints His wondrous images. Man, uncertainly balanced between heaven and hell, part-angel and part-demon, somewhat god-like and somewhat a rapacious beast, is perhaps the most wonderful of them.

Everything perceived actually exists. Nothing in Reality is actually unreal and whatever is experienced is what there is to experience. Hunger is experienced by those who are actually hungry; who can doubt the pangs? Who can doubt the actual pain of human suffering, physical and mental, or the actuality of human love and compassion? Who can doubt the actual experience of Existence? We actually do live on the planet Earth. The sun actually does blaze in the sky, bathing us with its undeniable light and the moon actually does shine on us at night. Who can doubt life? It is not shadow play, as some would have it, but is Reality substantially actualized. It is a *māyā* illusion, but only in the sense of its illusory identity.

Each being, each entity and each phenomenon is an actual specificity in an actually existing world. All these beings, entities and phenomena are finite, temporal transients and, in that sense, are unreal. But they are nontheless actual aspects of Infinite, Eternal Reality. They are as the Creator made them, each a unique and perfect expression of His/Her/Its Infinite Creativity in which He/She/It is the only substantial Reality. The knowledge of this is implicit with the knowledge of "That." Knowing "That" by knowing "this" enables one to know oneself as a particular specification of "That," a particular personality and ego but one not set in concrete, not fixed in unchangeable eternity. Within our species there is the possibility for individuals to choose, to move, to grow, to realize their fullest potential, or to waste and wither. So much is mystery, but among what is known is the knowledge that no one is stuck for ever in a weary and suffering body. No one is trapped for ever in an unchanging dim-light of individual, incarnate half-awareness. After a time the compassionate and loving Creator wipes the slate clean and starts the joyous play again, gifting its players with new, fresh bodies and new, fresh playgrounds. It is a very big universe!

With the example of his saintly life, his teachings and his writings in general and these twenty-four *sūtra*s in particular, Narayana Guru provides the basis for an irrefutable intellectual conviction of the existence and nature of *Brahman*, the Absolute, the Self; of the existence of One, not many realities. But that intellectual conviction is not to be mistaken for actual perception of the Self. It is hearsay only; it is information given about *Brahman*. With his teaching the Guru provides a description and signpost of the destination to be sought, but not even he can gift its golden goal. It is for the seeker to desire, to strive for and attain.

To express his own experience of that attainment Narayana Guru wrote these words:

> Oh! till now we have been looking outwardly. Now we become turned inward. What an abode of divine wondrousness it is! Till now we were seeing ourselves only as reflections in a divine mirror. It (the mirror) indeed is our God! We had never beheld It thus before. No veiling now hinders our vision of this abode. We and our God are One! Now we become incapabale of uttering any word! Oh behold! we become merged in God![1]

---

1. *Ātmavilāsam* from *Sri Narayana Gurudeva Kṛtikal* (our translation), S.N.D.P. Yogam, Quilon, p. 216.

God is known to be the One Self, the Reality of everything. Thus it is known that other than *ātman*, other than *Brahman*, other than God, nothing exists.

auṁ tat sat

Appendix

The Works of Narayana Guru

(Published in the Malayalam language as "The Complete Works of Sri Narayana Guru" by the S.N.D.P. Yogam, Quilon, 1994.)

Sanskrit indicated by (S), Malayalam by (M) and Tamil by (T).

Hymns

ON VINĀYAKA OR GAṆAPATI

1. *Vināyakāṣṭakam* (S) (Eight Verses on Vināyaka).

ON VIṢṆU

2. *Śrī Vāsudevāṣṭakam* (S) (Eight Verses on Vāsudeva-Viṣṇu).
3. *Viṣṇuāṣṭakam* (S) (Eight Verses on Viṣṇu).
4. *Śrī Kriśṇadarśanam* (M) (A Vision of Śrī Kṛṣṇa).

ON ŚIVA

5. *Śivaprasāda Pañcakam* (M) (Five Verses on Śiva's Grace).
6. *Sadāśiva Darśanam* (M) (A Vision of Sadāśiva).
7. *Śiva Śatakam* (M) (One Hundred Verses on Śiva).
8. *Ardhanārīśvara Stavam* (M) (Hymn on the Androgynous God).
9. *Mananātītam* (M) (Beyond Comprehension).

10. *Cijjaḍa-Cintanam* (M) (Reflections on Mind and Matter).
11. *Indriya Vairāgyam* (M) (Detachment from Sense Pleasure).
12. *Kuṇḍalinī Pāttu* (M) (Song on Kuṇḍalinī Snake).
13. *Prapañca Sṛṣṭi* (M) (Creation of the world).
14. *Kolatīreśa Stavam* (M) (Hymn on Kolatīreśa — A Hymn on the deity of Śiva installed by the Guru at Kolathukara or Kolatīra).
15. *Svānubhava Gīti* (M) (Lyric of Ecstatic Self-Experience).
16. *Piṇḍanandī* (M) (Prenatal Gratitude).
17. *Cidambarāṣṭakam* (S) (Eight Verses on Chidambara or Mental Space).
18. *Tevāra Patikankaḷ* (T) (Four Tamil Songs of Ten Verses, each praising Śiva).
19. A Tamil Single Verse.

ON DEVĪ, THE MOTHER GODDESS

20. *Devī Stavam* (M) (Hymn on Devī).
21. *Maṇṇamtala Devī Stavam* (M) (Hymn on the Devī of Mannamthala — Mannamthala is a place near Trivandrum where the Guru installed an image of Devī).
22. *Kālī Nāṭakam* (M) (The Dance-Drama of Kālī).
23. *Jananī Navaratna Mañjarī* (M) (A Nine-Gemmed Bouquet on Mother).
24. *Devī Praṇāmāṣṭakam* (S) (Eight Verses Prostrating to Devī).
25. *Bhadrakālyāṣṭakam* (S) (Eight Verses on Bhadra Kālī).

ON SUBRAHMAṆYA

26. *Ṣaṇmukha Stotram* (M) (Hymn on Ṣaṇmukha, the Six-Headed God).

27. *Ṣaṇmukha Daśakam* (M) (Ten Verses on Ṣaṇmukha, the Six-Headed God).
28. *Ṣāṇmātura Stavam* (S) (Hymn on Ṣāṇmātura, the Six-Mothered God).
29. *Subrahmaṇya Kīrtanam* (M) (In Praise of Subrahmaṇya).
30. *Navamañjarī* (M) (A Bouquet of Nine Verses).
31. *Guhāṣṭakam* (S) (Eight Verses on Guha-Subrahmaṇya).
32. *Bāhuleyāṣṭakam* (S) (Eight Verses on Bāhulaya-Subrahmaṇya).
33. *Subrahmaṇya Stuti* (M) (A Hymn of Sixty Verses on Subrahmaṇya).

Philosophical Poems

34. *Ātmopadeśa-Śatakam* (M) (One Hundred Verses of Self-Instruction).
35. *Advaita-Dīpikā* (M) (The Lamp of Non-Duality).
36. *Aṛivu* (M) (Knowledge-Consciousness-Gnosis).
37. *Daiva Daśakam* (M) (Ten Verses on God — A Universal Prayer).
38. *Darśana-Mālā* (S) (A Garland of Visions of The Absolute — One Hundred Verses).
39. *Brahmavidyā-Pañcakam* (S) (Brahmavidyā in Five Verses).
40. *Nirvṛtti-Pañcakam* (S) (Five Verses on Final Absorption).
41. *Ślokatrayī* (S) (A Work of Three Verses).
42. *Vedānta-Sūtras* (S) The Philosophy of Vedānta, in aphorisms.
43. *Homa-Mantram* (S) (A *Mantra* for Burnt Sacrifice).

Instructive Compositions

44. *Jīvakāruṇya-Pañcakam* (M) (Five Verses on Kindness to Life).

45. *Anukampā-Daśakam* (M) (Ten Verses on Mercy).
46. *Jāti-Nirṇayam* (S and M) (A Critique of Caste).
47. *Jāti-Lakṣaṇam* (M) (Definition of Kind).
48. *Sadācāram* (M) (Pattern of Good Behaviour).
49. *Municaryā-Pañcakam* (S) (Five Verses on The Behaviour of a Recluse).
50. *Āśramam* (S) (Five Verses on how to run an *Āśram*).
51. *Dharmam* (S) (One Verse on *Dharma*).
52. An Obituary of Two Verses on Chattambi Swami.
53. Filling of an Incomplete Verse (M).
54. Greetings to the *Dharmakumāran*, Monthly (M).

Translations

55. *Tirukkuṛal* — Tamil to Malayalam.
56. *Īśa Upaniṣad* — Sanskrit to Malayalam.

Prose Work

57. *Cijjaḍa-Cintanam* (M) (Reflections on Mind and Matter).
58. *Daiva Cintanam*-I (M) (Reflections on God).
59. *Daivacintanam*-II (M) (Reflections on God).
60. *Gadya-Prārthanā* (M) (A Prayer in prose form).
61. *Ātmavilāsam* (M) (Self's self-manifestation).

Glossary

Abhāva : Non-existence. The opposite of *bhāva*. Non-existence has two main divisions:

(1) The absence of one entity in another (*saṁsarga-abhāva*) which is of three kinds:

(a) prior non-existence (*prāg-abhāva*)

(b) annihilative non-existence (*pradhvaṁśa-abhāva*)

(c) absolute non-existences (*atyanta-abhāva*)

(2) One object not being another (*anyonya-abhāva)* or reciprocal non-existences.

Adhyāsa : Superimposition; false attribution; illusion.

Advaita : Non-duality, the transcendence of experiencing every form of duality or multiplicity.

Advaitin : A proponent of the *Advaita* philosophy.

Āgama : A synonym of any ancient scripture, particularly the Vedas. There are non-Vedic *āgama*s also, like *Śaivāgama, Vaiṣṇavāgama, Jaināgama,* etc.

Ajāta-vāda : The theory that no creation takes place. Only what exists gets transformed into new forms.

Akṣaram : The imperishable. Refers to the Ultimate Reality, *Brahman*.

Amṛta : Immortality or the Immortal Reality. Poetically imagined as the elixir in a golden pot that emerged from the Milk Ocean when the *deva*s and the *asura*s churned it together.

Amṛtatva : The state of being immortal.

Ānanda (*Ānandam*) : Bliss. To be understood in the context of the Good in Western philosophy as a supreme value. *Sat, cit* and *ānanda* are terms conjointly used to describe the Absolute (*Brahman*) in Vedānta. Concerning an individual being, it is to be understood as the value consciousness that enables one to evaluate his own experiences either as pleasant or unpleasant.

Anātmā (*Anātman*) : Non-self.

Antarikṣa : Literally, that which is perceived in the middle. The middle world conceived in the Vedas as existing between earth and heaven.

Aṇu : Atom. Literally, the indivisible.

Anubhava : Experience.

Anumāna : Inference. One of the *pramāṇa*s.

Anupalabdhi : Non-apprehension. One of the *pramāṇa*s (valid means of knowledge).

Anvaya : Stating the positive reason for an inference (*anumāna*), e.g. there is fire where there is smoke. Stating the negative for the same inference is known as *vyatireka*, e.g. there will be no smoke where there is no fire. An inference becomes fully valid when both these conditions agree.

Aṛivu : A Malayalam word for knowledge. Narayana Guru prefers this word, especially when he refers to Pure Consciousness. The word could also be used to denote any kind of knowledge.

Arthāpatti : Presumption. One of the *pramāṇa*s.

Asat : Non-existence, the non-existent, that which is morally void.

Asti : See *ṣaḍ-bhāva*.

Atala : One of the seven lower worlds.

Ātmā (*Ātman*) : The self (from the root *āt*, to pervade). The invisible reality or stuff that pervades any visible form. Often confused with *jīva*, the soul. Used in slightly altered senses according to the context. The simplest meaning of the word is "I" or "oneself."

Ātmajñāna : The knowledge of the self, self-knowledge, to know oneself.

Avasthātraya : *Avasthā* — states, *traya* — three. The three states of consciousness, viz. *jāgrat* (wakefulness), *svapna* (dreaming state) and *suṣupti* (deep-sleep).

Avatāra : Incarnation of God, a concept of Vaiṣṇavism that Viṣṇu incarnates from time to time to save the world from evil forces. Ten such incarnations are believed in — nine of the past and one yet to come.

Avidyā : Nescience or ignorance. Taking the unreal as the real and the real as the unreal. The root cause of all illusions and sufferings.

Bhakti : Devotedness. Derived from the root *bhaj*, meaning to meditate constantly on something. It can either be fully supported by wisdom (*jñāna*) or be of the form of full surrender to God with no understanding as such. The latter form is known as *prapatti*. A devotee is called *bhakta*.

Bhāva : Becoming. Any manifest form of that which exists (*sat*). Derived from the root *bhū*, to become.

Bhūloka : Another name for the Earth. *Bhū*, the Earth, *loka*, world.

Bhūmi : Another name for the Earth.

Bhuvarloka : The intermediate world according to the Indian mythological concept of cosmology. Also known as *antarikṣa*.

Brahmajijñāsā : The desire to have the wisdom of the Absolute.

Brahman : The Absolute. Derived from the root *bṛh*, to grow constantly. Literally, that which grows constantly.

Caitanya : *Cit* in its functional state.

Cidambaram : *Cit* + *ambaram*. Consciousness + Space. Space of consciousness. Also, the place in Tamil Nadu where the deity of Śiva in the form of Naṭarāja (the King of Dance) is installed.

Cijjaḍa : *Cit* + *jaḍa*, mind-matter duality.

Cit : Literally, consciousness. The imperishable Reality pervading all the perishable and visible forms is pure consciousness in essence. Hence *Brahman* is designated as *cit*. See *sat* and *ānanda* also.

Dama	:	Checking and turning away of the senses from distractions. One of the prerequisite mental preparations for attaining the wisdom of the Absolute.
Darśana	:	Literally, vision. The Indian equivalent to "philosophy." Vision of Reality as seen from the point of view of a given system of philosophy. Nyāya, Vaiśeṣika, Sāṁkhya, Yoga, Pūrva Mīmāṁsā and Uttara Mīmāṁsā are the six such systems of Indian philosophy. Narayana Guru in his *Darśana-Mālā* uses this word to mean any particular point of view of the non-dual Reality, of which he presents ten in the work, strung together systematically.
Deha	:	Physical body.
Dehoham buddhi	:	Self-identity with the physical body.
Devas	:	Gods. Inhabitants of Vedic heaven.
Dharma	:	Derived from the root *dhṛ*, to support. The universal functional system that sustains the world and life. Righteous way of life fully in harmony with the universal order.
Dravya	:	Any substance that inheres qualities.
Dṛk	:	Eye, the viewing person, the knower, the knowing personal consciousness.
Dṛśya	:	The visible objective world, any object of knowledge.
Eṣaṇā	:	Desire. Most common worldly interests which are *putreṣaṇā* (interest in one's children), *vitteṣaṇā* (interest in wealth) and *dāreṣaṇā* (interest in wife). These are the strongest binding forces in worldly life.
Gandharva	:	A type of heavenly beings presiding over human interests in fine arts, especially music.
Gauṇa	:	That which is related to qualities (*guṇas*). The power of words to be meaningful, especially in the Vedic context.
Guha	:	Cave, secret hiding place. In the Upaniṣads, the word stands for the mysterious abode of the Self.

Guṇas	:	The triple modalities of nature, originally conceived by Kapila in *Sāṁkhya-pravacana-sūtras*: *sattva* (pure), *rajas* (active), *tamas* (dark-inert).
Idam	:	This. Stands for "this world," the world here and now.
Idanta	:	This-sense, referring to the sense of objectivity as against subjectivity (*ahanta*).
Īśa (+*Īśvara*)	:	The Sanskrit equivalent to god. Literally, one who controls. It refers to the principle that controls the integral law that sustains each entity as a particular mode of expression of the universal being.
Īṣṭa	:	That which is dear and favourable. Its opposite is *aniṣṭa*.
Itihāsa	:	The Sanskrit word for epic. Defined as the narration of ancient historical events in order to teach the four basic human values, viz. *dharma* (righteousness), *artha* (wealth), *kāma* (desire, erotics) and *mokṣa* (final liberation).
Jagat	:	The world. Literally, that which is always on the move.
Jāgrat	:	See *avasthātraya*.
Janaloka	:	See *lokas*.
Jijñāsā	:	The desire to know, inquisitiveness.
Jijñāsuḥ	:	One who is desirous of knowledge.
Jīva	:	The Sanskrit equivalent to soul. Literally, a being that sustains through breathing. Often confused with *ātmā*, the self.
Jīvātmā (*Jīvātman*)	:	Individual soul, as against the universal soul, (*paramātman*) in Śaṅkara's school of Vedānta.
Jīvātma-buddhi	:	The sense of self-identity with the soul.
Jñāna (*Jñānam*)	:	Wisdom. In the Vedāntic context, the Wisdom of the non-difference of oneself from the universal Reality. The way of *jñāna* (*jñāna mārga*) is contrasted with that of rituals and actions (*karma mārga*).
Jñānī (*jñānin*)	:	One who possesses Wisdom.

Jñātā (jñātṛ) : The knower, the subject as against object (*jñeya*).

Jyotiḥ : Light, brightness, fire, any luminary.

Kāraṇa : Cause. Gold is cause and ornament is effect. What really exists is gold alone. Similarly, what really exists in the world is *Brahman* alone, which is its cause. This way of thinking is called *sat-kāraṇa-vāda* (argument giving primacy to cause). Indians distinguish two kinds of causes, viz. *upādāna-kāraṇa* (material cause) like clay for pots and *nimitta-kāraṇa* (incidental cause) like the potter and his tools.

Kāraṇa bhāna : Specially used by Narayana Guru to denote that specific mode of consciousness at deep-sleep in which one is ignorant of everything.

Kāraṇa śarīra : The body with the help of which consciousness remains fully ignorant in deep-sleep state.

Karma : All actions in general. Philosophically the creative urge inherent in the Imperishable Reality, causing the emergence of all manifest forms. In the Vedic context, the ritual of burnt-sacrifice enjoined by the Vedas. As a religious belief of the Hindus, the incipient memory factors clinging to the souls as a result of their deeds in previous births. All are bound to enjoy or suffer the fruits of their deeds, and will have to reincarnate for this purpose. One might be accumulating more *karma*s in the new birth. This vicious chain of action goes on till one attains final release. Such *karma*s are divided into three categories — *sañcita karma* (the actions accumulated in all the previous births), *āgāmi karma* (fresh actions to be done in the present lifetime) and *prārabdha karma* (actions already initiated but the eating of their fruits is not finished with).

Kartā (Kartṛ) : The doer of *karma*s, the agency of actions.

Kinnara : A heavenly being imagined to have a human body and a horse's head.

Kriyā : Another word for *karma*.

Kṛti : Another word for *karma*. Any work or creation.

Kṣetra-kṣetrajña : The field and the knower of the field. *Kṣetra* defined as body in the *Bhagavad-Gītā* includes in it everything that is changeful, both physical and mental. *Kṣetrajña* is the consciousness that witnesses all that happens in the realm of *kṣetra*. The entire chapter XIII of the *Bhagavad-Gītā* is devoted to a discussion of this, one of the central problems of philosophy.

Lakṣaṇam : Precise definition of any concept.

Lakṣaṇārtha : Indirect meaning as against the direct literal meaning (*vācyārtha*).

Līlā : Sport. The world considered as the expression of the divine sporting or the cosmic dance of God, the Absolute.

Lokas : The worlds. Indian mythology conceives of seven upper worlds and seven lower worlds. The following are the upper worlds.

1. *Bhūloka* — the earth inhabited by human beings.
2. *Bhuvarloka* — the intermediate world of stars and planets.
3. *Svarloka* — inhabited by gods (*devas*).
4. *Maharloka* — of Viṣṇu.
5. *Janaloka* — the world of procreation.
6. *Tapoloka* — of *ṛṣis*.
7. *Satyaloka* — of Brahmā, the Creator.

The seven lower worlds are as follows:

1. *Atala,* the abode of Vala, the son of Yama, the God of death.
2. *Vitala,* the abode of Śiva.
3. *Sutala,* of Mahābali.
4. *Rasātala,* of *rākṣasas,* the devilish monsters.
5. *Talātala,* of Māyāmayī.
6. *Mahātala,* the world of serpents.
7. *Pātāla,* the world of snakes.

All these stand for different value worlds.

Maharṣi	:	*Mahā* + *ṛṣi*. A great *ṛṣi* or seer.
Mahāvākyas	:	Literally, the great sentences. Applied to the conclusive formulae of Vedāntic wisdom, such as *tat tvam asi* (that thou art), *aham brahma asmi* (I am *Brahman*), *Prajñānam brahma* (consciousness is *Brahman*), *ayam ātmā brahma* (this Self is *Brahman*), *auṁ tat sat* (*auṁ*, that is what is real), *sarvam-khalvidam brahma* (everything here is *Brahman* indeed).
Maheśa (*Maheśvara*)	:	Another name of Śiva. Literally, the great God.
Mama-kāra	:	"Mine"-sense that always follows "I"-sense (*ahaṁkāra*).
Manana	:	Intense cogitation of what is directly heard of a Guru (*śravaṇa*) leading finally to full conviction and realization (*nididhyāsana*).
Māyā	:	Connotes a factor of epistemological and methodological importance in Śaṅkara's Vedānta especially, and in the Upaniṣadic lore generally. Whatever is postulated as the cause of the unreal, spoken of in the most generic of categorical terms in philosophy, as against theology, is to be laid at the door of *māyā*. It is the basis of duality or synergic antinomies. The nearest Western equivalent is the Negativität of Hegel's system.
Māyāvin	:	The wielder of *māyā*, an epithet of God.
Mokṣa	:	Final liberation. Literally, freedom. Also called *mukti*.
Mumukṣutva (*mumukṣutā*)	:	The state of being a restless aspirant for liberation through wisdom.
Nāma	:	Name. *Nāma* along with *rūpa* (form) distinguish every individual entity in this world.
Nididhyāsana	:	See *manana*.
Nimitta kāraṇa	:	See *kāraṇa*.
Nirupādhika jñāna	:	Unconditioned knowledge. Knowledge not conditioned by the senses of subject and object. Knowledge so conditioned is called *sopādhika jñāna*.
Niṣkāma-karma	:	Actions not motivated by personal benefits, but

		performed as part of the creative function of nature with full sense of detachment. Such actions keep its doer always liberated from all bondages.
Pāpa	:	Sin.
Parā	:	The transcendental.
Para-Brahman	:	The higher *Brahman*. Śaṅkara conceives of two aspects of *Brahman*. The lower *Brahman* (*Apara Brahman*) is the ultimate Reality having forms of the world for its attributes. The higher *Brahman* is attributeless, and hence is inconceivable.
Parā-jñāna	:	The transcendental knowledge indicated by the words *auṁ tat sat*, with no function of mental faculties, as defined by Narayana Guru in his *Darśana Mālā*.
Paramārtha	:	The Ultimate meaning. The Ultimate meaning of life, connoting *Brahman*.
Paramātman	:	The supreme or Transcendental Self. See *jīvātman*.
Parīkṣā	:	Any test to verify the infallibility of a definition.
Pariṇāma-vāda	:	The theory of evolution. The theory that the world came into being through a gradual process of evolution as from a "big-bang," a modern scientific concept.
Parokṣa jñāna	:	An indirect knowledge differentiated from direct perceptual knowledge (*pratyakṣa jñāna*).
Pātāla	:	See *lokas*.
Pradhāna	:	Another name for *prakṛti*, of the *prakṛti-puruṣa* dual concepts of the Sāṁkhya philosophy. Literally, the important.
Prakṛti	:	Nature. Literally, that which is always in an active state. This activeness is inherent in the ultimate Reality or *Brahman*. *Brahman* in an active state is called *prakṛti*.
Pramā	:	Certitude arrived at through valid means or *pramāṇa*.
Pramāṇas	:	Any valid means of certitude (*pramā*). Six of them are recognized by Vedāntins, whose validity is only in worldly knowledge. They are *pratyakṣa* (perception), *anumāna* (inference), *upamāna*

(comparison or analogy), *śabda* (scriptures), *arthāpatti* (presumption) and *anupalabdhi* (non-apprehension).

Pramāṇa-caitanya : Consciousness conditioned as the means of acquiring knowledge. An offshoot of the concept that pure Consciousness is the one and only Reality and everything apparent emanates from it as its conditioned mode of expression.

Pramātā (*Pramātṛ*) : The knower. The subject.

Pramātṛ-caitanya : Consciousness conditioned as the subject. See *pramāṇa-caitanya.*

Prāṇa : The vital breath. The functions of vital breath are identified as five, namely *prāṇa* (going upward), *apāna* (going downward), *vyāna* (that which takes vitality to every part of the body), *samāna* (that which keeps the balance of the body) and *udāna* (that which leaves the body at death).

Praṇava : Another word for *auṁ*. Literally "the ever new."

Pratibimba : Reflected form, like a mirror reflection. Madhva's concept is that all the souls are reflected forms of God the original (*bimba*).

Pratyag-ātmā; Pratyak + ātmā : *Pratyak,* the most interior or backward, *ātmā* the self. The most interior self-experience where subject becomes object, and their duality vanishes.

Pratyakṣa : See *pramāṇas*.

Pratipat : Another word for *cit*.

Priyam : That which is dear. The feeling of dearness.

Puṇya : Merit as against *pāpa* (sin).

Purāṇa : Literally, the ancient. The collection of legends of antiquity, meant mainly for teaching the common man, the philosophy of the Upaniṣads with the help of numerous tales.

Pūrva Mīmāṁsā : See *darśana.*

Rajas (*Rajoguṇa*) : See *guṇas*.

Ṛṣi : A seer. A wise sage of ancient India who lived generally in the seclusion of forests. They wrote all the hymns of the Vedas as well as the Upaniṣads. They were not necessarily monks and many of them had families.

Rudra : An epithet of Śiva. Literally, one who makes the evil weep. The Rudra concept belongs to Vedism and Śiva concept to pre-Vedism. Later these two got merged.

Rudratva : The state of being Rudra, the source of sufferings.

Śabda : Literally, any sound. Any word. In the philosophical context any scriptural utterance, one of the *pramāṇas*, the only means that leads to transcendental knowledge. Also called *āgama* and *śruti*.

Saccidānanda (*sat* + *cit* + *ānanda*) : Existence-Consciousness-Value experience, the only positive definition of *Brahman*. See *sat, cit* and *ānanda*.

Ṣaḍa-bhāva : The six states of existence in a cycle of life, namely, *asti* (existence), *janma* (birth), *vṛddhi* (growth), *pariṇāma* (evolution), *apakṣaya* (degeneration) and *vināśa* (destruction).

Sādhana-catuṣṭaya : The common name of the four principal prerequisite qualifications of a seeker. They are *nitya-anitya-vastu viveka* (discrimination of the eternal and transient values), *vairāgya* (sense of detachment towards transient values), the six disciplines beginning with *śama*, and *mumukṣutva*. The six disciplines are *śama, dama, uparati, titikṣā, śraddhā, samādhāna* (see *śama*).

Śama : Checking the mind and turning it away from distractions. One of the six qualities to be developed by self-effort as part of the spiritual discipline. The other five are *dama* (self-restraint by withdrawing sense-organs from their objects), *uparati* (non-dependence on the external), *titikṣā* (endurance), *śraddhā* (full faith in the words of one's Guru and of the scriptures) and *samādhāna* (having the thought of *Brahman* always in mind).

Samādhāna	:	See *śama.*
Sambhūti	:	Becoming. Any emergence of a new form as part of the creative unfoldment of *Brahman.*
Saṁhāra	:	Dissolution. The function of Śiva. It happens constantly as the reverse of *sambhūti.*
Sāṁkhya	:	See *darśana.*
Saṁvit	:	Another word for *cit.* Pure Consciousness.
Saṁvit sāgara	:	The ocean of Consciousness in which everything takes place as part of the self-unfoldment of *saṁvit.* Used as a synonym of God.
Sat	:	That which exists always. The subsisting reality in all the transient forms of the visible world, even as gold is the subsisting reality in all ornaments. *Brahman* as this subsisting Reality is designated as *sat.* See *ānanda* and *cit* also.
Sat-kāraṇa-vāda	:	The theory that cause alone is Real and all effects are mere superimpositions projected on to *sat,* and therefore all appearances are unreal. This is the theory of Śaṅkara.
Sat-kārya-vāda	:	The theory that effect is as real as cause — Rāmānuja's theory.
Sattva	:	See *guṇa*s.
Satya loka	:	See *loka*s.
Satya-dharman	:	Term found in the *Īśa Upaniṣad* which indicates the seeker of Truth (*satya*) from which *dharma* (see *dharma*) is inseparable.
Satya (satyam)	:	Reality, Truth, the truthful way of living.
Siddhi	:	Attainment. Supra-mundane attainments gained through certain yogic practices. Eight such attainments are referred to by Patañjali in his *Yoga-Sūtras.*
Śiva	:	Literally, the auspicious. The ancient hero-god, of prehistorical times, associated with radical virility and renunciation. He is an unconventional god like Dionysius, wearing skins and dancing in ecstasy, drunk with cosmic consciousness. He is the most ancient and the most important figure

of the Indian pantheon, and occupies his seat in Benares in the plains, and Kailāsa in the Himālayas.

Śivatva : The state of being Śiva, the most auspicious.

Sopādhika-jñāna : Knowledge conditioned by subject-sense and object-sense as against *nirupādhikājñāna.*

Sphoṭa : The name of the Indian theory of semantics. Literally, bursting out. Meaning bursts out in mind just on hearing the utterance of a word.

Śraddhā : One of the prerequisites on the part of a seeker. Willingness to have full faith in the truthfulness of the word of the Guru and of the scriptures. A necessary stepping stone for *manana* (see *manana*).

Śravaṇa : See *manana.*

Sṛṣṭi : Creation. The Vedāntic concept of creation is that all the world of appearances emerge out of the one *sat, Brahman,* as a result of its own creative urge. Mythologically, Brahmā is conceived as the God of creation.

Sthiti : Sustenance of this world. Viṣṇu is considered the God of sustenance, or rather the urge in the *sat* to sustain its own appearances is called Viṣṇu.

Sthūla-bhāna : The concretised manifestation of consciousness, the Reality, resulting in the experience of the gross (*sthūla*) world.

Sthūla-śarīra : The gross body with the help of which consciousness in its wakeful state becomes aware of the gross world.

Sukha : Another word for *ānanda.*

Sūkṣma-śarīra : The subtle body with the help of which consciousness creates and enjoys dreams.

Suṣupti : See *avasthātraya.*

Sutala : See *lokas.*

Svadharma : External behaviour pattern and way of life fully in harmony with one's inner nature. This harmony results in self-contentment in life, which in essence is not different from final liberation, according to the *Bhagavad-Gītā.*

Svapna : See *Avasthātraya*.

Svarūpa-lakṣaṇam : The positive definition of something, clarifying the essential nature and content of what is defined, as distinguished from *vyāvartaka lakṣaṇam* (see *vyāvartaka lakṣaṇam*).

Svarga : Heaven, one of the *lokas*. The Vedic heaven or paradise, inhabited by *devas* (gods) whose chief is Indra.

Talātala : See *lokas*.

Tamas (tamoguṇa) : See *guṇas*.

Tapoloka : See *lokas*.

Tattva-darśin : A visionary of basic principle or basic Reality, of the oneness of *tat* (That) and *tvam* (You or oneself).

Tejas : Brightness, fire.

Titikṣā : Endurance of the trouble incidental in life, without petulance or self-pity. One of the pre-requisite qualities of a seeker.

Triguṇas : See *guṇas*.

Trikālātīta : Beyond the past, present and future. The timeless.

Tripuṭi : The aspects involved in the event of knowing something, namely the knower, the known and the act of knowing. Literally, the three-petalled one.

Turīya : Literally, the fourth. The transcendental state of Consciousness in which the *tripuṭi* merges in the all-engulfing Self-radiance. Narayana Guru defines it as, "to know that which is bottomless and topless, from top to bottom."

Turīya-bhāna : The mode of consciousness in which one is fully aware, "I am *Brahman* indeed."

Upādāna kāraṇa : See *kāraṇa*.

Upamāna : See *pramāṇas*.

Upamiti-jñāna : Knowledge acquired through *upamāna* as a *pramāṇa*.

Upaniṣad : When the chapter of *karma* or ritualistic action has been transcended by a religious student or *brahmacārin*, he is ready to receive the posterior philosophical teachings which constitute the Vedānta (i.e., "the end of the Vedas"). The Vedānta is non-theological; concerned with the Absolute or the *Brahman*. The word is said to be derived from *upa*, beside and *niṣad*, sitting near, so that it is a teaching received by a disciple when he is allowed to sit and listen to philosophical teachings near or by the side of the *guru*.

Uparati : The disposition of not being influenced by external matters and considerations in deciding what to do and how to do in the course of life.

Vaiśvānara : The name given to the individuated self in which one is conscious of the external objects in the wakeful state. Literally, the universal man.

Vartamāna : The present. Literally, the state in which all measures (*māna*) are functionally existent (*varta*).

Vināśa : See *ṣaḍ-bhāva*s.

Viṣaya : Any object of knowledge.

Viṣaya caitanya : Consciousness transformed into the form of the object to be known.

Vitala : See *loka*s.

Vivarta-vāda : The theory that what seems to be creation is only the appearance of forms, effecting no intrinsic change in the causal Reality, the one Pure Consciousness or *Brahman*. Thus creations are mere illusory appearances.

Vṛddhi : See *ṣaḍ-bhāva*s.

Vyatireka : See *anvaya*.

Vyāvartaka lakṣaṇam : To define something by differentiating it from other definable entities (see *svarūpa-lakṣaṇam*).

Yajña : Sacrifice. Vedic fire-sacrifice. To offer what is considered as possessed by an individual back to the universal *prakṛti* to which everything, including ourselves, belongs.

Yoga : (from the root *yuj*, to join). Psychic union of oneself with the Self, just as an ornament finds its oneness with gold. As a contemplative method of self-enquiry, the way of expressing an inexpressible reality by allowing it to be viewed from two opposite sides and leaving the unitive meaning to be understood by the reader or seeker. For example, "attaining immortality" and "crossing over death" are two expressions meaning the same. But these two expressions are opposite in nature. They have in between them a meaning that cannot be expressed as it is.

Different systems of *yoga* have been developed in India, each giving emphasis to a particular pair to be joined together. Patañjali's *Yoga-Sutras* is the basic source book on *Yoga*. Patañjali's system is also known as *Rāja Yoga*. The names *Haṭha Yoga, Karma Yoga, Jñāna Yoga, Bhakti Yoga* are popular. Each of the eighteen chapters of the *Bhagavad-Gītā* is also named a *Yoga*. The *Bhagavad-Gītā* itself claims to be a *Yoga Śāstra* (textbook on the science of *Yoga*).

Yoga buddhi : The awareness attained by the method of *Yoga* (see *Yoga*).

Yogī (Yogin) : One who is adept in *Yoga*.

Yukti : The state of being a *yogin*. Also means logical reasoning.

Index